A View of the State of Ireland

To David and Mary Yarnold

EDMUND SPENSER

A View of the
State of Ireland

From the first printed edition (1633)

Edited by
*Andrew Hadfield and
Willy Maley*

Copyright © Blackwell Publishers Ltd, 1997

First published 1997

2 4 6 8 10 9 7 5 3 1

Blackwell Publishers Ltd
108 Cowley Road
Oxford OX4 1JF
UK

Blackwell Publishers Inc.
350 Main Street
Malden, Massachusetts 02148
USA

British Library Cataloguing-in-Publication Data
A CIP catalogue record for this book is available from the British Library.

Library of Congress Cataloging in Publication Data

Spenser, Edmund, 1552?–1599.
    A view of the state of Ireland : from the first printed edition
(1633) / Edmund Spenser; edited by Andrew Hadfield and Willy Maley.
      p.   cm.
    Includes bibliographical references and index.
    ISBN 0-631-20534-9 (hbk : alk. paper). — ISBN 0-631-20535-7 (pbk:
alk. paper)
    1. Ireland—Politics and government—1172–1603. 2. Ireland–
–Description and travel—Early works to 1800.   I. Hadfield, Andrew.
II. Maley, Willy.   III. Title.
DA937.S64 1997
941.5—dc21
                                   97–2338
                                      CIP

Typeset in 10 on 12½ pt Galliard
by Ace Filmsetting Ltd, Frome, Somerset
Printed in Great Britain by Hartnolls, Bodmin, Cornwall

This book is printed on acid-free paper

Contents

Acknowledgements

We would like to thank the all the academics who supported this project and so made it possible; Andrew McNeillie for similar help and for seeing it through the press; Telferin Pritchard for answering queries so promptly and helpfully; Johns Hopkins University Press for permission to use material from *The Works of Edmund Spenser: A Variorum Edition.* ed. Edwin Greenlaw et al. (1932–49), vol. X, pp. 519–23. Appendix II is based on this original research. We would also like to thank Alison, Lucy, Patrick and Maud Hadfield, and Geraldine Gallagher, for their encouragement and support over the years.

Andrew Hadfield and Willy Maley
November 1996

Framework of Events

1577   If the account of the execution of Murrogh O'Brien in the *View* is autobiographical, then Spenser was in Ireland during this year.

1579   Anonymous publication of Spenser's *The Shepheardes Calender*. Outbreak of the Desmond Rebellion.

1580   Spenser arrives in Ireland as secretary to Lord Grey, the Lord Deputy of Ireland. Massacre of Spanish garrison at Smerwick.

1581   Spenser acquires land in Wexford and serves as Clerk of Faculties in the Irish Court of Chancery. Publication of John Derricke's *The Image of Ireland*.

1582   Spenser acquires a house in Dublin and land in Kildare. Grey is recalled.

1583   Spenser serves as Deputy Clerk of the Council of Munster; appointed commissioner for musters in Kildare. Death of the Earl of Desmond.

1584   Sir John Perrot appointed Lord Deputy of Ireland.

1585   Scheme for Munster plantation devised.

1586   Spenser is found to be in arrears on property attached to Limerick Cathedral. The parliamentary attainder of Desmond and supporters clears the way for the Munster Plantation.

1587   Execution of Mary Stuart (Mary, Queen of Scots).

1588   Wreck of the Spanish Armada. Sir William Fitzwilliam appointed Lord Deputy.

1589   Spenser obtains official possession of 3,000-acre estate of Kilcolman in Co. Cork on the Munster Plantation. Sir Walter Raleigh visits him there.

1590   Publication of *The Faerie Queene* Books I–III.

1591   Spenser is granted £50 annual pension by Elizabeth; publication of *Complaints*.

1593   Opening of Trinity College, Dublin. Death of Lord Grey.

1594   Spenser serves as Queen's Justice for Cork. Publication of Richard Beacon's Irish dialogue, *Solon His Follie*, at Oxford. Outbreak of the Nine Years' War. Sir William Russell appointed Lord Deputy.

1595   Publication of *Amoretti* and *Epithalamion*, and *Colin Clouts Come Home Againe*.

1596   Publication of *The Faerie Queene*, Books I–VI. James VI attacks Book V because of its slander of his mother, figured as Duessa.

1597   Thomas, Lord Burgh, appointed Lord Deputy.

1598   *A View* entered in the Stationers' Register. English forces crushed by the Irish at the Yellow Ford. Spenser nominated Sheriff of Cork. Munster Plantation overthrown. Spenser flees to England.

1599   Spenser dies in London, 'for lack of bread', according to Ben Jonson. Appointment of the Earl of Essex as Lord Lieutenant of Ireland.

1600   Charles Blount, Lord Mountjoy, appointed Lord Deputy.

1601   Defeat of Irish and Spanish forces at Kinsale. Execution of the Earl of Essex.

1603   The Earl of Tyrone submits to Lord Mountjoy. End of Nine Years' War. Death of Elizabeth I. Accession of James I.

1605   Sir Arthur Chichester appointed Lord Deputy.

1606   Sir John Davies appointed Attorney General.

1607   'Flight of the Earls' as Gaelic lords abandon Ireland, and their lands are seized by the English Crown.

1608   Survey of six escheated counties in Ulster.

1609   Publication of the first folio edition of *The Faerie Queene*, complete with the 'Cantos of Mutabilitie' which contain significant Irish material.

1610   Publication of Barnaby Rich's *New Description of Ireland*.

1611   First folio edition of Spenser's collected works, excluding the *View*.

1612   Publication of Sir John Davies' *A Discovery of the True Causes why Ireland was never entirely Subdued, nor brought under Obedience of the Crowne of ENGLAND, untill the Beginning of his Majesties happie Raigne.*

1613   First survey of the Ulster Plantation.

1616   Death of Hugh O'Neill in Rome.

1621   Publication of Philip O'Sullivan Bear's *History of Ireland* in Lisbon.

1625   Death of James I. Accession of Charles I.

1633   Appointment of Thomas, Viscount Wentworth, as Lord Deputy. Publication of Ware's edition of the *View*, dedicated to Wentworth. Anonymous publication of Thomas Stafford's *Pacata Hibernia*.

1634   Completion of Geoffrey Keating's history of Ireland. *Foras Feasa ar Éirinn.*

1636   Completion of the *Annals of the Four Masters* by Michael Ó Cléirigh and others.

1640   Wentworth created Earl of Strafford.

1641   Execution of Strafford. Outbreak of Ulster Rising.

Introduction

In 1596, the same year that he published the second edition of *The Faerie Queene*, Edmund Spenser, a dutiful colonial servant who had acquired a substantial estate in Ireland and who also had a certain fame as an English poet, began work on a long treatise which was designed to help rescue his adopted home from the chaos to which he felt it had degenerated. *A View of the Present State of Ireland* was completed some time before 1598, when it was entered into the Stationers' Register by one of Spenser's publishers, the proper channel for anyone seeking to have a work licensed by the authorities and have it registered as their property. Although the tract circulated extensively in manuscript and was clearly read by many important political figures of the day, it did not appear in print until 1633, in an edition of *Ancient Irish Chronicles* collected by the Dublin antiquarian and historian, Sir James Ware (1594–1666). This was the edition of Spenser's treatise which was used by all subsequent readers before the twentieth century, and it is arguable that until Spenser became a central figure in the canon of English poetry in the early eighteenth century, he was as well-known to many readers as the author of *A View* as *The Faerie Queene*. *A View* was read by such central literary figures as Milton, Wordsworth and Yeats, who all commented carefully on Spenser's opinions, and was certainly an instrumental work in establishing the staunchly Protestant identity of the Anglo-Irish in the seventeenth century.[1] Its influence on Anglo-Irish

---

1 Willy Maley, 'How Milton and some contemporaries read Spenser's *View*', in Brendan Bradshaw, Andrew Hadfield and Willy Maley (eds), *Representing Ireland: literature and the origins of conflict, 1534–1660* (Cambridge: Cambridge University Press, 1993),

politics of the 1590s has been disputed by historians; it has been claimed that Spenser was too obscure and confused to be persuasive and that it is only his posthumous reputation which has misled commentators into taking his ideas seriously; alternatively, *A View* has been read as the expression of the aggressive Protestant mentality of the New English who insisted that only violence would subdue the recalcitrant native Irish and the Old English settlers who had chosen to adopt their lifestyle and manners; more recently a case has been made that *A View* was instrumental in forcing the Queen to reintroduce martial law into Ireland after she had made great efforts to abandon such draconian measures and return to the normality of the common law.[2] Whether read as the eloquent expression of communal beliefs or as a unique text, commentators agree on the powerful rhetoric of the work and its ability to disturb – often to shock – the reader.

Spenser in Ireland

Spenser has most usually been read – certainly until recently – either within the history of English literary development, or within the context of Elizabeth's England. It was Spenser's reputation as the loyal, courtly servant of his Queen which led Karl Marx to brand him 'Elizabeth's arse-kissing poet'.[3] However, Spenser spent virtually all his creative adult life in Ireland, away from the English court, returning only briefly to petition the Queen and oversee the publication of his poetry,

pp. 191–208; E. Wayne-Marjoram, 'Wordsworth's View of the State of Ireland', *PMLA*, 55 (1940), pp. 608–11; W. B. Yeats, 'Edmund Spenser', in *Essays and Introductions* (London: Macmillan, 1969), pp. 356–83; Nicholas Canny, 'Edmund Spenser and the development of an Anglo-Irish identity', *Yearbook of English Studies*, 13 (1983), pp. 1–19.

2 Ciarán Brady, 'Spenser's Irish crisis: humanism and experience in the 1590s', *Past and Present*, 111 (May 1986), pp. 17–49; Brendan Bradshaw, 'Sword, word and strategy in the Reformation in Ireland', *Historical Journal*, 21 (1978), pp. 475–502; David Edwards, 'Martial law and Spenser's *Vewe* of Ireland' (paper presented at *The Faerie Queene* in the World Symposium, Yale Center for British Art, Sept. 1996).

3 Cited in David Norbrook, *Poetry and Politics in the English Renaissance* (London: Routledge, 1984), p. 311. For a representative example of such scholarship see Robin Headlam Wells, *Spenser's* Faerie Queene *and the Cult of Elizabeth* (London: Macmillan, 1983).

a fact which surely casts doubt on the assumptions made in such analyses. Spenser was a permanent resident of Ireland from 1580, when he went to serve as secretary to the Lord Deputy, Arthur, Lord Grey de Wilton. Spenser may have been keen to leave England because he had offended Lord Burghley in his early satire *Mother Hubberds Tale*, but his move to Ireland can be seen just as plausibly as a means of forwarding a career and attaining the status of a landed gentleman.[4] Certainly Spenser was not the only literary figure to seek his fortune in Ireland: others who followed the same path include Sir Walter Raleigh, Sir John Harington, Sir Geoffrey Fenton, Barnaby Rich, Thomas Churchyard, Barnaby Googe and Sir John Davies. It should also be noted that in 1594 Spenser married Elizabeth Boyle a 'kinswoman' of Richard Boyle, the Earl of Cork, who had already procured a spectacular fortune and was to become the richest man in the British Isles.[5] Ireland possessed the advantages and disadvantages of the colonial world: on one hand great wealth, power and influence were available to those who would be excluded in the metropolis; on the other, the price was isolation from the 'real' centres of power, a crisis of identity and the constant threat of danger. Such balanced concerns permeate the arguments of *A View*.

As secretary to Grey, Spenser probably witnessed the notorious massacre at Smerwick in 1580, when Lord Grey slaughtered the Spanish and Papal forces in the Fort d'Oro during the Desmond Rebellion, after they had surrendered.[6] Grey's actions apparently horrified courtiers close to the Queen and led to his recall in 1582, although Spenser vigorously defended his erstwhile employer in *A View* (see below, pp. 103–5). After a series of appointments in and around Dublin, Spenser moved down to Munster around 1584; there he played a prominent role in the newly established provincial council. By about 1588 he had become a substantial landowner, occupying the ruined Norman castle of Kilcolman with an estate of over 3000 acres, part of the land confiscated after the Desmond Rebellion which went to form the basis for the ambitious Munster Plantation, a scheme in which English settlers were encour-

4 For a recent analysis of Spenser's life and career, see Richard Rambuss, *Spenser's Secret Career* (Cambridge: Cambridge University Press, 1993).
5 Nicholas Canny, *The Upstart Earl: a study of the social and mental world of Richard Boyle, first Earl of Cork, 1566–1643* (Cambridge: Cambridge University Press, 1982).
6 For details see Alfred O'Rahilly, *The Massacre at Smerwick (1580)* (Cork: Cork University Press, 1938).

aged to colonize south-west Ireland in order to make the land more civil and governable.[7] But which land? A key feature of English colonial ventures in the period is the way in which the state supported or countenanced projects that offered an opportunity to subdue and placate restless natives at home and abroad. The younger sons of the lesser gentry who planted themselves in Ireland may have proved a nuisance had they remained in England. In Spenser's case, the acquisition of an Irish estate transformed him into a landowning gentleman, but also led to a protracted law-suit with the Anglo-Irish Lord Roche, whose sons were eventually to come out in rebellion.

Spenser continued with his official duties in various capacities, purchasing more land and eventually becoming a sufficiently senior figure to be made sheriff of Cork in 1598. Throughout the 1590s most of his major works were published, culminating in the second edition of *The Faerie Queene* in 1596. The rebellion of Hugh O'Neill (the Nine Years' War), the most threatening event of Elizabeth's last decade, which almost succeeded in wresting Ireland from the grasp of the English monarch and placing it under Spanish control, broke out in 1594.[8] Kilcolman was sacked and burnt in 1598, and Spenser fled to England with dispatches from the governor of Munster for the Privy Council. He died in Westminster in January 1599, 'for lack of bread', according to Ben Jonson.

The Contexts of *A View*

It would appear from this brief summary of Spenser's life that he was deeply involved in Ireland, as a politician, writer, colonist and civil servant.[9] As a result, *A View* should not be left as a marginal and little read appendage to his more interesting poetry, but regarded as central to his concerns as a writer. Nobody undertakes such an elaborate, carefully

---

7 For further detail see Michael MacCarthy-Morrogh, *The Munster Plantation: English migration to Southern Ireland, 1583–1641* (Oxford: Clarendon Press, 1986).

8 See Hiram Morgan, *Tyrone's Rebellion: the outbreak of the Nine Years War in Tudor Ireland* (Woodbridge: Boydell Press/Royal Historical Society, 1993).

9 For further details see Willy Maley, *A Spenser Chronology* (Basingstoke: Macmillan, 1994).

written, well recognized generic form – the dialogue – of such length, unless they expect it to have some audience and influence. Until recently, *A View* has generally been used by literary scholars to help decode the allegory of Book V of *The Faerie Queene*, which has usually been considered the least interesting section of the poem because it is the most historical. Given the impetus of recent critical developments – partly centred around the contexts of Spenser's life and writings – and much exciting work on the series of Irish references throughout the poem, it might be suggested that each work be used to illuminate the other, rather than privileging the poetry and relegating the prose to 'background information'.[10] Furthermore, perhaps we ought to widen our notions of which texts are worth studying in the early modern period, when the boundaries and categories of literature were quite fluid. Such a recognition might place a greater burden on the student of Renaissance culture, but undoubtedly it makes the subject more open-ended and fascinating.

However, *A View* does not simply demand to be read by those committed to the study of Spenser's voluminous writings. As the lively debates among historians have demonstrated, it is a key text for the interpretation of late sixteenth-century Irish cultural and political history.[11] As such, it should not be ignored by students of British or colonial history, specifically during the Renaissance, but later periods also. Edward Said, in his pioneering study, *Culture and Imperialism*, has pointed out Spenser's relevance to contemporary analyses of imperialism and the lack of awareness of this connection among readers of his poetry: 'it is generally true that literary historians who study the great sixteenth-century poet Edmund Spenser, for example, do not connect his bloodthirsty plans for Ireland, where he imagined a British army virtually exterminating the native inhabitants, with his poetic achievement or with the history of British rule over Ireland, which continues

10 See Stephen Greenblatt, *Renaissance Self-Fashioning: from More to Shakespeare* (Chicago: University of Chicago Press, 1980), ch. 4; Richard A. McCabe, 'Edmund Spenser, Poet of Exile', *Proceedings of the British Academy*, 80 (1991), pp. 73–103.
11 See, for example, Ciarán Brady and Nicholas Canny, 'Debate: Spenser's Irish crisis', *Past and Present*, 120 (1988), pp. 201–15; Brendan Bradshaw, 'Robe and sword in the conquest of Ireland', in Claire Cross, David Loades and J. J. Scarisbrick (eds)., *Law and Government under the Tudors: essays presented to Sir Geoffrey Elton on his retirement* (Cambridge: Cambridge University Press, 1988), pp. 139–62.

today.'[12] Said's wider purpose is to demonstrate 'the involvements of culture with expanding empires', and within such a project Spenser must clearly be regarded as a pivotal figure, hence the importance *A View* must possess for scholars of colonialism and post-colonialism. The terms of post-colonial theory, most notably ambivalence, hybridity, and the role of the diaspora, are central motifs in Spenser's Irish treatise. More than any other early modern English text on Ireland, its concerns are with ethnography, genealogy, degeneracy and cultural formation. While critics have long seen Shakespeare's *The Tempest* as an exemplary colonial document, *A View* is arguably the most sustained and sophisticated treatment of Renaissance concepts of race and identity by a major canonical author.

In connecting this crucial text to a continuing Irish history, Said further points out the interconnection between a wider colonial framework and a supposedly 'internal' history of the British Isles and British literature.[13] As J. G. A. Pocock recognized without developing the point, *A View* raises important questions concerning political and legal history, so it should be available to students of these disciplines.[14] The recent historiographical interest in the 'British Problem' would benefit from the exploration of a tract written by an Englishman in Ireland whose epic poem about a Welsh prince was attacked by a Scottish monarch. *A View* rehearses and elaborates the vexed issues of sovereignty, subjection and statehood that impinge upon the nascent British polity. All of which argues that it is little short of scandalous that there has been no readily available edition of the work for readers to use and that the work has often been known through the circulation of the same small pool of quotations, giving a skewed and superficial account of a

12   Edward Said, *Culture and Imperialism* (London: Vintage, 1994), p. 5. For an analysis of Said's comments see Andrew Hadfield, *Edmund Spenser's Irish Experience: Wilde Fruit and Salvage Soyl* (Oxford: Clarendon Press, 1997), 'Introduction: Spenser, Colonialism, and National Identity'.

13   See H. F. Kearney, 'The making of an English Empire', in *The British Isles: a history of four nations* (Cambridge: Cambridge University Press, 1989), ch. 7. More generally, see Robert Crawford, *Devolving English Literature* (Oxford: Clarendon Press, 1992).

14   J. G. A. Pocock, *The Ancient Constitution and the Feudal Law: a study of English historical thought in the seventeenth century* (Cambridge: Cambridge University Press, rev. edn, 1987), p. 263. See also Hans S. Pawlisch, *Sir John Davies and the Conquest of Ireland: a study in legal imperialism* (Cambridge: Cambridge University Press, 1985).

highly stratified text. The most familiar passage, and the one most frequently cited, is the infamous description of the Munster famine (see below, pp. 101–2).[15]

The Argument of *A View*

A View is a prose dialogue of some 65,000 words between Eudoxus, a rational Englishman, interested in politics but largely ignorant of Ireland, and Irenius, who is clearly speaking from a position of knowledge and probably represents one of the New English colonists, like Spenser himself.[16] Unlike other contemporary dialogues, no time is taken up with formalities or the establishment of the fictional setting, but the two figures plunge straight into the argument with Eudoxus' perplexed observation that if Ireland is 'of so goodly and commodious a soyle' as Irenius claims, why has nothing been done to transform 'that nation to better government and civility'? Irenius answers that Ireland is doomed if left to its own devices, perhaps owing to 'the very *Genius* of the soyle, or influence of the starres' or, worse still, a curse, which will stretch over the Irish Sea and damn England as well: 'for some secret scourge, which shall by her come unto *England*'.

The opening speeches set the tone for the rest of the dialogue. Eudoxus asks the questions and Irenius provides the answers, often at great length and in the form of what appear to be digressions from the subject, so that it is he who dominates the dialogue. Irenius' words also establish the fear, frequently expressed in English works on Ireland in the 1590s, that if nothing is done, then Ireland will ruin England too. Ireland serves as the limit and boundary of the spread of English political culture, always threatening to overturn the values which the English regard as their defining characteristics – liberalism, tolerance, justice, fairness – a role now filled by the taboo figure of the Northern Irish statelet. The

15 For recent uses of this passage in critical and imaginative writing, see Maud Ellman, *The Hunger Artists: starving, writing & imprisonment* (London: Virago, 1993), p. 11; Seamus Heaney, 'Bog Oak', in *New Selected Poems, 1966–87* (London: Faber, 1990), pp. 19–20; Robert Welch, *The Kilcolman Notebook* (Dingle, Co. Kerry: Brandon, 1994), pp. 84–93.

16 The names might be glossed as 'of good repute' or 'good thought', and 'man of peace' or, more likely, 'man of Ireland', respectively.

words of Mr. 'Whisky' Sisodia in Salman Rushdie's *The Satanic Verses,* 'The trouble with the Engenglish is that their hiss history happened overseas, so they dodo don't know what it means,' can be applied with bitter irony to Ireland, a land which is indeed, 'overseas', but which has always existed within and without the state as both a colony and a British kingdom ruled by the English monarch.[17]

A View can be divided up into two approximately equal sections: in the first, Irenius outlines the abuses and cultural inferiority of the Irish. Irenius catalogues the habits and practices of Irish life, condemning their primitive mode of agriculture whereby they follow wandering herds of cattle ('bollying') instead of cultivating crops; their inadequate and socially divisive system of land distribution and government ('tanistry' and 'gavelkind'); their incestuous marriages and fostering out of children to wet nurses; their heretical and primitive form of Catholicism; the subversive works of their poets ('bards'); their inability to use the vast resources at their disposal; even their clothes ('mantles') and hairstyles ('glibs') are designed to aid rebellion and oppose civilized life. Irenius, in probably the longest digression in the dialogue, also establishes that the Irish are descended from the ancient Scythians, a barbarous race, opposed to civilized values.

Few of these observations and opinions in *A View* are original. Most can be seen to stem from the writings of Gerald of Wales, the medieval commentator who provided eye-witness accounts of the Irish at the time of Henry II's original conquest in the late twelfth century, and whose writings were generally copied by all subsequent English observers until they were supplanted by *A View* in the seventeenth century.[18] What does tend to distinguish Spenser's work is the rhetorical sophistication of the arguments, the sheer length and elaborate construction of the treatise, and the often unexpected – and quite horrifying – conclusions.

This first section closes with the two speakers having agreed that the Irish are so savage and resistant to the spread of civil order that only the

---

17 Salman Rushdie, *The Satanic Verses* (London: Viking, 1988), p. 343. On the anomalous constitutional status of Ireland, see Nicholas Canny, *Kingdom and Colony: Ireland in the Atlantic World, 1560–1800* (Baltimore, MD: Johns Hopkins University Press, 1988).

18 See Gerald of Wales, *The History and Topography of Ireland*, trans. J. J. O'Meara (Harmondsworth: Penguin, 1951); David Beers Quinn. *The Elizabethans and the Irish* (Ithaca, NY: Cornell University Press, 1966).

most drastic of solutions can reform them and transform their nation. Eudoxus is invariably shocked by Irenius' proposals, most notably at the moment when Irenius tries to persuade him that only the use of the sword can effect change, as the imposition of English law in Ireland simply will not work (p. 93). Eventually, Eudoxus accedes to Irenius' superior logic based on his experience in Ireland, and accepts that only ruthless violence will solve the problems. It is a major theme reiterated time and again throughout *A View* that only those familiar with Ireland know how to reform it, an argument which clearly privileges the experience of the New English over those at court who instinctively shudder at the costs, both human and financial. The case is that, in order to protect civilized values from the attacks of hostile savages, savage methods will have to be used, which raises the troubling possibility that one may not be able to distinguish the problem from the solution with any degree of confidence. *A View* defends the policies of Lord Grey, who appeared to those at court as 'a bloodie man' who had disgraced Elizabeth in so far as he 'regarded not the life of her subjects no more then dogges' (p. 103). The Lord Deputy is vindicated in Spenser's dialogue on the grounds that his methods actually helped to establish a secure platform for reform, unlike less ruthless English viceroys such as Sir John Perrot.

② Having separated the bad people from the good land, the second section then provides Irenius' proposed solution to this situation. A huge English army of 11,000 men will be placed in garrisons constructed throughout Ireland and an ultimatum will be issued demanding the surrender of all Irish rebels. When a suitable period of time has elapsed, the armies will complete the final conquest of Ireland, defeating such rebels as remain. Part of this process will be the destruction of all fertile land and all goods and cattle, even those of the Irish who had already surrendered, in order to prevent the surviving rebels from using them for sustenance. Irenius estimates that the war and the subsequent famine will take about a year. Peace will be maintained by the transplantation of many of those who had submitted to different provinces of Ireland (rebels from Ulster and Leinster will change places). These will be given lands run by English landlords. The garrisons will be maintained through a tax levied on all the colonies established to pay for their own security, thus creating the self-sufficient units that the metropolitan government both feared and desired; feared because self-sufficiency bordered on autonomy, but desired because financial constraints were the greatest obstacle to colonial expansion.[19]

The logic of Irenius' harsh proposals is perhaps best illustrated in his infamous description of the effects of the Munster famine during the Desmond Rebellion, an account made all the more harrowing owing to Irenius' claim to have been an eye-witness to the conflict ('as I saw by proofe in *Desmonds* warres' (p. 100)):

> Out of every corner of the woods and glynnes they came creeping forth upon their hands, for their legges could not beare them, they looked like anatomies of death, they spake like Ghosts crying out of their graves, they did eate the dead Carrions, happy were they could finde them, yea, and one another soone after, insomuch as the very carcasses they spared not to scrape out of their graves, and if they found a plot of water-cresses or Shamrocks, there they flocked as to a feast for the time, yet not able long to continue therewithall, that in short space there were none almost left, and a most populous and plentifull countrey suddainely left voyde of man and beast, yet sure in all that warre, there perished not many by the Sword, but all by the extremitie of famine, which they themselves had wrought. (pp. 101–2)

This traumatic passage is an important crux in a variety of ways. It provides a key to how Spenser/Irenius anticipates the final conquest of Ireland will function when, presumably, the same process will take place. If this appears too much for tender stomachs to digest, then the revelation that the Irish are implacably barbarous descendants of the Scythians, as well as the extensive analysis of their diverse social practices, should persuade the reader that Irenius' proposals are reasonable ones. Furthermore, the powerful rhetoric works in the opposite way to that one might expect from the start of the description. The last sentence reveals that it is the Irish who are really to blame for their own fate, 'which they themselves had wrought', so that the revolting images of cannibalism – traditionally regarded as the sign that the boundary separating human from animal status had been crossed[20] – have to make sense as a sign that the Irish are akin to the lowest form of savages in their resistance to the

---

19 For analysis see Brady, 'Spenser's Irish crisis', pp. 30–3.
20 See Bernard W. Sheehan, *Savagism and Civility: Indians and Englishman in Colonial Virginia* (Cambridge: Cambridge University Press, 1980), ch. 2.

spread of English law. To adopt a term from literary criticism, they have become 'self-consuming artefacts', actually nourishing the body politic in the process.

Irenius/Spenser's political analysis is vitiated by an apparent contradiction. On one hand, the attempt appears to be to convince the reader that Ireland is not beyond reform and that the land can be salvaged from its current abject situation. On the other, the argument seems to cast the Irish as irredeemably 'other', implacably opposed to such English efforts by dint of their being Irish and wanting to remain that way. In terms of this second language, the only way that the situation can change is if the Irish cease to be Irish and if Ireland, as a contemporary treatise puts it, becomes 'mearely a West England'.[21]

However, the text of *A View*, the varieties of representations and discourses it employs, make it far more sophisticated than this straightforward – and frequently repeated – contradiction would imply. In his catalogue of Irish social practices, Irenius provides Eudoxus with a detailed account of the Irish bards with whose literary craft he is highly impressed, declaring that the verses he has had translated 'savoured of sweet wit and good invention . . . sprinkled with some pretty flowres of their naturall device, which gave good grace & comlinesse unto them' (p. 77). Irenius is also struck by the social standing and political influence of the bards. When their works are recited at meetings, 'their verses are taken up with a generall applause' and even the singers 'receive for the same, great rewards and reputation amongst them'. Moreover, 'none dare displease them for feare to runne into reproach through their offence, and to bee made infamous in the mouthes of all men' (p. 75). The problem with the bards is that they are on the wrong side and praise miscreants rather than men of virtue: 'whomsoever they finde to be most licentious of life, most bolde and lawlesse in his doings, most dangerous and desperate in all parts of dis-obedience and rebellious disposition, him they set up and glorifie in their Rithmes, him they praise to the people, & to yong men make an example to follow' (p. 76).

The value of the bards in Irish society would appear to stand as a

21 D. B. Quinn (ed.), ' "A Discourse of Ireland" (circa 1599): a sidelight on English colonial policy', *Proceedings of the Royal Irish Academy*, 47, Sect. C (1942), pp. 151–66, esp. p. 166.

pointed contrast to the situation of the poet, Bonfont, in *The Faerie Queene*, whose tongue is nailed to a post and whose name is changed to 'Malfont' for his (unspecified) criticisms of the Queen, Mercilla: 'For that therewith he falsely did reuyle,/ And foule blaspheme that Queene for forged guyle' (V.ix.25). Irenius' description perhaps also recalls Sir Philip Sidney's castigation of England for neglecting its poets in *An Apology for Poetry*, a neglect which contrasts unfavourably with the value placed on poetry among 'the most barbarous and simple Indians', Turks and Irish: 'In our neighbour country Ireland, where truly learning goeth very bare, yet are their poets held in a devout reverence.'[22] In making similar judgements, Spenser would appear to be admitting that a simple polarity between the civilized English and barbarous Irish cannot adequately account for the complexities of the colonial scene in early modern Ireland. Not only could the English learn from their neighbours, but criticizing imperial English authority could place the New English in an analogous position to the Irish rebels, exposing their bodies to the same forms of spectacular public torture.

Censorship?

It has often been assumed that because *A View* did not appear after it was entered into the Stationers' Register, it must have been censored by the English authorities. Some have suggested that this was because *A View* was simply too offensive in its anti-Irish prejudice and recommendation of draconian measures for the reform of Ireland; others, because it exposed government policy in Ireland or revealed information which might have been useful for enemies of the Crown, notably the Spanish.[23] Such claims are by no means implausible, but all are based on supposition and require that the insubstantial surviving evidence be interpreted unambiguously.

22 Sir Philip Sidney, *An Apology for Poetry*, ed. Geoffrey Shepherd (Manchester: Manchester University Press, 1965), pp. 97–8.
23 See, for example, Brady, 'Spenser's Irish crisis', p. 25; David J. Baker, ' "Some Quirk, Some Subtle Evasion": legal subversion in Spenser's *A View of the Present State of Ireland*', *Spenser Studies*, 6 (1986), pp. 147–63; Jonathan Goldberg, *James I and the Politics of Literature: Jonson, Shakespeare and their contemporaries* (Baltimore: Johns Hopkins University Press, 1983), p. 9.

What we know for certain is that on 14 April 1598, the printer Matthew Lownes entered into the Stationers' Register 'a booke intituled A viewe of the present state of Ireland. Discoursed by way of a Dialogue betwene EUDOXUS and IRENIUS. uppon Condicion that hee gett further aucthoritie before yt be prynted'.[24] Its subsequent non-appearance until Ware's edition of *Ancient Irish Histories* (1633), and the nervousness displayed by that editor regarding some of Spenser's more forceful judgements (see below, p. xxiv), is the sole basis for the belief that Spenser's work was as difficult to stomach in its day as it has been ever after.

However, the evidence is not so secure as it might seem. It has to be remembered that the primary purpose of the Stationers' Company was not to serve as official censors, but to register works as the property of individual printers and their clients, an early form of copyright law.[25] Works were supposedly vetted by the authorities, but the wording of the entry was by no means unusual and may be the result of confusions regarding the rights to *A View*. Matthew Lownes was, in fact, in dispute with the more powerful William Ponsonby over a number of texts, and it is possible that the work failed to appear on his insistence, as he certainly had the power in 1598 to prevent Lownes publishing a work by one of his major clients.[26]

Nevertheless, it would be wrong to regard such evidence as conclusive. It is still likely that *A View* may have failed to appear in print because it was deemed to be a subversive work. One should note the lack of books on Ireland published in the whole of Elizabeth's reign, but especially in the late 1590s when the danger from Hugh O'Neill's rebellion was at its height. Writing to Humphrey Galdelli in Venice in July 1599, Francis Cordale lamented that he 'could send no news of the Irish wars, all advertisements thence being prohibited, and such news as comes to Council carefully concealed'.[27] It is strange that anyone should have attempted to publish a work such as *A View* in 1598 as it would appear to be unlikely that the authorities would have allowed such a

---

24 Edward Arber (ed), *A Manuscript of the Stationers' Register, 1554–1640*, 5 vols (Birmingham: Privately printed, 1875–94), vol III, p. 34.

25 John Feather, *A History of British Publishing* (London: Croom Helm, 1988), ch. 3.

26 See Michael Brennan, 'William Ponsonby', in *The Spenser Encyclopedia*, ed. A. C. Hamilton (London: Routledge, 1990), pp. 554–5.

27 Cited in *Calendar of State Papers, Domestic Series, 1598–1601*, ed. Mary Anne Everett Green (London: Longman, 1869), p. 251.

frank discussion of Irish issues to be aired in print, whatever the actual substance of the arguments. It is most plausible, then, to assume that *A View* aroused official ire because of its subject-matter rather than any particular point in the argument. Censors are notorious today either for reading carelessly or for not reading 'subversive' books at all, and it may well be that Elizabethan censors were no different.[28]

Ware's Edition

The eventual publisher of the work, Sir James Ware, clearly felt uneasy about Spenser's text, including it in a selection of antiquarian works when, despite its wealth of detailed comment on Irish genealogy, its main thrust is towards an analysis of contemporary Irish society. Ware suggests in his preface that the work has no relevance to the Ireland of the 1630s, a bitter irony in the light of the subsequent events of 1641.[29] Ware commented that 'we may wish that in some passages it had bin tempered with more moderation', and he blamed Spenser's harshness on '[t]he troubles and miseries of the time' and alleged that

> if he had lived to see these times, and the good effects which the last 30 yeares peace have produced in this land, both for obedience to the lawes, as also in traffique, husbandry, civility, and learning, he would have omit-ted those passages which may seeme to lay either any particular aspersion upon some families, or generall upon the Nation.

Ware obligingly cut out references to major Anglo-Irish magnates whom Spenser had attacked (notably, the Earl of Ormond), and some of his harsher judgements on the native Irish, Old and New English inhabit-ants of Ireland in order to render the text of *A View* less offensive and (supposedly) less anachronistic.

28 For a more elaborate argument see Andrew Hadfield, 'Was Spenser's *View of the Present State of Ireland* censored? A review of the evidence', *Notes and Queries*, 239 (1994), pp. 459–63.

29 See Raymond Gillespie, 'The end of an era: Ulster and the outbreak of the 1641 uprising', in Ciarán Brady and Raymond Gillespie (eds)., *Natives and Newcomers: the making of Irish colonial society, 1534–1641* (Dublin: Irish Academic Press, 1986), pp. 191–213.

Ware's edition is therefore not a representation of a text that Spenser necessarily authorized, a marked contrast to the authoritative texts of much of his poetry, which Spenser saw into print and for which there remain no extant manuscripts. Both major twentieth-century editions of *A View* have been composite texts, the Variorum edition based on Ellesmere MS 7041 in the Huntington Library and W. L. Renwick's edition of 1934 on MS Rawlinson B 3478 in the Bodleian Library.[30] On the last page of the second manuscript, Thomas Man, Warden of the Stationers' Company (1597–8) has written 'Master Collinges I pray enter this Copie for mathew Lownes to be prynted whenever he do bringe other attoryte', an endorsement which suggests that perhaps Spenser was not party to the entering of the manuscript for publication as it is by no means the most obvious text for a final edition.

The problem with the production of composite texts is that what the modern reader is given is a text which never actually existed for contemporary readers, a work which was never actually read until assembled by the editor in question. In the absence of a critical consensus as to the manuscript which approximated most closely to Spenser's designs, this edition reproduces what is arguably the most significant text of *A View*. Ware's text is important for a number of obvious reasons. First, it was the text which was most widely known after 1633; second, Ware has regularized much of Spenser's spelling and punctuation, a labour he would surely have undertaken himself had he planned to see the work into print, so that the work is much more accessible to a modern reader than the convoluted and arcane style and irregular orthography reproduced in the Variorum text; third, Ware includes certain sections which have the appearance of great importance yet which do not appear in all manuscripts, notably the passage concerning the matter of Britain preserved only in the manuscript in the State Papers, surely a significant detail, and much of the Scottish material (see pp. 44–6). Clearly such arguments are not conclusive, but they do suggest that Ware's version of *A View* should not be dismissed as simply a corrupt text; it has a claim to stand as an important document of early modern England and Ireland. Indeed, the search for a fugitive holograph manuscript has devalued Ware's edition, and resulted in a situation in which *A View* is much cited but little read.

30 For a discussion of the manuscripts see the Variorum edition, Appendix III, Sect. C, pp. 506–24

In one area the first published text is obviously 'corrupt', rather than simply being out of agreement with the various manuscripts which other editors have judged to be more authoritative, namely the excisions performed by Ware to neutralize *A View*'s capacity to offend its readers.[31] Accordingly, we have included an appendix of these omissions based on the list provided in the Variorum edition, rather than cluttering up the text with these included in square brackets and so depart from our principle of providing a text which actually existed. We have attempted to keep notes to a minimum so that the text can stand as a narrative in its own right and explain itself wherever possible. Ware's footnotes are included in the text, marked by asterisks; his substantial annotations are included in Appendix I. We have, however, provided a glossary so that readers can familiarize themselves with obscure or difficult words, a framework of the major events, and a summary of much important criticism in the form of an annotated bibliography as a guide to further reading.

---

31 We have used the 1809 reprint of Ware's edition, which contains some minor modifications in terms of punctuation and capitalization.

Point of Dunluce

The Scots

ANTRIM

MacNeils

Knockfergus ▲

DONEGAL
(TYRCONNELL)

COLRANE

Castleliffer ■
Castlefinn ■ Strabane

Belfast ▲ □ The Ardes

ULSTER

O'Donnells

TYRONE

O'Neils

Blackfort ■

Armagh ●

Fertoghe

Savages
(The Little
Ardes

DOWN

Ballyshannon ▲
Bundroise ■
Belleek ▲

*Lough
Erne*

FERMANAGH

O'Rourkes

Enniskillen ▲

Blackwater

Armagh ●

ARMAGH

Newry ▲

Carlingford ●
Greencastle ●
Cattletown ●

CONNAUGHT

SLIGO

*Clan
MacCostulagh*

MAYO

*Burkes of
MacWilliam
Euter*

Cuillens

LEITRIM

The Breny

ROSCOMMON

O'Connor Roo

Moneveur ●

O'Farrells

MONAGHAN

MacMahons

Monaghan ▲▲

Magures

Belturbet ■

CAVAN

O'Reillys

Lough Sheelin

LONGFORD
(THE ANALY)

**WEST
MEATH**

Fertullagh

Mullingar ●

Dundalk ▲

LOUTH

Ardy ●

Kells ●

Drogheda ●

EAST MEATH

MEATH

ULSTER

House
of
Roscommon ●

Castle of
Athlone ▲ Athlone

Trim ●

GALWAY
(CLANRICKARD)

*Bermighams
Burkes of
MacWilliam
Eighter*

Garendow ●

Galway ●

Corrandoo ●

KINGS
(OFFALY)

Philipstown ●
(Fort of Offaly)

MacCoghlans

KILDARE

DUBLIN

Dublin ●

Three Castles ●
WICKLOW
O'Byrnes

CLARE
(THOMOND)

O'Connors

O'Molloys

Maryborough ●
(Fort of Leix)

QUEENS
(LEIX)

O'Moores

Athy ●

Talbotstown ■
O'Tooles
Ballinecor ▲▲

*Western
Sea*

CONNAUGHT

O'Briens

MacNemaras
(Mortimer's country)

Clare Castle ●

Killaloe ▲
(Clarifort)

O'Carrols

TIPPERARY
(LIBERTY AND CROSS)

Upper Ossery ●

CARLOW

KnoKloc ▲
▲

Keatings

Cavanaghs

ArKlow ●

Shillelagh ●

FERNS

MacMahone

Limerick ●

Thurles ●

Cashel ●

Butlers

Butlers

Kilkenny ●

Fern
Castle ▲

MacSheehys

LIMERICK

Kilmarnock ●

Aheulow ●

Kilpatrick ●

KILKENNY

New Ross ●

WEXFORD

Wexford ●

KERRY

Smerwick ●

Castlemaine ▲

Kilmore ● Kilcolman ●

Suttevant ●

White
Knight's
Country

Roches

Burkes

WATERFORD

LEINSTER

Binglecush ●

DESMOND

MacSweenys

CORK

Mourne ●

Cork ●

Youghal ●

Macarthy Mores
The Bantry ▲

Kinsale ●
Courcys ▲

MUNSTER

Arundel Castle ●

MUNSTER

*Southern
Sea*

Boundaries of provinces ━ ━ ━
Established counties ┈┈┈┈┈
Hypothetical counties ─ ─ ─
Sixteenth-century English Pale ★★★★
Temporary garrisons ■
Permanent garrisons ▲
Other places ●

A View of the
State of Ireland

TO THE

RIGHT HONORABLE

THOMAS LO. VISCOVNT WENTWORTH,[1]

LO. DEPVTY GENERALL

OF

IRELAND,

LO. PRESIDENT OF HIS MAIESTIES COVNCELL ESTABLISHED IN THE NORTH
PARTS OF ENGLAND, AND ONE OF HIS MAIESTIES MOST HONORABLE
PRIVIE COVNCELL.

RIGHT HONORABLE,

The sense of that happy peace, which by the divine providence this Kingdome hath enjoyed, since the beginning of the raigne of his late Majestie of ever sacred memory, doth then take the deeper impression, when these our halcyon dayes are compared with the former turbulent and tempestuous times, and with the miseries (of severall kindes) incident unto them. Those calamities are fully set out, and to the life by Mr. Spenser, with a discovery of their causes, and remedies, being for the most part excellent grounds of reformation. And so much may be justly expected from him in regard of his long abode and experience of this Kingdome. In these respects, and for other

1   Sir Thomas Wentworth, Earl of Strafford (1593–1641). Ruthless Lord Deputy of
Ireland (1633–41), notable for attempting to make as much money for the Crown as
possible and playing off Catholics against Protestants in order to secure New English
rule in Ireland. He was impeached and executed in 1641 after his Irish enemies
presented their grievances to the Long Parliament, a prelude to the English Civil
War.

good uses, which the collections (now communicated) doe afford for matter of history and policy, I am incouraged to dedicate them to your Lordship, and humbly to desire your favourable acceptance of them, and of

> *Your Lordships ever*
>
> *humbly devoted,*
>
> JAMES WARE.

The Preface

How far these collections may conduce to the knowledge of the *antiquities* and *state* of this Land, let the fit reader judge: yet something I may not passe by touching Mr. *Edmund Spenser* & the worke it selfe, lest I should seeme to offer injury to his worth, by others so much celebrated. Hee was borne in *London* of an ancient and noble family, and brought up in the Vniversitie of *Cambridge*, where (as the fruites of his after labours doe manifest) he mispent not his time. After this he became Secretary to *Arthur* Lord *Grey* of *Wilton*, Lord Deputy of *Ireland*;[2] a valiant and worthy Governour; and shortly after for his services to the Crowne, he had bestowed upon him by Queene *Elizabeth*, 3000 acres of land in the Countie of *Corke*. There hee finished the latter part of that excellent poem of his *Faery Queene*, which was soone after unfortunately lost by the disorder and abuse of his servant, whom he had sent before him into *England*, being then *á rebellibus* (as *Camdens** words are) *è laribus ejectus & bonis spoliatus*.[3] He deceased at *Westminster* in the year 1599. (others have it wrongly 1598.) soone after his returne into *England*, and was buried according to his owne desire, in the collegiat Church there, neere unto *Chaucer*, whom he worthily imitated, (at the costes of *Robert* Earle of *Essex*,)[4] whereupon this Epitaph was framed,

---

*   *Annal. rer. Anglic. & Hibern. pag. 729, edit. 1625.*

2   Arthur, Lord Grey De Wilton (1536–93). Lord Deputy of Ireland (1580–2). Spenser served as his secretary and later defended Grey from charges of ruthless cruelty (see below).

3   'Ejected from his home and deprived of his property' (we owe this translation to Mr R. T. Pritchard).

4   Robert Devereux. Second Earl of Essex (1566–1601). Courtier and soldier who was

Hîc prope Chaucerum *situs est* Spenserius, *illi proximus ingenio, proximus
     ut tumulo.*
Hîc prope Chaucerum Spensere *poeta poetam conderis, & versu quàm
     tumulo propior.*
Anglica te vivo vixit plausitq poesis, nunc moritura timet te moriente mori.[5]

As for his worke now published,* although it sufficiently testifieth his
learning and deepe judgement, yet we may wish that in some passages it
had bin tempered with more moderation. The troubles and miseries of
the time when he wrote it, doe partly excuse him, And surely wee may
conceive, that if hee had lived to see these times, and the good effects
which the last 30 yeares peace have produced in this land, both for obedience to the lawes, as also in traffique, husbandry, civility, & learning,
he would have omitted those passages which may seeme to lay either
any particular aspersion upon some families, or generall upon the Nation. For now we may truly say, *jam cuncti gens una sumus,*[6] and that
upon just cause those ancient statutes, wherein the natives of *Irish* descent were held to be, and named *Irish* enemies, and wherein those of
English bloud were forbidden to marry and commerce with them, were
repealed by act of Parlament,† in the raigne of our late Soveraigne King
JAMES of ever blessed memory.[7]

   His proofes (although most of them conjecturall) concerning the
originall of the language, customes of the Nations, and the first peopling
of the severall parts of the Iland, are full of good reading; and doe shew
a sound judgement. They may be further confirmed by comparing them

---

*   *Ex Bibliotheca Remi in Christo patris D. Jacobi Vsserij Archisp Armachani.*
†   *Vid. lib. Statut. edit. Dubl. an. 1621. pag. 427.*

   Lord Lieutenant of Ireland (1599–1600). Generally thought to have been Spenser's
   last patron. Executed after his rebellion in 1601, which followed on from his un-
   satisfactory campaign against Hugh O'Neill.

5   'Here, near Chaucer, lies Spenser, closest to him in ability, and next to him in his
   grave. Here, you the best poet, Spenser, are interred near the poet Chaucer, and
   closer to him in poetry than in the grave. While you were alive, English poetry was
   alive and celebrated itself, now it fears death because it is about to die' (we owe this
   translation to Mr R. T. Pritchard).

6   'Now we are all one nation' (we owe this translation to Mr R. T. Pritchard).

7   Ware is referring to the Statutes of Kilkenny (1366), which forbade English and Irish
   to mix or to intermarry.

with *Richard Creagh's* Booke *de linguâ Hibernicâ*, which is yet extant in the originall manuscript, & althogh mixed with matter of story, leaning too much to some fabulous traditions, yet in other respects worthy of light.

Touching the generall scope intended by the author for the reformation of abuses and ill customes, This we may say, that although very many have taken paines in the same subject, during the raigne of Queene *Elizabeth*, and some before, as the author of the booke intituled *Salus populi**, and after him *Patrick Finglas*†,[8] cheife Baron of the Exchequer here, and afterwardes cheife Justice of the common pleas, yet none came so neere to the best grounds for reformation, a few passages excepted, as *Spenser* hath done in this. Some notes I have added, although not intending any, untill the fourth part of the Booke was printed.

---

*   *Floruit sub. initium reg. Edw. 4.*

†   *Floruit sub. Hen. 8.*

8   Sir Patrick Finglas, Chief Baron of the Exchequer, author of a treatise on the reformation of Ireland in the late 1520s.

Ancient Irish Histories.

A
View
of the
State of Ireland,

WRITTEN

Dialogue-wise,

BETWEENE

EUDOXUS and IRENÆUS.

BY

EDMUND SPENSER, Esq.
In the Yeare
1596.

Dublin:
Printed by the Society of Stationers,
M.DCXXXIII.

A View of the State of Ireland,

WRITTEN DIALOGUE-WISE BETWEENE EUDOXUS AND IRENÆUS.

Eudox. But if that countrey of Ireland, whence you lately came,[9] be of so goodly and commodious a soyl, as you report, I wonder that no course is taken for the turning thereof to good uses, and reducing that nation to better government and civility.

Iren. Marry so there have bin divers good plottes devised, and wise councels cast already about reformation of that realme, but they say, it is the fatall destiny of that land, that no purposes whatsoever which are meant for her good, will prosper or take good effect, which, whether it proceed from the very genius of the soyle, or influence of the starres, or that Almighty God hath not yet appointed the time of her reformation, or that hee reserveth her in this unquiet state still for some secret scourge, which shall by her come unto England, it is hard to be knowne, but yet much to be feared.

Eudox. Surely I suppose this but a vaine conceipt of simple men, which judge things by their effects, and not by their causes; for I would rather thinke the cause of this evill, which hangeth upon that countrey, to proceed rather of the unsoundnes of the councels, and plots, which you say have bin often-times laid for the reformation, or of faintnes in following and effecting the same, then of any such fatall course appointed of God, as you misdeem; but it is the manner of men, that when they are fallen into any absurdity, or their actions succeede not as they would, they are alwayes readie to impute the blame thereof

9 *A View* is not set in Ireland, but, presumably, England.

unto the heavens, so to excuse their owne follies and imperfections. So have I heard it often wished also, (even of some whose great wisedomes in opinion should seeme to judge more soundly of so weighty a consideration) that all that land were a sea-poole; which kinde of speech, is the manner rather of desperate men farre driven, to wish the utter ruine of that which they cannot redress, then of grave councellors, which ought to think nothing so hard, but that thorough wisedome, it may be mastered and subdued, since the Poet saith, that "the wise man shall rule even over the starres," much more over the earth; for were it not the part of a desperate phisitian to wish his diseased patient dead, rather then to apply the best indeavour of his skill for his recovery.[10] But since we are so farre entered, let us, I pray you, a little devise of those evils, by which that country is held in this wretched case, that it cannot (as you say) be recured. And if it be not paineful to you, tell us what things during your late continuance there, you observed to bee most offensive, and greatest impeachment to the good rule and government thereof.

Iren. Surely Eudox. The evils which you desire to be recounted are very many, and almost countable with those which were hidden in the basket of Pandora. But since you please, I will out of that infinite number, reckon but some that are most capitall, and commonly occurrant both in the life and conditions of private men, as also in the managing of publicke affaires and pollicy, the which you shall understand to be of divers natures, as I observed them: for some of them are of verie great antiquitie and continuance; others more late and of lesse indurance; others dayly growing and increasing continuallie by their evill occasions, which are every day offered.

Eudox. Tell them then, I pray you, in the same order that you have now rehearsed them; for there can be no better method then this which the very matter itselfe offereth. And when you have reckoned all the evils, let us heare your opinion for the redressing of them: after which there will perhaps of it selfe appeare some reasonable way to settle a sound and perfect rule of government, by shunning the former evils, and following the offered good. The which method we may learne of the wise Phisitians, which first require that the malady be knowne thoroughly, and discovered: afterwards to teach how to cure

10   It was common in the Renaissance to describe the State as a body: elsewhere in *A View* Spenser uses the same comparison.

and redresse it: and lastly doe prescribe a dyet, with straight rule and orders to be dayly observed, for feare of relapse into the former disease, or falling into some other more dangerous then it.

Iren.   I will then according to your advisement begin to declare the evils, which seeme to me most hurtfull to the common-weale of that land; and first, those (I say) which were most auncient and long growne. And they also are of three sorts: The first in the Lawes, the second in Customes, and the last in Religion.

Eudox.   Why, Irenæus, can there be any evill in the Lawes; can things, which are ordained for the good and safety of all, turne to the evill and hurt of them? This well I wote both in that state, and in all other, that were they not contained in duty with feare of law, which restraineth offences, and inflicteth sharpe punishment to misdoers, no man should enjoy any thing; every mans hand would be against another. Therefore, in finding fault with the lawes, I doubt me, you shall much overshoote your selfe, and make me the more dislike your other dislikes of that government.

Iren.   The lawes Eudox. I doe not blame for themselves, knowing right well that all lawes are ordained for the good of the common-weale, and for repressing of licentiousness and vice; but it falleth out in lawes, no otherwise then it doth in physick, which was at first devised, and is yet daylie ment, and ministred for the health of the patient. But neverthelesse we often see, that either thorough ignorance of the disease, or thorough unseasonablenesse of the time, or other accidents comming betweene, in stead of good, it worketh hurt, and, out of one evill, throweth the patient into many miseries. So the lawes were at first intended for the reformation of abuses, and peaceable continuance of the subject; but are sithence either disannulled, or quite prevaricated thorough change and alteration of times, yet are they good still in themselves; but, in that commonwealth which is ruled by them, they worke not that good which they should, and sometimes also that evill which they would not.

Eudox.   Whether doe you mean this by the common-lawes of that realme, or by the Statute Lawes, and acts of Parliaments?

Iren.   Surely by them both; for even the common law being that which William of Normandy brought in with his conquest,[11] and laid upon

11   Irenius is referring to the introduction of the Common Law by William the Conqueror in the late eleventh century.

the neck of England, though perhaps it fitted well with the state of England then being, and was readily obeyed thorough the power of the commander, which had before subdued the people unto him, and made easie way to the setling of his will, yet with the state of Ireland peradventure it doth not so well agree, being a people very stubborne, and untamed, or if it were ever tamed, yet now lately having quite shooken off their yoake, and broken the bonds of their obedience. For England (before the entrance of the Conqueror) was a peaceable kingdome, and but lately inured to the milde and goodly government of Edward, surnamed the Confessor; besides now lately growne into a loathing and detestation of the unjust and tyrannous rule of Harold an usurper, which made them the more willing to accept of any reasonable conditions and order of the new victor, thinking surely that it could be no worse then the latter, and hoping well it would be as good as the former; yet what the proofe of first bringing in and establishing of those lawes was, was to many full bitterly made knowne. But with Ireland it is farre otherwise; for it is a nation ever acquainted with warres, though but amongst themselves, and in their owne kinde of military discipline, trayned up ever from their youthes, which they have never yet beene taught to lay aside, nor made to learn obedience unto lawes, scarcely to know the name of law, but in stead thereof have alwayes preserved and kept their owne law, which is the Brehon law.

Eudox. What is that which you call the Brehon law? it is a word unto us altogether unknowne.

Iren. It is a rule of right unwritten, but delivered by tradition from one to another, in which oftentimes there appeareth great shew of equity, in determining the right betweene party and party, but in many things repugning quite both to Gods law, and mans: As for example in the case of Murder, the Brehon, that is their judge, will compound betweene the murderer, and the friends of the party murdered, which prosecute the action, that the malefactor shall give unto them, or to the child, or wife of him that is slain a recompence, which they call an Eriach: By which vilde law of theirs, many murders amongst them are made up, and smothered. And this judge being as hee is called the Lords Brehon, adjudgeth for the most part, a better share unto his Lord, that is the Lord of the soyle, or the head of that sept, and also unto himselfe for his judgement a greater portion, then unto the plaintiffes or parties grieved.

Eudox.   This is a most wicked law indeed: but I trust it is not now used in Ireland, since the kings of England have had the absolute dominion thereof, and established their owne lawes there.

Iren.   Yes truly; for there be many wide countries in Ireland, which the lawes of England were never established in, nor any acknowledgment of subjection made, and also even in those which are subdued, and seeme to acknowledge subjection; yet the same Brehon law is practised among themselves, by reason, that, dwelling as they doe, whole nations and septs of the Irish together, without any Englishman amongst them, they may doe what they list, and compound or altogether conceale amongst themselves their owne crimes, of which no notice can be had, by them which would and might amend the same, by the rule of the lawes of England.

Eudox.   What is this which you say? And is there any part of that realme, or any nation therein, which have not yet beene subdued to the crowne of England? Did not the whole realme universally accept and acknowledge our late Prince of famous memory Henry the viiith for their onely King and Liege Lord?[12]

Iren.   Yes verily: in a Parliament holden in the time of Sir Anthony Saint-Leger, then Lord Deputy, all the Irish Lords and principall men came in, and being by faire meanes wrought thereunto, acknowledged King Henry for their Soveraigne Lord, reserving yet (as some say) unto themselves all their owne former priviledges and seignories inviolate.

Eudox.   Then by that acceptance of his soveraignty they also accepted of his lawes. Why then should any other lawes be now used amongst them?

Iren.   True it is that thereby they bound themselves to his lawes and obedience, and in case it had beene followed upon them, as it should have beene, and a government thereupon setled among them agreeable thereunto, they should have beene reduced to perpetuall civilitie, and contained in continuall duty. But what bootes it to break a colte, and to let him straight runne loose at randome. So were these people

---

12   Eudoxus is referring to the Act which declared Henry VIII King of Ireland in the Irish Parliament, 18 June 1541. Hitherto, Ireland had been a lordship of the English crown; henceforth it was a kingdom ruled by the English monarch. Irenius is arguing that this was merely a cosmetic change.

at first well handled, and wisely brought to acknowledge allegiance to the Kings of England: but, being straight left unto themselves and their owne inordinate life and manners, they eftsoones forgot what before they were taught, and so soone as they were out of sight, by themselves shook of their bridles, and beganne to colte anew, more licentiously than before.

Eudox.   It is a great pittie, that so good an opportunity was omitted, and so happie an occasion foreslacked, that might have beene the eternall good of the land. But doe they not still acknowledge that submission?

Iren.   No, they doe not: for now the heires and posterity of them which yeelded the same, are (as they say) either ignorant thereof, or do wilfully deny, or steadfastly disavow it.

Eudox.   How can they so doe justly? Doth not the act of the parent in any lawfull graunt or conveyance, bind their heires for ever thereunto? Sith then the auncestors of those that now live, yeelded themselves then subjects and liegemen, shall it not tye their children to the same subjection?

Iren.   They say no: for their auncestors had no estate in any their lands, seigniories, or hereditaments, longer then during their owne lifes, as they alledge, for all the Irish doe hold their land by Tanistrie; which is (say they) no more but a personall estate for his life time, that is, Tanist, by reason that he is admitted thereunto by election of the countrey.

Eudox.   What is this which you call Tanist and Tanistry? They be names and termes never heard of nor knowne to us.

Iren.   It is a custome amongst all the Irish, that presently after the death of any of their chiefe Lords or Captaines, they doe presently assemble themselves to a place generally appointed and knowne unto them to choose another in his steed, where they doe nominate and elect for the most part, not the eldest sonne, nor any of the children of the Lord deceased, but the next to him of blood, that is the eldest and worthiest, as commonly the next brother unto him if he have any, or the next cousin, or so forth, as any is elder in that kinred or sept, and then next to him doe they choose the next of the blood to be Tanist, who shall next succeed him in the said Captainry, if he live thereunto.

Eudox.   Doe they not use any ceremony in this election? for all barbarous nations are commonly great observers of ceremonies and superstitious rites.

Iren. They use to place him that shalbe their Captaine, upon a stone alwayes reserved for that purpose, and placed commonly upon a hill: In some of which I have seen formed and ingraven a foot, which they say was the measure of their first Captaines foot, whereon hee standing, receives an oath to preserve all the auncient former customes of the countrey inviolable, and to deliver up the succession peaceably to his Tanist, and then hath a wand delivered unto him by some whose proper office that is: after which, descending from the stone, he turneth himselfe round, thrice forward, and thrice backward.

Eudox. But how is the Tanist chosen?

Iren. They say he setteth but one foot upon the stone, and receiveth the like oath that the Captaine did.

Eudox. Have you ever heard what was the occasion and first beginning of this custome? for it is good to know the same, and may perhaps discover some secret meaning and intent therein, very materiall to the state of that government.

Iren. I have heard that the beginning and cause of this ordinance amongst the Irish, was specially for the defence and maintenance of their lands in their posteritie, and for excluding all innovation or alienation thereof unto strangers, and specially to the English. For when their Captaine dieth, if the signiorie should descend to his child, and he perhaps an infant, another might peradventure step in between, or thrust him out by strong hand, being then unable to defend his right, or to withstand the force of a forreiner; and therefore they doe appoint the eldest of the kinne to have the signiorie, for that he commonly is a man of stronger years, and better experience to maintain the inheritance, and to defend the countrey, either against the next bordering Lords, which use commonly to incroach one upon another, as one is stronger, or against the English, which they thinke lye still in waite to wype them out of their lands and territoryes. And to this end the Tanist is alwayes ready knowne, if it should happen the Captaine suddenly to dye, or to be slaine in battell, or to be out of the countrey, to defend and keepe it from all such doubts and dangers. For which cause the Tanist hath also a share of the countrey allotted unto him, and certaine cuttings and spendings upon all the inhabitants under the Lord.

Eudox.　When I hear this word Tanist, it bringeth to my remembrance what I have read of Tania, that it should signifie a province or seigniorie, as Aquitania, Lusitania, and Britania, the which some thinke to be derived of Dania, that is, from the Danes, but, I think, amisse. But sure it seemeth, that it came anciently from those barbarous nations that over-ranne the world, which possessed those dominions, whereof they are now so called. And so it may well be that from thence the first originall of this word Tanist and Tanistry came,* and the custome thereof hath sithence, as many others else beene continued. But to that generall subjection of the land, whereof wee formerly spake, me seems that this custome or tenure can be no barre nor impeachment, seeing that in open Parliament by their said acknowledgement they waved the benefite thereof, and submitted themselves to the benefite of their new Soveraigne.

Iren.　Yea, but they say, as I earst tolde you, that they reserved their titles, tenures, and seigniories whole and sound to themselves, and for proof alledge, that they have ever sithence remained to them untouched, so as now to alter them, should, (say they) be a great wrong.

Eudox.　What remedie is there then, or meanes to avoide this inconvenience? for, without first cutting of this dangerous custome, it seemeth hard to plant any sound ordinance, or reduce them to a civill government, since all their ill customes are permitted unto them.

Iren.　Surely nothing hard: for by this Act of Parliament whereof wee speake, nothing was given to King Henry which he had not before from his auncestors, but onely the bare name of a King; for all other absolute power of principality he had in himselfe before derived from many former Kings, his famous progenitours and worthy conquered of that and. The which, sithence they first conquered and by force subdued unto them, what needed afterwards to enter into any such idle termes with them to be called their King, when it is in the power of the conqueror to take upon himself what title he will, over his dominions conquered. For all is the conquerours, as Tully to Brutus saith.[13] Therefore (me seemes) instead of so great and meritorious a

---

*　See whether it may not be more fitly derived from Thane, which word was commonly used among the Danes, and also among the Saxons in England, for a noble man, and a principall officer.

13　This reference has not been traced.

service as they boast they performed to the King, in bringing all the Irish to acknowledge him for their Liege, they did great hurt unto his title, and have left a perpetuall gall in the minde of the people, who before being absolutely bound to his obedience, are now tyed with but termes, whereas else both their lives, their lands, and their liberties were in his free power to appoint what tenures, what lawes, what conditions hee would over them, which were all his: against which there could be no rightfull resistance, or if there were, he might, when he would, establish them with a stronger hand.

Eudox.   Yea, but perhaps it seemed better unto that noble King to bring them by their owne accord to his obedience, and to plant a peaceable government amongst them, then by such violent means to pluck them under. Neither yet hath he thereby lost any thing that he formerly had; for, having all before absolutely in his owne power, it remaineth so still unto him, he having thereby neither forgiven nor forgone any thing thereby unto them, but having received somthing from them, that is, a more voluntary and loyall subjection. So as her Majesty may yet, when it shall please her, alter any thing of those former ordinances, or appoint other lawes, that may be more both for her owne behoofe, and for the good of that people.

Iren.   Not so: for it is not so easie, now that things are growne unto an habit, and have their certaine course to change the channell, and turne their streames another way, for they may have now a colorable pretence to withstand such innovations, having accepted of other lawes and rules already.

Eudox.   But you say they do not accept of them, but delight rather to leane to their old customes and Brehon lawes, though they be more unjust and also more inconvenient for the common people, as by your late relation of them I have gathered. As for the lawes of England they are surely most just and most agreeable, both with the government and with the nature of the people. How falls it then that you seeme to dislike of them, as not so meete for that realme of Ireland, and not onely the common Law, but also the Statutes and Actes of Parliament, which were specially provided and intended for the onlie benefit thereof?

Iren.   I was about to have told you my reason therein, but that your selfe drew me away with other questions, for I was shewing you by what meanes, and by what sort the positive lawes were first brought

in and established by the Norman Conquerour: which were not by
him devised nor applyed to the state of the realme then being, nor as
yet might best be, (as should by lawgivers principally be regarded)
but were indeed the very lawes of his owne countrey of Normandie.
The condition whereof, how farre it differeth from this of England, is
apparent to every least judgement. But to transferre the same lawes
for the governing of the realme of Ireland, was much more inconvenient and unmeete; for he found a better advantage of the time, then
was in the planting of them in Ireland, and followed the execution of
them with more severity, and was also present in person to overlooke
the Magistrates, and to overawe these subjects with the terrour of his
sword, and countenance of his Majesty. But not so in Ireland, for they
were otherwise affected, and yet doe so remaine, so as the same lawes
(me seemes) can ill fit with their disposition, or worke that reformation that is wished. For lawes ought to be fashioned unto the manners
and conditions of the people, to whom they are meant, and not to be
imposed upon them according to the simple rule of right, for then (as
I said) in stead of good they may worke ill, and pervert iustice to
extreame iniustice. For hee that transferres the lawes of the
Lacedemonians to the people of Athens, should finde a great absurditie
and inconvenience. For those lawes of Lacedemon were devised by
Licurgus as most proper and best agreeing with that people, whom
hee knew to be enclined altogether to warres, and therefore wholly
trained them up even from their cradles in armes and military exer-
cises, cleane contrary to the institution of Solon, who, in his lawes to
the Athenians, laboured by all meanes to temper their warlike courages
with sweet delightes of learning and sciences, so that asmuch as the
one excelled in armes, the other exceeded in knowledge.[14] The like
regard and moderation ought to be had in tempering, and managing,
this stubborne nation of the Irish to bring them from their delight of

14 Solon (*c*.640–*c*.558 BC), established most of Athens' laws. He was also a poet. Rich-
     ard Beacon's treatise on the reformation of Ireland, probably written just before
     Spenser's, was entitled *Solon his Follie* (1594). Beacon, like Spenser, was an English
     settler on the Munster Plantation. The Lacedemonians are better known as the
     Spartans, a warlike and ascetic people of Greece who have given their name to the
     modern adjective, 'Spartan'. Lycurgus was their legendary ancient law-giver, about
     whom nothing is known. The Spartan constitution was famed for encouraging
     citizens to obey the law, and avoid corruption and selfish luxury.

licentious barbarisme unto the love of goodnes and civilite.

Eudox. I cannot see how that may better be then by the discipline of the lawes of England: for the English were, at first, as stoute and warlike a people as ever the Irish, and yet you see are now brought unto that civillity, that no nation in the world excelleth them in all goodly conversation, and all the studies of knowledge and humanitie.

Iren. What they now be, both you and I see very well, but by how many thornie and hard wayes they are come thereunto, by how many civill broiles, by how many tumultuous rebellions, that even hazzarded oftentimes the whole safety of the kingdome, may easily be considered: all which they neverthelesse fairely overcame, by reason of the continuall presence of their King; whose onely person is oftentimes in stead of an army, to containe the unrulie people from a thousand evill occasions, which this wretched kingdome, for want thereof, is dayly carried into. The which, whensoever they make head, no lawes, no penalties, can restraine, but that they doe, in the violence of that furie, tread downe and trample under foote all both divine and humane things, and the lawes themselves they doe specially rage at, and rend in peeces, as most repugnant to their libertie and naturall freedome, which in their madnes they affect.

Eudox. It is then a very unseasonable time to plead law, when swords are in the hands of the vulgar, or to thinke to retaine them with feare of punishments, when they looke after liberty, and shake off all government.

Iren. Then so it is with Ireland continually, Eudoxus; for the sword was never yet out of their hand, but when they are weary of warres, and brought downe to extreame wretchednesse; then they creepe a little perhaps and sue for grace, till they have gotten new breath and recovered their strength againe. So as it is vaine to speake of planting lawes, and plotting pollicie, till they be altogether subdued.

Eudox. Were they not so at the first conquering of them by Strongbowe,[15] in the time of King Henry the second? was there not a thorough way then made by the sword, for the imposing of the lawes

---

15 Richard de Clare, Earl of Pembroke, known as Strongbow. He came to Ireland in 1170, on the invitation of Dermot MacMurrogh, King of Leinster, whose daughter he married. The Norman invasion of Ireland dates from 1169. Henry established English law during his expedition to Ireland in 1172.

upon them? and were they not then executed with such a mightie hand as you said was used by the Norman Conquerour? What oddes is there then in this case? why should not the same lawes take as good effect in that people as they did here, being in like sort prepared by the sword, and brought under by extreamity? and why should they not continue in as good force and vigour for the containing of the people?

Iren.   The case yet is not like, but there appeareth great oddes betweene them: for, by the conquest of Henry the second, true it is that the Irish were utterly vanquished and subdued, so as no enemy was able to hold up head against his power, in which their weaknes hee brought in his lawes, and settled them as now they there remaine; like as William the Conquerour did; so as in thus much they agree; but in the rest, that is the chiefest, they varie: for to whom did King Henry the second impose those lawes? not to the Irish, for the most part of them fled from his power, into deserts and mountaines, leaving the wyde countrey to the conquerour: who in their stead eftsoones placed English men, who possessed all their lands and did quite shut out the Irish, or the most part of them. And to those new inhabitants and colonies he gave his lawes, to wit, the same lawes under which they were borne and bred, the which it was no difficultie to place amongst them, being formerly well inured thereunto; unto whom afterwards there repaired diverse of the poore distressed people of the Irish, for succour and reliefe; of whom, such as they thought fit for labour, and industriously disposed, as the most part of their baser sort are, they received unto them as their vassalls, but scarcely vouchsafed to impart unto them the benefit of those lawes, under which themselves lived, but every one made his will and commandement a law unto his owne vassall: thus was not the law of England ever properly applyed unto the Irish nation, as by a purposed plot of government, but as they could insinuate and steale themselves under the same, by their humble carriage and submission.

Eudox.   How comes it then to passe, that having beene once so low brought, and thoroughly subjected, they afterwards lifted up themselves so strongly againe, and sithence doe stand so stiffely against all rule and government?

Iren.   They say that they continued in that lowlinesse, untill the time that the division betweene the two houses of Lancaster and York arose for the crowne of England: at which time all the great English Lords and Gentlemen, which had great possessions in Ireland, repaired over hither into England, some to succour their friends here, and to strengthen their partie for to obtain the crowne; others to defend their lands and possessions here against such as hovered after the same upon hope of the alteration of the kingdome, and successe of that side which they favoured and affected.[16] Then the Irish whom before they had banished into the mountaines, where they lived onely upon white meates, as it is recorded, seeing now their lands so dispeopled, and weakened, came downe into all the plaines adjoyning, and thence expelling those few English that remained, repossessed them againe, since which they have remained in them, and, growing greater, have brought under them many of the English, which were before their Lords. This was one of the occasions by which all those countreys, which lying neere unto any mountaines or Irish desarts, had beene planted with English, were shortly displanted and lost. As namely in Mounster all the lands adjoyning unto Slewlogher, Arlo, and the bog of Allon.[17] In Connaght all the Countries bordering upon the Curlues, Mointerolis, and Orourkes countrey. In Leinster all the lands bordering unto the mountaines of Glanmalour, unto Shillelah, unto the Brackenah, and Polmonte. In Ulster, all the countreys near unto Tirconnel, Tyrone, and the Scottes.

Eudox. Surely this was a great violence: but yet by your speach it seemeth that onely the countreys and valleyes neere adjoining unto those mountaines and desarts, were thus recovered by the Irish: but how comes it now that we see almost all that realme repossessed of them? Was there any more such evill occasions growing by the troubles of England? Or did the Irish, out of those places so by them gotten, break further and stretch themselves out thorough the whole land? for now, for ought that I can understand, there is no part but the bare English Pale, in which the Irish have not the greatest footing.

Iren. Both out of these small beginnings by them gotten neare to the

16 The Wars of the Roses were the most important civil wars in English political memory and led to the establishment of the Tudor dynasty in 1485. They were a series of interrelated battles and civil disturbances from *c.*1450 to 1487, concerning the question of who should rule England and how, fought between varying factions of nobles.

17 Spenser includes the areas surrounding his own estate. Arlo Hill (Galtymore) overlooked Kilcolman. He refers to the Bog of Allen and Arlo Hill in *The Faerie Queene*.

mountaines, did they spread themselves into the inland; and also, to their further advantage, there did other like unhappy accidents happen out of England; which gave heart and good opportunity to them to regaine their old possessions: For, in the raigne of King Edward the fourth, things remained yet in the same state that they were after the late breaking out of the Irish, which I spake of; and that noble Prince began to cast an eye unto Ireland, and to minde the reformation of things there runne amisse: for he sent over his brother the worthy Duke of Clarence, who having married the heire of the Earle of Ulster, and by her having all the Earledome of Ulster, and much in Meath and in Mounster, very carefully went about the redressing of all those late evills, and though he could not beate out the Irish againe, by reason of his short continuance, yet hee did shut them up within those narrow corners and glennes under the mountaines foote, in which they lurked, and so kept them from breaking any further, by building strong holdes upon every border, and fortifying all passages. Amongst the which hee repaired the castle of Clare in Thomond, of which countrey he had the inheritance, and of Mortimers lands adjoyning, which is now (by the Irish) called Killaloe. But the times of that good King growing also troublesome, did lett the thorough reformation of all things. And thereunto soone after was added another fatall mischiefe, which wrought a greater calamity then all the former. For the said Duke of Clarence, then Lord Lieutenant of Ireland, was, by practise of evill persons about the King, his brother, called thence away: and soone after, by sinister meanes, was cleane made away. Presently after whose death, all the North revolting, did set up Oneale for their Captaine, being before that of small power and regard: and there arose in that part of Thomond, one of the O-Briens, called Murrogh en-Ranagh, that is, Morrice of the Ferne, or wast wilde places, who, gathering unto him all the reliques of the discontented Irish, eftsoones surprised the said castle of Clare, burnt, and spoyled all the English there dwelling, and in short space possessed all that countrey beyond the river of Shanan and neere adjoyning: whence shortly breaking forth like a suddaine tempest he over-ran all Mounster and Connaght; breaking downe all the holds and fortresses of the English, defacing and utterly subverting all corporate townes, that were not strongly walled: for those he had no meanes nor engines to overthrow, neither indeed would hee stay at all about them, but speedily ran forward, counting his suddennesse his most advantage, that he might overtake the English before they could fortifie or gather themselves together. So in short space hee cleane wyped out many great townes, as first Inchequin, then Killalow, before called Clariford, also Thurles, Mourne, Buttevant, and many others, whose names I cannot remember, and of some of which there is now no memory nor signe remaining. Upon report whereof there flocked unto him all the scumme of the Irish out of all places, that ere long he had a mighty army, and thence marched foorth into Leinster, where he wrought great out-rages, wasting all the countrey where he went; for it was his policie to leave no hold behinde him, but to make all plaine and waste.[18] In which he soone after created himselfe King, and was called King of all Ireland; which before him I doe not reade that any did so generally, but onely Edward le Bruce.[19]

Eudox. What? was there ever any generall King of all Ireland? I never heard it before, but that it was alwayes (whilst it was under the Irish) divided into foure, and sometimes into five kingdomes or dominions. But this Edward le Bruce, what was hee, that could make himselfe King of all Ireland?

Iren. I would tell you, in case you would not challenge me anon for forgetting the matter which I had in hand, that is, the inconvenience and unfitnesse which I supposed to be in the lawes of the land.

Eudox. No surely, I have no cause, for neither is this impertinent thereunto; for sithence you did set your course (as I remember in your first part) to treate of the evils which hindered the peace and good ordering of that land, amongst which, that of the inconvenience in the lawes, was the first which you had in hand, this discourse of the over-running and wasting of the realme, is very materiall thereunto, for that it was the begining of al the other evils, which sithence have

---

18 Spenser's history of Irish rebellion from the twelfth century contains a number of inaccuracies; he has confused the Duke of Clarence who married the daughter of the Earl of Ulster with his ancestor, and, as a result, he misdates the rebellion of Murrogh en Ranagh, who died in 1383, as occurring in the fifteenth century. The recovery of the Irish really happened in the thirteenth century, not the Wars of the Roses. Spenser probably relied on his memory and oral sources for his history, as well as the chronicles he undoubtedly consulted.

19 Kings of Ireland actually existed much earlier, as English chronicles acknowledged. Edward the Bruce invaded Ireland from Scotland in 1315.

afflicted that land, and opened a way unto the Irish to recover their possession, and to beat out the English which had formerly wonne the same. And besides, it will give a great light both unto the second and third part, which is the redressing of those evils, and planting of some good forme or policy therin, by renewing the remembrance of these occasions and accidents, by which those ruines hapned, and laying before us the ensamples of those times, to be compared to ours, and to be warned by those which shall have to doe in the like. Therefore I pray you tell them unto us, and as for the point where you left, I will not forget afterwards to call you backe againe thereunto.

Iren. This Edw. le Bruce was brother of Robert le Bruce, who was King of Scotland, at such time as King Edward the second raigned here in England, and bare a most malicious and spightfull minde against King Edward, doing him all the scathe that hee could, and annoying his territoryes of England, whilest he was troubled with civill warres of his Barons at home. Hee also, to worke him the more mischiefe, sent over his said brother Edward with a power of Scottes and Red-shankes into Ireland, where, by the meanes of the Lacies, and of the Irish with whom they combined, they gave footing, and gathering unto him all the scatterlings and outlawes out of all the woods and mountaines, in which they long had lurked, marched foorth into the English Pale, which then was chiefly in the North, from the point of Donluce, and beyond unto Dublin: having in the middest of her Knockfergus, Belfast, Armagh, and Carlingford, which are now the most outbounds and abandoned places in the English Pale, and indeede not counted of the English Pale at all: for it stretcheth now no further then Dundalke towardes the North. There the said Edward le Bruce spoyled and burnt all the olde English Pale inhabitants, and sacked and rased all citties and corporate townes, no lesse then Murrough en Ranagh, of whom I earst tolde you: For hee wasted Belfast, Green-Castle, Kelles, Bellturbut, Castletowne, Newton, and many other very good townes and strong holdes: he rooted out the noble families of the Audlies, Talbotts, Tuchets, Chamberlaines, Maundevills, and the Savages[20] out of Ardes, though of the Lo. Savage their remaineth yet

---

20   The Savages, like the Lacys, were families of Anglo-Norman descent who came over in the wake of Henry II's invasion, and now made up the community of Old English.

an heire, that is now a poore gentleman of very meane condition, yet dwelling in the Ardes. And coming lastly to Dundalke, hee there made himselfe King, and raigned the space of one whole yeare, untill that Edward King of England, having set some quiet in his affaires at home, sent over the Lord Iohn Birmingham to be Generall of the warres against him, who, incountering him neere to Dundalke, over-threw his army, and slew him. Also hee presently followed the victory so hotly upon the Scottes, that hee suffered them not to breathe, or gather themselves together againe, untill they came to the sea-coast. Notwithstanding all the way that they fledde, for very rancor and despight, in their returne, they utterly consumed and wasted whatsoever they had before left unspoyled, so as of all townes, castles, forts, bridges, and habitations, they left not any sticke standing, nor any people remayning; for those few, which yet survived, fledde from their fury further into the English Pale that now is. Thus was all that goodly countrey utterly wasted. And sure it is yet a most beautifull and sweet countrey as any is under heaven, being stored throughout with many goodly rivers, replenished with all sorts of fish most abundantly, sprinkled with many very sweet ilands and goodly lakes, like little inland seas, that will carry even shippes upon their waters, adorned with goodly woods even fit for building of houses and ships, so commodiously, as that if some Princes in the world had them, they would soone hope to be lords of all the seas, and ere long of all the world: also full of very good ports and havens opening upon England, as inviting us to come unto them, to see what excellent commodities that countrey can afford, besides the soyle it selfe most fertile, fit to yeeld all kinde of fruit that shall be committed thereunto. And lastly, the heavens most milde and temperate, though somewhat more moist then the parts towards the West.

Eudox. Truly Iren. What with your praises of the countrey, and what with your discourse of the lamentable desolation therof, made by those Scottes, you have filled mee with a great compassion of their calamities, that I doe much pity that sweet land, to be subject to so many evills as I see more and more to be layde upon her, and doe halfe beginne to thinke, that it is (as you said at the beginning) her fatall misfortune above all other countreyes that I know, to bee thus miserably tossed and turmoyled with these variable stormes of affliction. But since wee are thus far entred into the consideration of her mishaps, tell mee, have there beene any more such tempests, as you term them, wherein she hath thus wretchedly beene wracked?

Iren.   Many more, God wot, have there beene, in which principall parts have beene rent and torne asunder, but none (as I can remember) so universall as this. And yet the rebellion of Thomas Fitz Garret[21] did well-nye stretch it selfe into all parts of Ireland. But that, which was in the time of the government of the Lord Grey, was surely no lesse generall then all those; for there was no part free from the contagion, but all conspired in one, to cast off their subiection to the crowne of England.[22] Neverthelesse thorough the most wise and valiant handling of that right noble Lord, it got not the head which the former evills found; for in them the realme was left like a ship in a storm, amidst all the raging surges, unruled, and undirected of any: for they to whom she was committed, either fainted in their labour, or forsooke their charge. But hee (like a most wise pilote,) kept her course carefully, and held her most strongly even against those roaring billowes, that he safely brought her out of all; so as long after, even by the space of 12 or 13 whole yeares, she roade at peace, thorough his onely paines and excellent indurance, how ever Envy list to blatter against him. But of this wee shall have more occasion to speak in another place. Now (if you please) let us returne againe unto our first course.[23]

Eudox.   Truely I am very glad to heare your iudgement of the government of that honourable man so soundly; for I have heard it oftentimes maligned, and his doings depraved of some, who (I perceive) did rather of malicious minde, or private grievance, seeke to detract from the honour of his deeds and counsels, then of any just cause: but he was neverthelesse, in the iudgements of all good and wise men, defended and maintained. And now that he is dead,[24] his immortall fame

---

21   Thomas Fitzgerald, tenth Earl of Kildare, was executed after his rebellion in 1535.

22   Grey had to deal with rebellion in the Pale led by William Nugent and Thomas, Viscount Baltinglas, as well as the Desmond Rebellion in Munster. Spenser gained property from confiscated land after both revolts.

23   As Grey's term of office finished in 1582, the 12–13 years spoken of here would argue that *A View* may have been started as early as 1595. The use of the verb 'blatter' (from the Latin, *blatero*, 'to babble or speak loudly') links this defence of Grey's actions in Ireland to the appearance of the Blatant Beast in *The Faerie Queene*, V, xii, 37, also after slanderous attacks on Artegall/Grey's Irish campaigns.

24   Grey died in October 1593.

surviveth, and flourisheth in the mouthes of all people, that even those which did backbite him, are checked with their owne venome, and breake their galls to heare his so honourable report. But let him rest in peace; and turne we to our more troublesome matters of discourse, of which I am right sorry that you make so short an end, and covet to passe over to your former purposes; for there be many other parts of Ireland, which I have heard have bin no lesse vexed with the like stormes, then these which you have treated of, as the countreyes of the Birnes and Tooles near Dublin, with the insolent out-rages and spoyles of Feagh mac Hugh, the countreyes of Catherlagh, Wexford, and Waterford, by the Cavenaghes. The countreyes of Leix, Kilkenny, and Kildare by the O Moores. The countreyes of Ofaly and Longford by the Connors. The countreyes of Westmeath, Cavan, and Lowth, by the O Relyes, and the Kellyes, and many others, so as the discoursing of them, besides the pleasure which would redound out of their history, be also very profitable for matters of policy.

Iren. All this which you have named, and many more besides, often times have I right well knowne, and yet often doe kindle great fires of tumultuous broyles in the countreyes bordering upon them. All which to rehearse, should rather bee to chronicle times, then to search into reformation of abuses in that realme; and yet very needfull it will bee to consider them, and the evills which they have often stirred up, that some redresse thereof, and prevention of the evills to come, may thereby rather be devised. But I suppose wee shall have a fitter opportunity for the same, when wee shall speake of the particular abuses and enormities of the government, which will be next after these generall defects and inconveniences which I saide were in the lawes, customes, and religion.

Eudox. Goe to them a Gods name, and follow the course which you have promised to your selfe, for it fitteth best, I must confesse, with the purpose of our discourse. Declare your opinion as you began about the lawes of the realme, what incommoditie you have conceived to bee in them, chiefly in the Common Law, which I would have thought most free from all such dislike.

Iren. The Common Law is (as I saide before) of itselfe most rightfull and very convenient (I suppose) for the kingdome, for which it was first devised: for this (I thinke) as it seemes reasonable, that out of your manners of your people, and abuses of your countrey, for which they were invented, they take their first beginning, or else they should bee most uniust; for no lawes of man (according to the straight rule of right) are iust, but as in regard of the evills which they prevent, and the safety of the commonweale which they provide for. As for example, in your true ballancing of iustice, it is a flat wrong to punish the thought or purpose of any before it bee enacted; for true iustice punisheth nothing but the evill act or wicked word, that by the lawes of all kingdomes it is a capitall crime to devise or purpose the death of your King:[25] the reason is, for that when such a purpose is effected, it should then bee too late to devise thereof, and should turne the commonwealth to more losse by the death of their Prince, then such punishment of the malefactors. And therefore the law in that case punisheth the thought; for better is a mischiefe, then an inconvenience. So that *ius politicum,*[26] though it bee not of it selfe iust, yet by application, or rather necessity, it is made iust; and this onely respect maketh all lawes iust. Now then, if these lawes of Ireland bee not likewise applyed and fitted for that realme, they are sure very inconvenient.

Eudox.   You reason strongly: but what unfitnesse doe you finde in them for that realme? shew us some particulars.

Iren.   The Common Law appointeth, that all tryalls, as well of crimes, as titles and rights, shall bee made by verdict of a iury, chosen out of the honest and most substantiall free-holders. Now, most of the free-holders of that realme are Irish, which when the cause shall fall betwixt an English-man and an Irish, or betweene the Queene and any free-holder of that countrey, they make no more scruple to passe against an Englishman, and the Queene, though it bee to strayn their oathes, then to drinke milke unstrayned. So that before the iury goe together, it is all to nothing what the verdict shall be. The tryall have I so often seene, that I dare confidently avouch the abuse thereof. Yet is the law, of itselfe, (as I said) good; and the first institution thereof being given to all Englishmen very rightfully, but now that the Irish have stepped into the very roomes of our English, wee are now to become heedfull and provident in iuryes.

---

25 After Henry VIII's break with the Papacy, the Treason Laws were revised and expanded in the 1530s to include the crime of imagining or 'compassing' the monarch's death.

26 Political law.

Eudox. In sooth, Iren. you have discovered a point worthy the consideration; for heereby not onely the English subiect findeth no
indifferencie in deciding of his cause, bee it never so iust; but the
Queene, aswell in all pleas of the crowne, as also in inquiries for
escheates, lands attainted, wardshipps, concealments, and all such like,
is abused and exceedingly damaged.

Iren. You say very true; for I dare undertake, that at this day there are
more attainted lands, concealed from her Majestie, then shee hath
now possessions in all Ireland; and it is no small inconvenience: for,
besides that shee looseth so much land as should turne to her great
profite, shee besides looseth so many good subiects, which might bee
assured unto her, as those landes would yeeld inhabitants and living
unto.

Eudox. But doth many of that people (say you) make no more conscience to perjure themselves in their verdicts, and damne their soules?

Iren. Not onely so in their verdicts, but also in all other their dealings;
especially with the English, they are most willfully bent: for though
they will not seeme manifestly to doe it, yet will some one or other
subtle-headed fellow amongst them put some quirke, or devise some
evasion, whereof the rest will likely take hold, and suffer themselves
easily to be led by him to that themselves desired. For in the most
apparent matter that may bee, the least question or doubt that may
bee mooved, will make a stoppe unto them, and put them quite out
of the way. Besides, that of themselves (for the most part) they are so
cautelous and wylie-headed, especially being men of so small experience and practice in law matters, that you would wonder whence they
borrow such subtiltyes and slye shifts.

Eudox. But mee thinkes this inconvenience might bee much helped in
the Iudges and Chiefe Magistrates which have the choosing and nomi-
nation of those iurors, if they would have dared to appoint either
most Englishmen, and such Irishmen as were of the soundest judgement and disposition; for no doubt but some there bee incorruptible.

Iren. Some there bee indeede as you say; but then would the Irish
partie crye out of partialitie, and complaine hee hath no iustice, hee is
not used as a subject; hee is not suffered to have the free benefite of
the law; and these outcryes the Magistrates there doe much shunne,
as they have cause, since they are readily hearkened unto heere; neither can it bee indeede, although the Irish party would bee so con-

tented to be so compassed, that such English freehoulders which are but few, and such faithfull Irish-men, which are indeede as few, shall alwayes bee chosen for tryalls; for being so few, they should bee made weary of their free-houldes. And therefore a good care is to bee had by all good occasions, to encrease their number, and to plant more by them. But were it so, that the iurors could bee picked out of such choyce men as you desire, this would neverthelesse bee as bad a corruption in the tryall; for the evidence being brought in by the baser Irish people, will bee as deceptfull as the verdict; for they care much lesse then the others, what they sweare, and sure their Lordes may compel them to say any thing; for I my selfe have heard, when one of the baser sort (which they call churles) being challenged, and reprooved for his false oath, hath answered confidently, That his Lord commaunded him, and it was the least thing that hee could doe for his Lord to sweare for him; so inconscionable are these common people, and so little feeling have they of God, or their owne soules good.

Eudox. It is a most miserable case, but what helpe can there bee in this? for though the manner of the trialls should bee altered, yet the proofe of every thing must needes bee by the testimony of such persons as the parties shall produce, which if they shall bee corrupt, how can there ever any light of the truth appeare, what remedy is there for this evill, but to make heavy lawes and penalties against iurors?

Iren. I thinke sure that will doe small good; for when a people be inclined to any vice, or have no touch of conscience, nor sence of their evill doings; it is bootelesse to thinke to restraine them by any penalties or feare of punishment, but either the occasion is to be taken away, or a more understanding of the right, and shame of the fault to be imprinted. For if that Licurgus should have made it death for the Lacedemonians to steale, they being a people which naturally delighted in stealth; or if it should bee made a capitall crime for the Flemmings to be taken in drunkennesse; there should have beene few Lacedemonians then left, and few Flemmings now. So unpossible it is, to remove any fault so generall in a people, with terrour of lawes or most sharpe restraints.

Eudox. What meanes may there be then to avoyde this inconvenience? for the case seemes very hard.

Iren. We are not yet come to the point to devise remedies for the evils, but only have now to recount them; of the which, this which I have told you is one defect in the Common Law.

Eudox. Tell us then (I pray you) further, have you any more of this sort in the Common Law?

Iren. By rehearsall of this, I remember also of an other like, which I have often observed in trialls, to have wrought great hurt and hinderance, and that is, the exceptions which the Common Law alloweth a fellon in his tryall; for he may have (as you know) fifty-six exceptions[27] peremptory against the iurors, of which he shal shew no cause. By which shift there being (as I have shewed you) so small store of honest iury-men, he will either put off his tryall, or drive it to such men as (perhaps) are not of the soundest sort, by whose meanes, if he can acquite himselfe of the crime, as he is likely, then will he plague such as were brought first to bee of his iurie, and all such as made any party against him. And when he comes forth, he will make their^j cowes and garrons to walke, if he doe no other harme to their persons.

Eudox. This is a slye devise, but I thinke might soone bee remedied, but we must leave it a while to the rest. In the meane-while doe you goe forwards with others.

Iren. There is an other no lesse inconvenience then this, which is, the tryall of accessaries to fellony; for, by the Common Law, the accessaries cannot be proceeded against, till the principall have received his tryall. Now to the case, how it often falleth out in Ireland, that a stealth being made by a rebel, or an outlawe, the stolne goods are conveyed to some husbandman or gentleman, which hath well to take to, and yet liveth most by the receipt of such stealthes, where they are found by the owner, and handled: whereupon the partie is perhaps appre-hended and committed to goal, or put upon sureties, till the sessions, at which time the owner preferring a bill of indictment, proveth suffi-ciently the stealth to have been committed upon him, by such an outlaw, and to have beene found in the possession of the prisoner, against whom, neverthelesse, no course of law can proceede, nor tryall can be had, for that the principall theife is not to be gotten, notwith-standing that he likewise, standing perhaps indicted at once, with the receiver, being in rebellion, or in the woods: where peradventure he is slaine before he can be gotten, and so the receiver cleane acquitted

---

27   This appears to be an exaggeration.

and discharged of the crime. By which meanes the theeves are greatly incouraged to steale, and their maintainers imboldened to receive their stealthes, knowing how hardly they can be brought to any tryall of law.

Eudox.   Truely this is a great inconvenience, and a great cause (as you say) of the maintenance of theeves, knowing their receivers alwayes ready; for, were there no receivers, there would be no theeves: but this (me seemes) might easily be provided for, by some Act of Parliament, that the receiver being convicted by good proofes might receive his tryall without the principall.

Iren.   You say very true Eudox. But that is almost impossible to be compassed: And herein also you discover another imperfection, in the course of the Common Law, and first ordinance of the realme: for you know that the said Parliament must consist of the peeres, gentlemen, freeholders, and burgesses of that realme it selfe. Now these being perhaps themselves, or the most part of them (as may seeme by their stiffe with-standing of this Act) culpable of this crime, or favourers of their friends, which are such, by whom their kitchins are sometimes amended, will not suffer any such Statute to passe. Yet hath it oftentimes beene attempted, and in the time of Sir Iohn Parrot[28] very earnestly (I remember) laboured, but could by no meanes be effected. And not onley this, but many other like, which are as needefull for the reformation of that realme.

Eudox.   This also is surely a great defect, but wee may not talke (you say) of the redressing of this, untill our second part come, which is purposely appointed thereunto. Therefore proceed to the recounting of more such evils, if at least, you have any more.

Iren.   There is also a great inconvenience, which hath wrought great dammage, both to her Majesty, and to that commonwealth, thorough close and colourable conveyances of the lands and goods of traytors, fellons, and fugitives. As when one of them mindeth to goe into rebellion, hee will convey away all his lands and lordships to feoffees in trust, wherby he reserveth to himselfe but a state for terme of life, which being determined either by the sword or by the halter, their lands straight commeth to their heire, and the Queen is defrauded of the intent of the law, which laide that grievous punishment upon traytors, to forfeite all their lands to the Prince; to the end that

---

28   Sir John Perrot (1527/8–92), Lord Deputy of Ireland, 1584–8.

men might the rather be terrified from committing treasons; for many which would little esteeme of their owne lives, yet for remorse of their wives and children would bee withheld from that haynous crime. This appeared plainely in the late Earle of Desmond.[29] For, before his break-ing forth into open rebellion, hee had conveyed secretly all his lands to feoffees of trust, in hope to have cut off her Maiestie from the escheate of his lands.

Eudox. Yea, but that was well enough avoided; for the Act of Parlia-ment, which gave all his lands to the Queene, did (as I have heard) cut off and frustrate all such conveyances, as had at any time by the space of twelve yeares before his rebellion, beene made; within the compasse whereof, the fraudulent feoffement, and many the like of others his accomplices and fellow-traytors, were contained.

Iren. Very true, but how hardly that Act of Parliament was wrought out of them, I can witnesse; and, were it to be passed againe, I dare undertake it would never be compassed. But were it also that such Acts might be easily brought to passe against traytors and fellons, yet were it not an endlesse trouble, that no traytour or fellon should be attainted, but a Parliament must be called for bringing of his lands to the Queene, which the Common-Law giveth her.

Eudox. Then this is no fault of the Common Law, but of the persons which worke this fraud to her Majestie.

Iren. Yes, marry; for the Common-Law hath left them this benefite, whereof they make advantage, and wrest it to their bad purposes. So as thereby they are the bolder to enter into evill actions, knowing that if the worst befall them, they shall lose nothing but themselves, whereof they seeme surely very carelesse.

Eudox. But what meant you of fugitives herein? Or how doth this concerne them?

Iren. Yes, very greatly, for you shall understand that there bee many ill disposed and undutifull persons of that realme, like as in this point there are also in this realme of England,[30] too many, which being men of good inheritance, are for dislike of religion, or danger of the law,

29 Gerald FitzJames Fitzgerald (*c.*1533–83). The Desmond Rebellion (1579–83) was probably the most significant threat to Tudor rule in Ireland before the Nine Years War and involved Papal and Spanish forces.

30 Another reminder that *A View* is set in England not Ireland.

into which they are run, or discontent of the present government, fled beyond the seas, where they live under Princes, which are her Maiesties professed enemies, and converse and are confederat with other traitors and fugitives which are there abiding. The which neverthelesse have the benefits and profits of their lands here, by pretence of such colourable conveyances thereof, formerly made by them unto their privie friends heere in trust, who privily doe send over unto them the said revenues wherwith they are there maintained and enabled against her Majestie.

Eudox.   I doe not thinke that there be any such fugitives, which are relieved by the profite of their lands in England, for there is a straighter order taken. And if there bee any such in Ireland, it were good it were likewise looked unto; for this evill may easily be remedied. But proceede.

Iren.   It is also inconvenient in the realme of Ireland, that the wards and marriages of gentlemens children should be in the disposition of any of those Irish Lords, as now they are, by reason that their lands bee held by knights service of those Lords. By which means it comes to passe that those gentlemen being thus in the ward of those Lords, are not onely thereby brought up lewdly, and Irish-like, but also for ever after so bound to their services, they will runne with them into any disloyall action.

Eudox.   This grievance Iren. is also complained of in England, but how can it be remedied? since the service must follow the tenure of the lands, and the lands were given away by the Kings of England to those Lords, when they first conquered that realme, and, to say troth, this also would be some prejudice to the Prince in her wardshipps.

Iren.   I doe not meane this by the Princes wards, but by such as fall into the hands of Irish Lords; for I could wish, and this I could enforce, that all those wardships were in the Princes disposition, for then it might be hoped, that she, for the universall reformation of that realme, would take better order for bringing up those wards in good nurture, and not suffer them to come into so bad hands. And although these things be already passed away, by her progenitours former grants unto those said Lords; yet I could finde a way to remedie a great part thereof, as hereafter, when fit time serves, shall appeare. And since we are entred into speech of such grants of former Princes, to sundry persons of this realme of Ireland, I will mention unto you some other, of like nature to this, and of like inconvenience, by which the former Kings of England passed unto them a great part of their prerogatives, which though then it was well intended, and perhaps well deserved of them which received the same, yet now such a gapp of mischeife lyes open thereby, that I could wish it were well stopped. Of this sort are the graunts of Counties Palatines in Ireland, which though at first were granted upon good consideration when they were first conquered, for that those lands lay then as a very border to the wild Irish, subject to continuall invasion, so as it was needfull to give them great priviledges for the defence of the inhabitants thereof: yet now that it is no more a border, nor frontired with enemies, why should such priviledges bee any continued?

Eudox. I would gladly know what you call a County Palatine, and whence it is so called.

Iren. It was (I suppose) first named Palatine of a pale, as it were a pale and defense to their inward lands, so as it is called the English Pale, and therefore is a Palsgrave named an Earle Palatine. Others thinke of the Latine, *palare*, that is, to forrage or out-run, because those marchers and borderers use commonly so to doe. So as to have a County Palatine is, in effect, to have a priviledge to spoyle the enemies borders adjoyning. And surely so it is used at this day, as a priviledge place of spoiles and stealthes; for the County of Tipperary, which is now the onely Countie Palatine in Ireland, is, by abuse of some bad ones, made a receptacle to rob the rest of the Counties about it, by meanes of whose priviledges none will follow their stealthes, so as it being situate in the very lap of all the land, is made now a border, which how inconvenient it is, let every man judge. And though that right noble man, that is the Lord of the liberty, do paine himselfe, all he may, to yeeld equall justice unto all, yet can there not but great abuses lurke in so inward and absolute a priviledge, the consideration whereof is to be respected carefully, for the next succession.[31] And much like

---

31   Thomas Butler, eleventh Earl of Ormond (1531–1614), a cousin and favourite of Elizabeth, held the Palatinate of Tipperary, the last such legally privileged area in Ireland. Ormond, a prominent Old English spokesman at Court, may have been instrumental in having Grey recalled in 1582, hence Spenser's attack on the abuses of the law that are implicit in such a jurisdiction (although Spenser would have had motive enough as a New English settler keen to oust his colonial rivals). Ormond was also the recipient of a dedicatory sonnet to *The Faerie Queene*.

unto this graunt, there are other priviledges granted unto most of the corporations there: that they shal not be bound to any other government then their owne, that they shall not be charged with garrisons, that they shall not be travailed forth of their owne franchises, that they may buy and sell with theeves and rebels, that all amercements and fines that shal be imposed upon them, shall come unto themselves. All which, though at the time of their first graunt they were tollerable, and perhaps reasonable, yet now are most unreasonable and inconvenient, but all these will easily be cut off with the superiour power of her Majesties prerogative, against which her own graunts are not to be pleaded or enforced.

Eudox.   Now truely Irenæus you have (me seemes) very well handled this point, touching inconveniences in the Common Law there, by you observed; and it seemeth that you have had a mindefull regard unto the things that may concerne the good of that realme. And if you can aswell goe thorough with the Statute Lawes of that land, I will thinke you have not lost all your time there. Therefore I pray you, now take them in hand, and tell us, what you thinke to bee amisse in them.

Iren.   The Statutes of that realme are not many, and therefore we shall the sooner runne thorough them. And yet of those few there are [some] impertinent and unnecessary: the which though perhaps at the time of the making of them, were very needfull, yet now thorough change of time are cleane antiquated, and altogether idle: As that which forbiddeth any to weare their beards all on the upper lippe, and none under the chinne. And that which putteth away saffron shirts and smockes. And that which restraineth the use of guilt bridles and petronels. And that which is appointed for the recorders and clerks of Dublin and Tredagh, to take but ijd. for the coppy of a plainte. And that which commaunds bowes and arrowes. And that which makes, that all Irishmen which shall converse among the English, shall be taken for spyes, and so punished. And that which forbids persons amesnable to law, to enter and distraine in the lands in which they have title; and many other the like, I could rehearse.

Eudox.   These truely, which yee have repeated, seeme very frivolous and fruitelesse; for, by the breach of them, little dammage or inconvenience, can come to the Common-wealth: Neither indeed, if any transgresse them, shall he seeme worthy of punishment, scarce of blame, saving but for that they abide by that name of lawes. But lawes ought to be such, as that the keeping of them should be greatly for the behoofe of the Common-weale, and the violating of them should be very haynous, and sharpely punishable. But tell us of some more weighty dislikes in the Statutes then these, and that may more behoofully import the reformation of them.

Iren. There is one or two Statutes which make the wrongfull distraining of any mans goods against the forme of Common Law, to be fellony. The which Statutes seeme surely to have beene at first meant for the good of that realme, and for restrayning of a foule abuse, which then raigned commonly amongst that people, and yet is not altogether laide aside: That when any one was indebted to another, he would first demand his debt, and, if he were not payed, hee would straight goe and take a distresse of his goods or cattell, where he could finde them, to the value; which he would keepe till he were satisfied, and this the simple churle (as they call him) doth commonly use to doe; yet thorough ignorance of his misdoing, or evill use, that hath long settled amongst them. But this, though it bee sure most unlawfull, yet surely (me seemes) too hard to make it death, since there is no purpose in the party to steale the others goods, or to conceale the distresse, but doth it openly, for the most part, before witnesses. And againe, the same Statutes are so slackely penned (besides the later of them is so unsensibly contryved, that it scarce carryeth any reason in it) that they are often and very easily wrested to the fraude of the subject, as if one going to distrayne upon his own land or tenement, where lawfully he may, yet if in doing therof he transgresse the least point of the Common Law, hee straight committeth fellony. Or if one by any other occasion take any thing from another, as boyes use sometimes to cap one another, the same is straight fellony. This a very hard law.

Eudox. Nevertheles that evill use of distrayning of another mans goods yee will not deny but it is to be abolished and taken away.

Iren. It is so, but not by taking away the subject withall, for that is too violent a medecine, especially this use being permitted, and made lawfull to some; and to other some death. As to most of the corporate townes there, it is graunted by their charter, that they may, every man by himselfe, without an officer (for that were more tolerable) for any debt, to distraine the goods of any Irish, being found within their liberty, or but passing thorough their townes. And the first permission of this, was for that in those times when that graunt was made, the Irish were not amesnable to law, so as it was not safety for the townes-man to goe to him forth to demaund his debt, nor possible to draw him into law, so that he had leave to bee his owne bayliffe, to arrest his said debters goods, within his owne franchese. The which the Irish seeing, thought it as lawfull for them to distrayne the townesmans goods in the countrey, where they found it. And so by ensample of that graunt to townes-men, they thought it lawfull, and made it a use to distrayne on anothers goods for small debts. And to say truth, mee thinkes it is hard for every trifling debt, of two or three shil. to be driven to law, which is so farre from them sometimes to be sought, for which me thinketh it too heavy an ordinance to give death, especially to a rude man that is ignorant of law, and thinketh, that a common use or graunt to other men, is a law for himselfe.

Eudox. Yea, but the iudge, when it commeth before him to triall, may easily decide this doubt, and lay open the intent of the law, by his better discretion.

Iren. Yea, but it is dangerous to leave the sence of the law unto the reason or will of the iudge, who are men and may bee miscarried by affections, and many other meanes. But the lawes ought to bee like stony tables, plaine, stedfast, and unmoveable. There is also such another Statute or two, which make Coigny and Livery to bee treason, no lesse inconvenient then the former, being as it is penned, how ever the first purpose thereof were expedient; for thereby now no man can goe into another mans house for lodging, nor to his owne tenants house to take victuall by the way, notwithstanding that there is no other meanes for him to have lodging, nor horse meate, nor mans meate, there being no innes, nor none otherwise to bee bought for money, but that he is endangered by that Statute for treason, whensoever he shall happen to fall out with his tennant, or that his said hoste list to complaine of greivance, as oftentimes I have seene them very malitiously doe thorough the least provocation.

Eudox. I doe not well know, but by ghesse, what you doe meane by these termes of Coigny and Livery, therefore I pray you explaine them.

Iren. I know not whether the words bee English or Irish, but I suppose them to bee rather auncient English,[32] for the Irishmen can make no derivation of them. What Livery is, wee by common use in England know well enough, namely, that it is allowance of horse-meate, as they commonly use the word in stabling, as to keepe horses at livery, the which word, I guesse, is derived of livering or delivering forth their nightly foode. So in great houses, the livery is said to be served up for all night, that is their evenings allowance for drinke: And Livery is also called, the upper weede which a serving man weareth, so called (as I suppose) for that it was delivered and taken from him at pleasure: so it is apparent, that, by the word Livery, is there meant horse-meate, like as, by the word Coigny, is understood mans meate; but whence the word is derived is hard to tell: some say of coine, for that they used commonly in their Coignies, not onely to take meate, but coine also; and that taking of money was speciallie meant to be prohibited by that Statute: but I thinke rather this word Coigny is derived of the Irish. The which is a common use amongst land-lords of the Irish, to have a common spending upon their tennants: for all their tennants, being commonly but tennants at will, they use to take of them what victuals they list: for of victuals they were wont to make small reckoning: neither in this was the tennant wronged, for it was an ordinary and knowne custome, and his Lord commonly used so to covenant with him, which if at any time the tennant disliked, hee might freely depart at his pleasure. But now by this Statute, the said Irish Lord is wronged, for that hee is cut off from his customary services, of the which this was one, besides many other of the like, as Cuddy, Coshery, Bonnaght, Shrah, Sorehin, and such others: the which (I thinke) were customes at first brought in by the English upon the Irish, for they were never wont, and yet are loath to yeeld any certaine rent, but only such spendings: for their common saying is, "Spend me and defend me."

Eudox. Surely I take it as you say, that therein the Irish Lord hath wrong, since it was an auncient custome, and nothing contrary to law, for to the willing there is no wrong done. And this right well I wot, that even heere in England, there are in many places as large

---

32 'Livery' appears to derive from Latin and French roots, 'coigne' from Irish: but Spenser is right to suggest that 'coigne and livery' was an English import into Ireland, not a native custom.

customes, as that of Coignie and Livery. But I suppose by your speach, that it was the first meaning of the Statute, to forbid the violent taking of victualls upon other mens tenants against their wills, which surely is a great out-rage, and yet not so great (me seems) as that it should be made treason: for considering that the nature of treason is concerning the royall estate or person of the Prince, or practizing with his enemies, to the derogation and danger of his crowne and dignitie, it is hardly wrested to make this treason. But (as you earst said) "better a mischiefe then an inconvenience."

Iren.   Another Statute I remember, which having beene an auncient Irish custome, is now upon advisement made a law, and that is called the Custome of Kin-cogish, which is, that every head of every sept, and every chiefe of every kindred or family, should be answereable and bound to bring foorth every one of that sept and kindred under it, at all times to be iustified, when he should be required or charged with any treason, felony, or other haynous crime.

Eudox.   Why? surely this seemes a very necessary law. For considering that many of them bee such losells and scatterlings, as that they cannot easily by any sheriffe, constable, bayliffe, or other ordinary officer bee gotten, when they are challenged for any such fact; this is a very good meanes to get them to bee brought in by him, that is, the head of that sept, or chiefe of that house; wherfore I wonder what just exception you can make against the same.

Iren.   Truely Eudoxus, in the pretence of the good of this Statute, you have nothing erred, for it seemeth very expedient and necessary; but the hurt which commeth thereby is greater then the good. For, whilest every chiefe of a sept standeth so bound to the law for every man of his blood or sept that is under him, he is made great by the commaunding of them all. For if hee may not commaund them, then that law doth wrong, that bindeth him to bring them foorth to bee iustified. And if hee may commaund them, then hee may commaund them as well to ill as to good. Hereby the lords and captaines of countreyes, the principall and heades of septs are made stronger, whome it should bee a most speciall care in policie to weaken, and to set up and strengthen diverse of his underlings against him, which whensoever hee shall swarve from duty, may bee able to beard him; for it is very dangerous to leave the commaund of so many as some septs are, being five or sixe thousand persons, to the will of one man, who may leade them to what he will, as he himselfe shall be inclined.

Eudox. In very deede Iren. it is very dangerous, seeing the disposition of those people is not alwayes inclineable to the best. And therefore I holde it no wisedome to leave unto them too much commaund over their kindred, but rather to withdrawe their followers from them asmuch as may bee, and to gather them under the commaund of law, by some better meane then this custom of Kin-cogish. The which word I would bee glad to know what it namely signifieth, for the meaning thereof I seeme to understand reasonably well.

Iren. It is a word mingled of English and Irish together, so as I am partly ledde to thinke, that the custome thereof was first English, and afterwardes made Irish; for such an other law they had heere in England, as I remember, made by King Alured, that every gentleman should bring foorth his kinred and followers to the law. So Kin is English, and Congish affinitie in Irish.

Eudox. Sith then wee that have thus reasonably handled the inconveniences in the lawes, let us now passe unto the second part, which was, I remember, of the abuses of customes; in which, mee seemes, you have a faire champian layde open unto you, in which you may at large stretch out your discourse into many sweete remembrances of antiquities, from whence it seemeth that the customes of that nation proceeded.

Iren. Indeede Eudox. You say very true; for all the customes of the Irish which I have often noted and compared with that I have read, would minister occasion of a most ample discourse of the originall of them, and the antiquity of that people, which in truth I thinke to bee more auncient then most that I know in this end of the world, so as if it were in the handling of some man of sound judgement and plentifull reading, it would bee most pleasant and profitable. But it may bee wee may, at some other time of meeting, take occasion to treate thereof more at large.[33] Heere onely it shall suffise to touch such customes of the Irish as seeme offensive and repugnant to the good government of the realme.

Eudox. Follow then your owne course, for I shall the better content

33   Such a work never appeared, although the promise is mentioned again at the very end of the work by Eudoxus.

my selfe to forbeare my desire now, in hope that you will, as you say,
some other time more aboundantly satisfie it.

Iren.   Before we enter into the treatie of their customes, it is first needfull
to consider from whence they first sprung; for from the sundry manners of the nations, from whence that people which now is called
Irish, were derived, some of the customes which now remain amongst
them, have been first fetcht, and sithence there continued amongst
them; for not of one nation was it peopled, as it is, but of sundry
people of different conditions and manners. But the chiefest which
have first possessed and inhabited it, I suppose to bee Scythians.[34]

Eudox.   How commeth it then to passe, that the Irish doe derive themselves from Gathelus the Spaniard?[35]

Iren.   They doe indeed, but (I conceive) without any good ground.
For if there were any such notable transmission of a colony hether out
of Spaine, or any such famous conquest of this kingdome by Gathelus
a Spaniard, as they would faine believe, it is not unlikely, but the very
Chronicles of Spaine (had Spaine then beene in so high regard, as
they now have it) would not have omitted so memorable a thing, as
the subduing of so noble a realme to the Spaniard, no more then they
doe now neglect to memorize their conquest of the Indians, especially in those times, in which the same was supposed, being nearer
unto the flourishing age of learning and writers under the Romanes.
But the Irish doe heerein no otherwise, then our vaine English-men
doe in the Tale of Brutus, whom they devise to have first conquered
and inhabited this land, it being as impossible to proove, that there
was ever any such Brutus of Albion or England, as it is, that there was
any such Gathelus of Spaine. But surely the Scythians (of whom I
earst spoke) at such time as the Northerne Nations overflowed all
Christendome, came downe to the sea-coast, where inquiring for other
countries abroad, and getting intelligence of this countrey of Ireland,
finding shipping convenient, passed thither, and arrived in the North-
part thereof, which is now called Ulster, which first inhabiting, and
afterwards stretching themselves forth into the land, as their numbers

---

34   The Scythians were a savage people from the ancient world who are described by all
     ancient geographers and historians. The lands they supposedly inhabited are never
     clearly defined, but they bordered Greece.

35   Gathelus lived in the time of Moses. He named his daughter Scotia, she gave her
     name to the Scots, the ancestors of both Irish and Scots.

increased, named it all of themselves Scuttenland, which more briefly is called Scutland, or Scotland.[36]

Eudox. I wonder (Irenaeus) whether you runne so farre astray; for whilest wee talke of Ireland, mee thinks you rippe up the originall of Scotland, but what is that to this?

Iren. Surely very much, for Scotland and Ireland are all one and the same.

Eudox. That seemeth more strange; for we all know right well they are distinguished with a great sea running between them; or else there are two Scotlands.

Iren. Never the more are there two Scotlands, but two kindes of Scots were indeed (as you may gather out of Buchanan) the one Irin, or Irish Scots, the other Albin-Scots; for those Scots are Scythians, arrived (as I said) in the North parts of Ireland, where some of them after passed into the next coast of Albine, now called Scotland, which (after much trouble) they possessed, and of themselves named Scotland; but in processe of time (as it is commonly seene) the dominion of the part prevaileth in the whole, for the Irish Scots putting away the name of Scots, were called only Irish, and the Albine Scots, leaving the name of Albine, were called only Scots. Therefore it commeth thence that of some writers, Ireland is called Scotia-major, and that which now is called Scotland, Scotia-minor.

Eudox. I doe now well understand your distinguishing of the two sorts of Scots, and two Scotlands, how that this which now is called Ireland, was anciently called Erin, and afterwards of some written Scotland, and that which now is called Scotland, was formerly called Albin, before the comming of the Scythes thither; but what other nation inhabited the other parts of Ireland?

Iren. After this people thus planted in the North, (or before,) for the certaintie of times in things so farre from all knowledge cannot be justly avouched, another nation comming out of Spaine, arrived in the West part of Ireland, and finding it waste, or weakely inhabited, possessed it: who whether they were native Spaniards, or Gaules, or Africans, or Gothes, or some other of those Northerne Nations which

---

36 Irenius' frequent references to the Scots and his stress on the connections between Scotland and Ireland illustrates Spenser's concern with contemporary Scottish involvement in Ireland.

did over-spread all Christendome, it is impossible to affirme, only some naked conjectures may be gathered, but that out of Spaine certainely they came, that do all the Irish Chronicles agree.

Eudox. You doe very boldly Iren. adventure upon the histories of auncient times, and leane too confidently on those Irish Chronicles which are most fabulous and forged, in that out of them you dare take in hand to lay open the originall of such a nation so antique, as that no monument remaines of her beginning and first inhabiting; especially having been in those times without letters, but only bare traditions of times and remembrances of Bardes, which use to forge and falsifie every thing as they list, to please or displease any man.

Iren. Truly I must confess I doe so, but yet not so absolutely as you suppose. I do herein rely upon those Bardes or Irish Chroniclers, though the Irish themselves through their ignorance in matters of learning and deepe judgement, doe most constantly beleeve and avouch them, but unto them besides I adde mine owne reading; and out of them both together, with comparison of times, likewise of manners and customes, affinity of words and names, properties of natures, and uses, resemblances of rites and ceremonies, monuments of churches and tombes, and many other like circumstances, I doe gather a likelihood of truth, not certainly affirming any thing, but by conferring of times, language, monuments, and such like, I doe hunt out a probability of things, which I leave to your judgement to believe or refuse.[37] Nevertheless there be some very auncient authors that make mention of these things, and some moderne, which by comparing them with present times, experience, and their owne reason, doe open a window of great light unto the rest that is yet unseene, as namely, of the elder times, Cæsar, Strabo, Tacitus, Ptolomie, Pliny, Pomponius Mela, and Berosus: of the later, Vincentius, Æneas Sylvius, Luidus, Buchanan, for that hee himselfe, being an Irish Scot or Pict by nation, and being very excellently learned, and industrious to seeke out the truth of all things concerning the originall of his owne people, hath both set downe the testimony of the auncients truely, and his owne opinion together withall very reasonably, though in some things he doth somewhat flatter. Besides, the Bardes and Irish Chroniclers themselves, though

---

37   This suggests that Spenser made use of Irish materials in his work (see the section on 'Language' in the Guide to Further Reading).

through desire of pleasing perhappes too much, and ignorances of arts, and purer learning, they have clauded the truth of those lines; yet there appeares among them some reliques of the true antiquitie, though disguised, which a well eyed man may happily discover and finde out.

Eudox. How can here be any truth in them at all, since the auncient nations which first inhabited Ireland, were altogether destitute of letters, much more of learning, by which they might leave the verity of things written. And those Bardes, comming also so many hundred yeares after, could not know what was done in former ages, nor deliver certainty of any thing, but what they fayned out of their unlearned heads.

Iren. Those Bardes indeed, Cæsar writeth, delivered no certaine truth of any thing, neither is there any certaine hold to be taken of any antiquity which is received by tradition, since all men be lyars, and many lye when they wil; yet for the antiquities of the written Chronicles of Ireland, give me leave to say something, not to justifie them, but to shew that some of them might say truth. For where you say the Irish have alwayes bin without letters, you are therein much deceived; for it is certaine, that Ireland hath had the use of letters very anciently, and long before England.

Eudox. It is possible? how comes it then that they are so unlearned still, being so old schollers? For learning (as the Poet saith) "Emollit mores, nec sinit esse feros:"[38] whence then (I pray you) could they have those letters?

Iren. It is hard to say: for whether they at their first comming into the land, or afterwards by trading with other nations which had letters, learned them of them, or devised them amongst themselves, is very doubtful; but that they had letters aunciently, is nothing doubtfull, for the Saxons of England are said to have their letters, and learning, and learned men from the Irish, and that also appeareth by the likenesse of the character, for the Saxons character is the same with the Irish. Now the Scythians, never, as I can reade, of old had letters amongst

38 'Softens manners, not suffers them to be wild' (Variorum translation). *A View* contains very few Latin quotations – although it does contain a large number of literary tropes and rhetorical flourishes – which suggests that it was intended to reach an audience not interested in the author's wealth of learning and polite culture.

them, therefore it seemeth that they had them from the nation which came out of Spaine, for in Spaine there was (as Strabo writeth) letters anciently used, whether brought unto them by the Phenicians, or the Persians, which (as it appeareth by him) had some footing there, or from Marsellis, which is said to have bin inhabited by the Greekes, and from them to have had the Greeke character, of which Marsilians it is said, that the Gaules learned them first, and used them only for the furtherance of their trades and privat busines; for the Gaules (as is strongly to be proved by many ancient and authentical writers) did first inhabite all the sea coast of Spaine, even unto Cales, and the mouth of the Straights, and peopled also a great part of Italy, which appeareth by sundry havens and cities in Spaine called from them, as Portugallia, Gallecia, Galdunum, and also by sundry nations therin dwelling, which yet have received their own names of the Gaules, as the Rhegni, Presamarci, Tamari, Cineri, and divers others. All which Pomponius Mela, being himselfe a Spaniard, yet saith to have descended from the Celts of France, whereby it is to be gathered, that that nation which came out of Spaine into Ireland, were anciently Gaules, and that they brought with them those letters which they had anciently learned in Spaine, first into Ireland, which some also say, doe much resemble the old Phenician character, being likewise distinguished with pricke and accent, as theirs aunciently, but the further enquirie hereof needeth a place of longer discourse then this our short conference.

Eudox. Surely you have shewed a great probability of that which I had thought impossible to have bin proved; but that which you now say, that Ireland should have bin peopled with the Gaules, seemeth much more strange, for all the Chronicles doe say, that the west and south was possessed and inhabited of Spaniards: and Cornelius Tacitus doth also strongly affirme the same, all which you must overthrow and falsifie, or else renounce your opinion.

Iren. Neither so, nor so; for the Irish Chronicles (as I shewed you) being made by unlearned men, and writing things according to the appearance of the truth which they conceived, doe erre in the circumstances, not in the matter. For all that came out of Spaine (they being no diligent searchers into the differences of the nations) supposed to be Spaniards, and so called them; but the ground-work thereof is neverthelesse true and certain, however they through ignorance disguise the same, or through vanity, whilst they would not seem to be ignorant, doe thereupon build and enlarge many forged histories of their owne antiquity, which they deliver to fooles, and make them believe for true; as for example, That first of one Gathelus the sonne' of Cecrops or Argos, who having married the King of Egypt his daughter, thence sailed with her into Spaine, and there inhabited: Then that of Nemedus and his sonnes, who comming out of Scythia, peopled Ireland, and inhabited it with his sonnes 250 yeares, until he was overcome of the Giants dwelling then in Ireland, and at the last quite banished and rooted out, after whom 200 yeares, the sonnes of one Dela, being Scythians, arrived there againe, and possessed the whole land, of which the youngest called Slanius, in the end made himselfe Monarch. Lastly, of the 4 sonnes of Milesius King of Spaine, which conquered the land from the Scythians, and inhabited it with Spaniards, and called it of the name of the youngest Hiberus, Hibernia: all which are in truth fables, and very Milesian lyes, as the later proverbe is: for never was there such a King of Spaine, called Milesius, nor any such colonie seated with his sonnes, as they faine, that can ever be proved; but yet under these tales you may in a manner see the truth lurke. For Scythians here inhabiting, they name and put Spaniards, whereby appeareth that both these nations here inhabited, but whether very Spaniards, as the Irish greatly affect, is no wayes to be proved.[39]

Eudox. Whence commeth it then that the Irish doe so greatly covet to fetch themselves from the Spaniards, since the old Gaules are a more auncient and much more honorable nation?

Iren. Even of a very desire of new fanglenes and vanity, for they derive themselves from the Spaniards, as seeing them to be a very honorable people, and neere bordering unto them: but all that is most vaine; for from the Spaniards that now are, or that people that now inhabite Spaine, they no wayes can prove themselves to descend; neither should it be greatly glorious unto them; for the Spaniard that now is, is come from as rude and savage nations as they, there being, as there may be gathered by course of ages, and view of their owne history, (though they therein labour much to enoble themselves) scarce any drop of

---

39 Irenius is concerned to link the Irish to the Scots as a British people and opposes all attempts to have the Irish and the Spanish equated, an obvious aim in the years after the Armada and in the light of Irish attempts in the 1590s to have their rebellion recognized as a Catholic crusade against English rule.

the old Spanish blood left in them; for all Spaine was first conquered by the Romans, and filled with colonies from them, which were still increased, and the native Spaniard still cut off. Afterwards the Carthaginians in all the long Punick Warres (having spoiled all Spaine, and in the end subdued it wholly unto themselves) did, as it is likely, root out all that were affected to the Romans. And lastly the Romans having againe recovered that countrey, and beate out Hannibal, did doubtlesse cut off all that favored the Carthaginians, so that betwixt them both, to and fro, there was scarce a native Spaniard left, but all inhabited of Romans. All which tempests of troubles being over-blowne, there long after arose a new storme, more dreadful then all the former, which over-ran all Spaine, and made an infinite confusion of all things; that was, the comming downe of the Gothes, the Hunnes, and the Vandals: And lastly all the nations of Scythia, which, like a mountaine flood, did over-flow all Spaine, and quite drowned and washt away whatsoever reliques there was left of the land-bred people, yea, and of all the Romans too. The which Northern Nations finding the nature of the soyle, and the vehement heat thereof farre differing from their constitutions, tooke no felicity in that countrey, but from thence passed over, and did spread themselves into all countryes of Christendome, of all which there is none but hath some mixture or sprinckling, if not throughly peopling of them. And yet after all these the Moores and the Barbarians, breaking over out of Africa, did finally possesse all Spaine, or the most part thereof, and did tread, under their heathenish feete, whatever little they found yet there standing. The which, though after they were beaten out by Ferdinando of Arragon and Elizabeth his wife, yet they were not so cleansed, but that through the marriages which they had made, and mixture with the people of the land, during their long continuance there, they had left no pure drop of Spanish blood, no more than of Roman or of Scythian. So that of all nations under heaven (I suppose) the Spaniard is the most mingled, and most uncertaine; wherefore most follishly doe the Irish thinke to enoble themselves by wresting their auncientry from the Spaniard, who is unable to derive himselfe from any in certaine.

Eudox. You speake very sharpely Iren. In dispraise of the Spaniard, whom some others boast to be the onely brave nation under the skie.

Iren. So surely he is a very brave man, neither is that any thing which

I speake to his derogation; for in that I said he is a mingled people, it is no dispraise, for I thinke there is no nation now in Christendome, nor much further, but is mingled, and compounded with others: for it was a singular providence of God, and a most admirable purpose of his wisedome, to draw those Northerne Heathen Nations downe into those Christian parts, where they might receive Christianity, and to mingle nations so remote miraculously, to make as it were one blood and kindred of all people, and each to have knowledge of him.

Eudox.   Neither have you sure any more dishonoured the Irish, for you have brought them from very great and ancient nations, as any were in the world, how ever fondly they affect the Spanish. For both Scythians and Gaules were two as mighty nations as ever the world brought forth. But is there any token, denomination or monument of the Gaules yet remaining in Ireland, as there is of the Scythians?

Iren.   Yea surely very many words of the Gaules remaining, and yet dayly used in common speech.

Eudox.   What was the Gaulish speech, is there any part of it still used among any nation?

Iren.   The Gaulish speech is the very British, the which was very generally used here in all Brittaine, before the comming of the Saxons: and yet is retained of the Welchmen, Cornishmen, and the Brittaines of France, though time working the alteration of all things, and the trading and interdeale with other nations round about, have changed and greatly altered the dialect thereof; but yet the originall words appeare to be the same, as who hath list to read in Camden and Buchanan, may see at large. Besides, there be many places, as havens, hills, townes, and castles, which yet beare the names from the Gaules, of the which Buchanan rehearseth above 500 in Scotland, and I can (I thinke) re-count neere as many in Ireland which retaine the old denomination of the Gaules, as the Menapii, Cauci, Venti, and others; by all which and many other reasonable probabilities (which this short course will not suffer to be laid forth) it appeareth that the chiefe inhabitants in Ireland were Gaules, comming thither first out of Spaine, and after from besides Tanais, where the Gothes, the Hunnes, and the Getes sate down; they also being (as it is said of some) ancient Gaules; and lastly passing out of Gallia it selfe, from all the sea-coast of Belgia and Celtica, into al the southerne coasts of Ireland, which they possessed and inhabited, whereupon it is at this day, amongst the Irish a common use, to call any stranger inhabitant there amongst them, Gald, that is, descended from the Gaules.

Eudox.   This is very likely, for even so did those Gaules anciently possesse all the southerne coasts of our Brittaine, which yet retaine their old names, as the Belgæ in Somerset-shire, Wilshire, and part of Hamshire, Attrebatii in Berkeshire, Regni in Sussex and Surry, and many others. Now thus farre then, I understand your opinion, that the Scythians planted in the North part of Ireland; the Spaniards (for so we call them, what ever they were that came from Spaine) in the West; the Gaules in the South: so that there now remaineth the East parts towards England, which I would be glad to understand from whence you doe think them to be peopled.

Iren.   Mary I thinke of the Brittaines themselves, of which though there be little footing now remaining, by reason that the Saxons afterwards, and lastly the English, driving out the inhabitants thereof, did possesse and people it themselves. Yet amongst the Tooles, the Birns, or Brins, the Cavenaghes, and other nations in Leinster, there is some memory of the Britans remayning. As the Tooles are called of the old British word Tol, that is, a Hill Countrey, the Brins of the British word Brin, that is, Woods, and the Cavenaghes of the word Caune, that is, strong; so that in these three people the very denomination of the old Britons doe still remaine. Besides, when any flieth under the succour and protection of any against an enemie, he cryeth unto him, Comericke, that is in the Brittish Helpe, for the Brittaine is called in their owne language, Comeroy. Furthermore to prove the same, Ireland is by Diodorus Siculus, and by Strabo, called Britannia, and a part of Great Brittaine.[40] Finally it appeareth by good record yet extant, that King Arthur, and before him Gurgunt, had all that iland under their alleagiance and subjection; hereunto I could add many probabilities of the names of places, persons, and speeches, as I did in the former, but they should be too long for this, and I reserve them for another.[41]

40   There is no evidence for this claim in either Strabo or Diodorus Siculus. Again, Spenser may be working from memory or forcing a genealogy.

41   Spenser is relying heavily on Geoffrey of Monmouth's *A History of the Kings of Britain* (*c.*1138), which narrates the history of the legendary British kings from Brutus, a descendant of Aeneas, to the last British king, Cadwallader, exiled to Brittany after the triumph of the Saxons. Geoffrey's work is the first substantial narration of the Arthurian legends, and he includes the story, often repeated, that Arthur conquered

And thus you have had my opinion, how all that realme of Ireland was first peopled, and by what nations. After all which the Saxons succeeding, subdued it wholly to themselves. For first Egfrid, King of Northumberland, did utterly waste and subdue it, as appeareth out of Beda's complaint against him; and after him, King Edgar brought it under his obedience, as appeareth by an auncient Record, in which it is found written, that he subdued all the islands of the North, even unto Norway, and brought them into his subjection.

Eudox. This ripping of auncestors, is very pleasing unto me, and indeede favoureth of good conceipt, and some reading withall. I see hereby how profitable travaile, and experience of forraine nations, is to him that will apply them to good purpose. neither indeede would I have thought, that any such antiquities could have beene avouched for the Irish, that maketh me the more to long to see some other of your observations, which you have gathered out of that country, and have earst half promised to put forth: and sure in this mingling of nations appeareth (as you earst well noted) a wonderfull providence and purpose of Almighty God, that stirred up the people in the furthest parts of the world, to seeke out their regions so remote from them, and by that meanes both to restore their decayed habitations, and to make himselfe knowne to the Heathen. But was there I pray you no more genrall employing of that iland, then first by the Scythians, which you say were the Scottes, and afterwards by the Spaniards, besides the Gaules, Brittaines, and Saxons?

Iren. Yes, there was another, and that last and greatest, which was by the English, when the Earle Strangbowe, having conquered that land, delivered up the same into the hands of Henry the Second, then King, who sent over thither great store of gentlemen, and other warlike people, amongst whom he distributed the land, and setled such a strong colonie therein, as never since could with all the subtle practices of the Irish be rooted out, but abide still a mighty people, of so many as remaine English of them.

Ireland and made it part of his empire, a feat repeated by Gurguntius. This would appear to contradict the assertion on p. 44 that the Irish in claiming Gathelus as an ancestor are no more foolish than the English in claiming Brutus. But there are doubts about the manuscript on which Ware based his text (see the Introduction, p. xxv).

Eudox. What is this that you say, of so many as remaine English of them? Why? are not they that were once English, English still?[42]

Iren. No, for some of them are degenerated and growne almost mere Irish, yea, and more malitious to the English then the Irish themselves.

Eudox. What heare I? And is it possible that an Englishman, brought up in such sweet civility as England affords, should find such likeing in that barbarous rudenes, that he should forget his owne nature, and forgoe his owne nation! how may this bee, or what (I pray you) may be the cause thereof?

Iren. Surely, nothing but the first evill ordinance and institution of that Common-wealth. But thereof here is no fit place to speake, least by the occasion thereof, offering matter of a long discourse, we might be drawne from this, that we had in hand, namely, the handleing of abuses in the customes of Ireland.

Eudox. In truth Iren. You doe well remember the plot of your first purpose; but yet from that (meseemes) ye have much swarved in all this long discourse, of the first inhabiting of Ireland; for what is that to your purpose?

Iren. Truely very materiall, for if you marked the course of all that speech well, it was to shew, by what meanes the customes, that now are in Ireland, being some of them indeede very strange and almost heathenish, were first brought in: and that was, as I said, by those nations from whom that countrey was first peopled; for the difference in manners and customes, doth follow the difference of nations and people. The which I have declared to you, to have beene three especially which seated themselves here: to wit, first the Scythian, then the Gaules, and lastly the English. Notwithstanding that I am not ignorant, that there were sundry nations which got footing in that land, of the which there yet remaine divers great families and septs, of whom I will also in their proper places make mention.

Eudox. You bring your selfe Iren. Very well into the way againe, notwithstanding that it seemeth that you were never out of the way, but now that you have passed thorough those antiquities, which I could

---

42   Eudoxus' shock or mock surprise at not being able to recognize the Old English as English is an exclamation designed to undermine the cause of the Old English, who are deemed to be worse than the Irish they imitate by dint of their wilful 'degeneration'. Presumably, the point is made for English readers.

have wished not so soone ended, begin when you please, to declare what customes and manners have beene derived from those nations to the Irish, and which of them you finde fault withall.

Iren. I will begin then to count their customes in the same order that I counted their nations, and first with the Scythian or Scottish manners. Of the which there is one use, amongst them, to keepe their cattle, and to live themselves the most part of the yeare in boolies, pasturing upon the mountaine, and waste wilde places; and removing still to fresh land, as they have depastured the former. The which appeareth plaine to be the manner of the Scythians, as you may read in Olaus Magnus, and Io. Bohemus, and yet is used amongst all the Tartarians and the people about the Caspian Sea, which are naturally Scythians, to live in heards as they call them, being the very same, that the Irish boolies are, driving their cattle continually with them, and feeding onely on their milke and white meats.

Eudox. What fault can you finde with this custome? for though it be an old Scythian use, yet it is very behoofefull in this country of Ireland, where there are great mountaines, and waste deserts full of grasse, that the same should be eaten downe, and nourish many thousands of cattle, for the good of the whole realme, which cannot (me thinks) well be any other way, then by keeping those boolies there, as yee have shewed.

Iren. But by this custome of boolying, there grow in the meane time many great enormityes unto that Common-wealth. For first if there be any out-lawes, or loose people, (as they are never without some) which live upon stealthes and spoyles, they are evermore succoured and finde releife only in these boolies, being upon the waste places, whereas else they should be driven shortly to starve, or to come downe to the townes to seeke releife, where by one meanes or other, they would soone be caught. Besides, such stealthes of cattle as they make, they bring commonly to those boolies, being upon those waste places, where they are readily received, and the theife harboured from danger of law, or such officers as might light upon him.[43] Moreover the people that thus live in those boolies, grow thereby the more barbarous, and live more licentiously than they could in townes, using what

---

43 Cattle raiding enjoyed a significant role in Irish culture and society. The greatest Irish epic, the *Táin Bó Cuailnge* ('Cattle Raid of Cooley'), as the title might suggest, centres around such an event.

manners they list, and practizing what mischeifes and villainies they will, either against the government there, by their combynations, or against private men, whom they maligne, by stealing their goods, or murdering themselves. For there they thinke themselves halfe exempted from law and obedience, and having once tasted freedome, doe like a steere, that hath beene long out of his yoke, grudge and repyne ever after, to come under rule again.

Eudox.   By your speech Iren. I perceive more evill come by this use of boolies, then good by their grasing; and therefore it may well be reformed: but that must be in his due course: do you proceed to the next.

Iren.   They have another custome from the Scythians, that is the wearing of Mantles, and long glibbes, which is a thicke curled bush of haire, hanging downe over their eyes, and monstrously disguising them, which are both very bad and hurtfull.

Eudox.   Doe you thinke that the mantle commeth from the Scythians? I would surely think otherwise, for by that which I have read, it appeareth that most nations of the world aunciently used the mantle. For the Iewes used it, as you may read of Elyas mantle, &c. The Chaldees also used it, as yee may read in Diodorus. The Egyptians likewise used it, as yee may read in Herodotus, and may be gathered by the description of Berenice, in the Greeke Commentary upon Callimachus. The Greekes also used it aunciently, as appeareth by Venus mantle lyned with starrs, though afterwards they changed the form thereof into their cloakes, called Pallia, as some of the Irish also use. And the auncient Latines and Romans used it, as you may read in Virgil, who was a very great antiquary: That Evander, when Æneas came to him at his feast, did entertaine and feast him, sitting on the ground, and lying on mantles. Insomuch as he useth the very word mantile for a mantle.

"—— Humi mantilia sternunt."[44]

So that it seemeth that the mantle was a generall habite to most nations, and not proper to the Scythians onely, as you suppose.

44   'They spread their cloaks on the ground' (we owe this translation to Mr R. T. Pritchard).

Iren. I cannot deny but that aunciently it was common to most, and yet sithence disused and laide away. But in this later age of the world, since the decay of the Romane empire, it was renewed and brought in againe by those Northerne Nations, when breaking out of their cold caves and frozen habitations, into the sweet soyle of Europe, they brought with them their usual weedes, fit to sheild the cold, and that continual frost, to which they had at home beene inured: the which yet they left not off, by reason that they were in perpetual warres, with the nations whom they had invaded, but, still removing from place to place, carried always with them that weed, as their house, their bed, and their garment; and, comming lastly into Ireland, they found there more special use thereof, by reason of the raw cold climate, from whom it is now growne into that general use, in which that people now have it. After whom the Gaules succeeding, yet finding the like necessite of that garment, continued the like use thereof.

Eudox. Since then the necessity thereof is so commodious, as you alledge, that it is instead of housing, bedding, and cloathing, what reason have you then to wish so necessarie a thing cast off?

Iren. Because the commoditie doth not countervaile the discommoditie; for the inconveniencies which thereby doe arise, are much more many; for it is a fit house for an out-law, a meet bed for a rebel, and an apt cloke for a theife. First the out-law being for his many crimes and villanyes banished from the townes and houses of honest men, and wandring in waste places, far from danger of law, maketh his mantle his house, and under it covereth himselfe from the wrath of heaven, from the offence of the earth, and from the sight of men. When it raineth it is his pent-house; when it bloweth it is his tent; when it freezeth it is his tabernacle. In Sommer he can wear it loose, in winter he can wrap it close; at all times he can use it; never heavy, never cumbersome. Likewise for a rebell it is as serviceable. For in his warre that he maketh (if at least it deserve the name of warre) when he still flyeth from his foe, and lurketh in the thicke woods and straite passages, waiting for advantages, it is his bed, yea and almost his houshold stuff. For the wood is his house against all weathers, and his mantle is his couch to sleep in. Therein he wrappeth himself round, and coucheth himselfe strongly against the gnats, which in that countrey doe more annoy the naked rebels, whilst they keepe the woods, and doe more sharply wound them then all their enemies swords, or spears, which can seldome come nigh them: yea and oftentimes their mantle serveth them, when they are neere driven, being wrapped about their left arme in stead of a target, for it is hard to cut thorough with a sword, besides it is light to beare, light to throw away, and, being (as they commonly are) naked, it is to them all in all. Lastly for a theife it is so handsome, as it may seem it was first invented for him, for under it he may cleanly convey any fit pillage that commeth handsomly in his way, and when he goeth abroad in the night in free-booting, it is his best and surest friend; for lying, as they often do, 2 or 3 nights together abroad to watch for their booty, with that they can prettily shroud themselves under a bush or a bank side, till they may conveniently do their errand: and when all is over, he can, in his mantle passe thorough any town or company, being close hooded over his head, as he useth, from knowledge of any to whom he is indangered. Besides this, he, or any man els that is disposed to mischief or villany, may under his mantle goe privily armed without suspicion of any, carry his head-peece, his skean, or pistol if he please, to be alwayes in readines. Thus necessary and fitting is a mantle, for a bad man, and surely for a bad huswife it is no lesse convenient, for some of them that bee wandring woe men, called of them Mona-shul, it is halfe a wardrobe; for in Summer you shal find her arrayed commonly but in her smock and mantle to be more ready for her light services: in Winter, and in her travaile, it is her cloake and safeguard, and also a coverlet for her lewde exercise. And when she hath filled her vessell, under it she can hide both her burden, and her blame; yea, and when her bastard is borne, it serves instead of swadling clouts. And as for all other good women which love to doe but little worke, how handsome it is to lye in and sleepe, or to louse themselves in the sun-shine, they that have beene but a while in Ireland can well witnes. Sure I am that you will thinke it very unfit for a good huswife to stirre in, or to busie her selfe about her huswifry in such sort as she should. These be some of the abuses for which I would thinke it meet to forbid all mantles.

Eudox. O evill minded man, that having reckoned up so many uses of a mantle, will yet wish it to be abandoned! Sure I thinke Diogenes dish did never serve his master for more turnes, notwithstanding that he made it his dish, his cup, his cap, his measure, his water-pot, then a mantle doth an Irish man. But I see they be most to bad intents, and therefore I will joyne with you in abolishing it. But what blame lay you to the glibbe? take heed (I pray you) that you be not too busie therewith for feare of your owne blame, seeing our Englishmen take it up in such a generall fashion to weare their haire so immeasurably long, that some of them exceed the longest Irish glibs.

Iren. I feare not the blame of any undeserved dislikes: but for the Irish glibbes, they are as fit maskes as a mantle is for a thiefe. For whensoever he hath run himselfe into that perill of law, that he will not be knowne, he either cutteth of his glibbe quite, by which he becommeth nothing like himselfe, or pulleth it so low downe over his eyes, that it is very hard to discerne his theevish countenance. And therefore fit to be trussed up with the mantle.

Eudox. Truly these three Scythian abuses, I hold most fit to bee taken away with sharpe penalties, and sure I wonder how they have beene kept thus long, notwithstanding so many good provisions and orders, as have beene devised for that people.

Iren. The cause thereof shall appeare to you hereafter: but let us now go forward with our Scythian customes. Of which the next that I have to treat of, is the manner of raising the cry in their conflicts, and at other troublesome times of uproare: the which is very natural Scythian, as you may read in Diodorus Siculus, and in Herodotus, describing the maner of the Scythians and Parthians comming to give the charge at battles: at which it is said, that they came running with a terrible yell as if heaven and earth would have gone together, which is the very image of the Irish hubub, which their kerne use at their first encounter. Besides, the same Herodotus writeth, that they used in their battles to call upon the names of their captains or generals, and somtimes upon their greatest kings deceased, as in that battle of Thomyris against Cyrus: which custome to this day manifestly appeareth amongst the Irish. For at their joying of battle, they lykewise call upon their captaines name, or the word of his auncestours. As they under Oneale cry Laundarg-abo, that is, the bloody hand, which is Oneales badge.[45] They under O Brien call Laun-laider, that is, the strong hand. And to their ensample, the old English also which there remayneth, have gotten up their cryes Scythian-like, as Crom-abo, and Butler-abo. And here also lyeth open an other manifest proofe,

45 The bloody hand is the traditional symbol of Ulster.

that the Irish bee Scythes or Scots, for in all their incounters they use one very common word, crying Ferragh, Ferragh, which is a Scottish word, to wit, the name of one of the first Kings of Scotland, called Feragus, or Fergus, which fought against the Pictes, as you may reade in Buchanan, de rebus Scoticis; but as others write, it was long before that, the name of their chiefe Captaine, under whom they fought against the Africans, the which was then so fortunate unto them, that ever sithence they have used to call upon his name in their battailes.

Eudox. Believe me, this observations of yours, Irenæus, is very good and delightfull; far beyond the blinde conceipt of some, who (I remember) have upon the same word Ferragh, made a very blunt conjecture, as namely Mr. Stanihurst, who though he be the same countrey man borne, that should search more neerly into the secret of these things; yet hath strayed from the truth all the heavens wyde, (as they say,) for he thereupon groundeth a very grosse imagination, that the Irish should descend from the Egyptians which came into that Island, first under the leading of one Scota the daughter of Pharaoh, whereupon the use (saith he) in all their battailes to call upon the name of Pharaoh, crying Ferragh, Ferragh. Surely he shootes wyde on the bow hand, and very far from the marke. For I would first know of him what auncient ground of authority he hath for such a senselesse fable, and if he have any of the rude Irish bookes, as it may be hee hath, yet (me seemes) that a man of his learning should not so lightly have bin carried away with old wives tales, from approvance of his owne reason; for whether it be a smack of any learned iudgment, to say, that Scota is like an Egyptian word, let the learned iudge. But his Scota rather comes of the Greek σχότος, that is, darknes, which hath not let him see the light of the truth.[46]

Iren. You know not Eudoxus, how well M. Stan. could see in the darke: perhaps he hath owles or cats eyes: but well I wot he seeth not well the very light in matters of more weight. But as for Ferragh I have told my coniecture only, and yet thus much I have more to prove a likelyhood, that there be yet at this day in Ireland, many Irish men

---

46 Eudoxus is disparaging 'The Description of Ireland' by Richard Stanihurst (1547–1618), included in the first edition of Holinshed's *Chronicles* (1577), the most popular of later Tudor historical collections. Spenser had read Holinshed by 1579 and may have had access to a copy in Ireland. Again, the motive appears to be a desire to discredit the Old English, this time by attacking their false histories.

(chiefly in the Northerne parts) called by the name of Ferragh. But let that now be: this only for this place suffiseth, that it is a word used in their common hububs, the which (with all the rest) is to be abolished, for that it discovereth an affectation to Irish captainry, which in this platform I indevour specially to beat down. There be other sorts of cryes also used among the Irish, which savour greatly of the Scythian barbarisme, as their lamentations at their buryals, with dispairfull out-cryes, and immoderate waylings, the which M. Stanihurst might also have used for an argument to proove them Egyptians. For so in Scrip-ture it is mentioned, that the Egyptians lamented for the death of Ioseph. Others thinke this custome to come from the Spaniards, for that they doe immeasurably likewise bewayle their dead. But the same is not proper Spanish, but altogether heathenish, brought in thither first either by the Scythians, or the Moores that were Africans, and long possessed that countrey. For it is the manner of all Pagans and Infidels to be intemperate in their waylings of their dead, for that they had no faith nor hope of salvation. And this ill custome also is spe-cially noted by Diodorus Siculus, to have beene in the Scythians, and is yet amongst the Northerne Scots at this day, as you may reade in their chronicles.

Eudox. This is sure an ill custome also, but yet doth not so much concerne civill reformation, as abuse in religion.

Iren. I did not reheerse it as one of the abuses which I thought most worthie of reformation; but having made mention of Irish cryes I thought this manner of lewd crying and howling, not impertinent to be noted as uncivill and Scythian-like: for by these old customes, and other like coniecturall circumstances, the descents of nations can only be proved, where other monuments of writings are not remayning.

Eudox. Then (I pray you) whensoever in your discourse you meet with them by the way, doe not shun, but boldly touch them: for besides their great pleasure and delight for their antiquity, they bring also great profit and helpe unto civility.

Iren. Then sith you will have it so, I will heere take occasion, since I lately spake of their manner of cryes in ioyning of battaile, to speake also somewhat of the manner of their armes, and array in battell, with other customes perhappes worthy the noting. And first of their armes and weapons, amongst which their broad swordes are proper Scythian, for such the Scythes used commonly, as you may read in Olaus Magnus.

And the same also the old Scots used, as you may read in Buchanan, and in Solinus, where the pictures of them are in the same forme expressed. Also their short bowes, and little quivers with short bearded arrowes, are very Scythian, as you may reade in the same Olaus. And the same sort both of bowes, quivers, and arrowes, are at this day to bee seene commonly amongst the Northerne Irish-Scots, whose Scottish bowes are not past three quarters of a yard long, with a string of wreathed hempe slackely bent, and whose arrowes are not much above halfe an ell long, tipped with steele heads, made like common broad arrow heades, but much more sharpe and slender, that they enter into a man or horse most cruelly, notwithstanding that they are shot forth weakely. Moreover their long broad shields, made but with wicker roddes, which are commonly used amongst the said Northerne Irish, but especially of the Scots, are brought from the Scythians, as you may read in Olaus Magnus, Solinus, and others: likewise their going to battle without armor on their bodies or heads, but trusting to the thicknes of their glibbs, the which (they say) will sometimes beare off a good stroke, is meere Scythian, as you may see in the said images of the old Scythes or Scots, set foorth by Herodianus and others. Besides, their confused kinde of march in heapes, without any order or array, their clashing of swords together, their fierce running upon their enemies, and their manner of fight, resembleth altogether that which is read in histories to have beene used of the Scythians. By which it may almost infallibly be gathered together, with other circumstances, that the Irish are very Scots or Scythes originally, though sithence intermingled with many other nations repairing and joyning unto them. And to these I may also adde another strong conjecture which commeth to my mind, that I have often observed there amongst them, that is, certain religious ceremonies, which are very superstitiously yet used amongst them, the which are also written by sundry authors, to have bin observed amongst the Scythians, by which it may very vehemently presumed that the nations were anciently all one. For Plutarch (as I remember) in his Treatise of Homer, indeavouring to search out the truth, what countryman Homer was, prooveth it most strongly (as he thinketh) that he was an Æolian borne, for that in describing a sacrifice of the Greekes, he omitted the loyne, the which all the other Grecians (saving the Æolians) use to burne in their sacrifices: also for that he makes the intralls to be rosted on five spits, which was the proper manner of the Æolians, who onely, of all the nations of Grecia, used to sacrifize in that sort. By which he inferreth necessarily, that Homer was an Æolian. And by the same reason may I as reasonably conclude, that the Irish are descended from the Scythians; for that they use (even to this day) some of the same ceremonies which the Scythians anciently used. As for example, you may reade in Lucian in that sweet dialogue, which is intitled Toxaris, or of friendship, that the common oath of the Scythians was by the sword, and by the fire, for that they accounted those two speciall divine powers, which should worke vengeance on the perjurers. So doe the Irish at this day, when they goe to battaile, say certaine prayers or charmes to their swords, making a crosse therewith upon the earth, and thrusting the points of their blades into the ground; thinking thereby to have the better successe in fight. Also they use commonly to sweare by their swords. Also the Scythians used, when they would binde any solemne vow or combination amongst them, to drink a bowle of blood together, vowing thereby to spend their last blood in that quarrell: and even so do the wild Scots, as you may read in Buchanan: and some of the Northerne Irish. Likewise at the kindling of the fire, and lighting of candles, they say certaine prayers, and use some other superstitious rites, which shew that they honour the fire and the light: for all those Northerne nations, having beene used to be annoyed with much colde and darkenesse, are wont therefore to have the fire and the sunne in great veneration; like as contrarywise the Moores and Egyptians, which are much offended and grieved with extreame heat of the sunne, doe every morning, when the sunne ariseth, fall to cursing and banning of him as their plague. You may also reade in the same booke, in the Tale of Arsacomas, that it was the manner of the Scythians, when any one of them was heavily wronged, and would assemble unto him any forces of people to joyne with him in his revenge, to sit in some publicke place for certaine dayes upon an oxe hide, to which there would resort all such persons as being disposed to take armes would enter into his pay, or joyne with him in his quarrel. And the same you may likewise reade to have beene the ancient manner of the wilde Scotts, which are indeed the very naturall Irish. Moreover the Scythians used to sweare by their Kings hand, as Olaus sheweth. And so do the Irish use now to sweare by their Lords hand, and, to forsweare it, holde it more criminall than to sweare by God.

Also the Scythians said, That they were once a yeare turned into wolves, and so it is written of the Irish: Though Master Camden in a better sense doth suppose it was a disease, called Lycanthropia, so named of the wolfe. And yet some of the Irish doe use to make the wolfe their gossip. The Scythians used also to seethe the flesh in the hide: and so doe the Northerne Irish. The Scythians used to draw the blood of the beast living. and to make meat thereof: and so do the Irish in the North still. Many such customes I could recount unto you, as of their old manner of marrying, of burying, of dancing, of singing, of feasting, of cursing, though Christians have wyped out the most part of them, by resemblance, whereof it might plainly appeare to you, that the nations are the same, but that by the reckoning of these few, which I have told unto you, I finde my speech drawne out to a greater length then I purposed. Thus much onely for this time I hope shall suffise you, to thinke that the Irish are anciently deduced from the Scythians.

Eudox.   Surely Iren. I have heard, in these few words, that from you which I would have thought had bin impossible to have bin spoken of times so remote, and customes so ancient: with delight whereof I was all that while as it were intranced, and carried so farre from my selfe, as that I am now right sorry that you ended so soone. But I marvaile much how it commeth to passe, that in so long a continuance of time, and so many ages come betweene, yet any jot of those olde rites and superstitious customes should remaine amongst them.

Iren.   It is no cause of wonder at all; for it is the maner of many nations to be very superstitious, and diligent observers of old customes and antiquities, which they receive by continuall tradition from their parents, by recording of their Bards and Chronicles, in their songs, and by daylie use and ensample of their elders.

Eudox.   But have you (I pray you) observed any such customes amongst them, brought likewise from the Spaniards or Gaules, as these from the Scythians? that may sure be very materiall to your first purpose.

Iren.   Some perhaps I have; and who that will by this occasion more diligently marke and compare their customes, shall finde many more. But there are fewer remayning of the Gaules or Spaniards, then of the Scythians, by reason that the partes, which they then possessed, lying upon the coast of the Westerne and Southerne Sea, were sithence visited with strangers and forraine people, repayring thither for trafficke, and for fishing, which is very plentifull upon those coasts: for the trade and interdeale of sea-coast nations one with another, worketh more civilitie and good fashions, (all sea men being naturally desirous of new fashions,) then amongst the inland folke, which are seldome seene of forrainers: yet some of such as I have noted, I will recount unto you. And first I will, for the better credit of the rest, shew you one out of their Statutes, among which it is enacted, that no man shall weare his beard onely on the upper lip, shaving all his chinne. And this was the auncient manner of the Spaniards, as yet it is of all the Mahometans to cut off all their beards close, save onelie their Muschachios, which they weare long. And the cause of this use, was for that they, being bred in a hot countrey, found much haire on their faces and other parts to be noyous unto them: for which cause they did cut it most away, like as contrarily all other nations, brought up in cold countreys, do use to nourish their haire, to keepe them the warmer, which was the cause that the Scythians and Scottes wore Glibbes (as I shewed you) to keepe their heads warme, and long beards to defend their faces from cold. From them also (I thinke) came saffron shirts and smocks, which was devised by them in those hot countryes, where saffron is very common and rife, for avoyding that evill which commeth by much sweating, and long wearing of linnen: also the woemen amongst the old Spaniards had the charge of all houshold affaires, both at home and abroad, (as Boemus writeth,) though now the Spaniards use it quite otherwise. And so have the Irish woemen the trust and care of all things, both at home, and in the field. Likewise round leather targets is the Spanish fashion, who used it (for the most part) painted, which in Ireland they use also, in many places, coloured after their rude fashion. Moreover the manner of their woemens riding on the wrong side of the horse, I meane with their faces towards the right side, as the Irish use, is (as they say) old Spanish, and some say African, for amongst them the woemen (they say) use so to ride: Also the deepe smocke sleive, which the Irish woemen use, they say, was old Spanish, and is used yet in Barbary: and yet that should seeme rather to be an old English fashion: for in armory the fashion of the Manche, which is given in armes by many, being indeede nothing else but a sleive, is fashioned much like to that sleive. And that Knights in auncient times used to weare their mistresses or loves sleive, upon their armes, as appeareth by that which is written of Sir Launcelot, that he wore the sleive of the faire Maide of

Asteloth, in a tourney, whereat Queene Gueneuer was much displeased.

Eudox.   Your conceipt is good, and well fitting for things so far growne from certainty of knowlege and learning, onely upon likelyhoods and conjectures. But have you any customes remaining from the Gaules or Brittaines?

Iren.   I have observed a few of either; and who will better search into them, may finde more. And first the profession of their Bardes was (as Cæsar writeth) usuall amongst the Gaules, and the same was also common amongst the Brittans, and is not yet altogether left off with the Welsh which are their posterity. For all the fashions of the Gaules and Brittaines; as he testifieth, were much like. The long darts came also from the Gaules, as you may read in the same Cæsar, and in Io. Boemus. Likewise the said Io. Boemus writeth, that the Gaules used swords a handfull broad, and so doe the Irish now. Also they used long wicker shields in battaile that should cover their whole bodies, and so doe the Northerne Irish. But I have not seene such fashioned targets used in the Southerne parts, but onely amongst the Northerne people, and Irish-Scottes, I doe thinke that they were brought in rather by the Scythians, then by the Gaules. Also the Gaules used to drinke their enemyes blood, and painte themselves therewith. So also they write, that the old Irish were wont, and so have I seene some of the Irish doe, but not their enemyes but friends blood. As namely at the execution of a notable traytor at Limericke, called Murrogh O-Brien, I saw an old woman, which was his foster mother, take up his head, whilst he was quartered, and sucked up all the blood that runne thereout, saying, that the earth was not worthy to drinke it, and therewith also steeped her face and breast, and tore her haire, crying out and shrieking most terribly.[47]

Eudox.   You have very well runne through such customes as the Irish have derived from the first old nations which inhabited the land; namely, the Scythians, the Spaniards, the Gaules, and the Brittaines. It now remaineth that you take in hand the customes of the old English which are amongst the Irish: of which I doe not thinke that you shall have much cause to finde fault with, considering that, by the

---

47   This took place on 1 July 1577. If it is an eye-witness account, as many commentators allege, then Spenser was clearly in Ireland before he went over with Lord Grey in 1580, probably as part of his service under the Earl of Leicester.

English, most of the old bad Irish customes were abolished, and more civill fashions brought in their stead.

Iren. You think otherwise, Eudox. then I doe, for the cheifest abuses which are now in that realme, are growne from the English, and some of them are now much more lawlesse and licentious then the very wilde Irish: so that as much care as was by them had to reforme the Irish, so and much more must now bee used to reforme them; so much time doth alter the manners of men.

Eudox. That seemeth very strange which you say, that men should so much degenerate from their first natures, as to grow wilde.

Iren. So much can liberty and ill examples doe.

Eudox. What liberty had the English there, more then they had here at home? Were not the lawes planted amongst them at the first, and had they not governours to curbe and keepe them still in awe and obedience?

Iren. They had, but it was, for the most part, such as did more hurt then good; for they had governours for the most part of themselves, and commonly out of the two families of the Geraldines and Butlers, both adversaries and corrivales one against the other. Who though for the most part they were but deputies under some of the Kings of Englands sonnes, brethren, or other neare kinsmen, who were the Kings lieutenants, yet they swayed so much, as they had all the rule, and the others but the title. Of which Butlers and Geraldynes, albeit (I must confesse) there were very brave and worthy men, as also of other the Peeres of that realme, made Lo: Deputies, and Lo: Iustices at sundry times, yet thorough greatnes of their late conquests and seignories they grew insolent, and bent both that regall authority, and also their private powers, one against another, to the utter subversion of themselves, and strengthning of the Irish againe.[48] This you may read plainely discovered by a letter written from the citizens of Cork out of Ireland, to the Earle of Shrewsbury then in England, and remaining yet upon record, both in the Towre of London, and also

---

48 Irenius is referring to the traditional rivalry between the Geraldines and the Butlers for control of Irish policy. Their conflict became less important after 1530 when Lord Deputies were sent over from England, ending the Crown's traditional reliance upon the Geraldines. The chief revolts against English government in the sixteenth century before O'Neill's rising – the Nine Years' War – were most frequently Old English reactions to loss of power and privileges.

among the Chronicles of Ireland. Wherein it is by them complained, that the English Lords and Gentlemen, who then had great possessions in Ireland, began, through pride and insolency, to make private warres one against another, and, when either part was weak, they would wage and draw in the Irish to take their part, by which meanes they both greatly encouraged and inabled the Irish, which till that time had beene shut up within the Mountaines of Slewlogher, and weakened and disabled themselves, insomuch that their revenues were wonderfully impaired, and some of them which are there reckoned to have been able to have spent 12 or 1300 pounds per annum, of old rent, (that I may say no more) besides their commodities of creekes and havens, were now scarce able to dispend the third part. From which disorder, and through other huge calamities which have come upon them thereby, they are almost now growne like the Irish; I meane of such English, as were planted above towards the West; for the English Pale hath preserved it selfe, thorough nearenes of the state in reasonable civilitie, but the rest which dwelt in Connaght and in Mounster, which is the sweetest soyle of Ireland, and some in Leinster and Ulster, are degenerate, yea, and some of them have quite shaken off their English names, and put on Irish that they might bee altogether Irish.

Eudox.   Is it possible that any should so farre growe out of frame that they should in so short space, quite forget their countrey and their owne names! that is a most dangerous lethargie, much worse than that of Messala Corvinus, who, being a most learned man, thorough sickenesse forgat his owne name. But can you count us any of this kinde?

Iren.   I cannot but by report of the Irish themselves, who report, that the Mac-mahons* in the North, were aunciently English, to wit, descended from the Fitz Ursulas, which was a noble family in England, and that the same appeareth by the signification of their Irish names: Likewise that the Mac-swynes, now in Ulster, were aunciently of the Veres in England, but that they themselves, for hatred of English, so disguised their names.

Eudox.   Could they ever conceive any such dislike of their owne natu-

---

*   These families of Mac-mahones and Mac-swines are by others held to be of the ancient Irish.

ral countryes, as that they would bee ashamed of their name, and byte at the dugge from which they sucked life?

Iren. I wote well there should be none; but proud hearts doe oftentimes (like wanton colts) kicke at their mothers, as we read Alcibiades and Themistocles did, who, being banished out of Athens, fled unto the Kings of Asia, and there stirred them up to warre against their country, in which warres they themselves were cheiftaines. So they say did these Mac-swines and Mac-mahons, or rather Veres and Fitz-Ursulaes, for private despight, turne themselves against England. For at such time as Robert Vere, Earl of Oxford, was in the Barons warres against King Richard the Second, through the mallice of the Peeres, banished the realme and proscribed, he with his kinsman Fitz-Ursula fled into Ireland, where being prosecuted, and afterwards in England put to death, his kinsman there remaining behinde in Ireland rebelled, and, conspiring with the Irish, did quite cast off both their English name and alleagiance, since which time they have so remained still, and have since beene counted meere Irish. The very like is also reported of the Mac-swines, Mac-mahones, and Mac-shehies of Mounster, how they likewise were aunciently English, and old followers to the Earle of Desmond, untill the raigne of King Edward the Fourth: at which time the Earle of Desmond that then was, called Thomas, being through false subornation (as they say) of the Queene for some offence by her against him conceived, brought to his death at Tredagh* most unjustly, notwithstanding that he was a very good and sound subject to the King: Thereupon all his kinsemen of the Geraldines, which then was a mighty family in Mounster, in revenge of that huge wrong, rose into armes against the King, and utterly renounced and forsooke all obedience to the Crowne of England, to whom the said Mac-swines, Mac-shehies, and Mac-mahones, being then servants and followers, did the like, and have ever sithence so continued. And with them (they say) all the people of Mounster went out, and many other of them, which were meere English, thenceforth joyned with the Irish against the King, and termed themselves very Irish, taking on them Irish habits and customes, which could never since be cleane wyped

---

* Others hould that he was beheaded at Tredagh, 15. Febr. 1467, by (the command of) Iohn Tiptoft Earle of Worcester, then Lo: Deputy of Ireland, for exacting of Coyne and Livery. Vid. Camden. Britan. pag. 738, edit. Londin. an. 1607.

away, but the contagion hath remained still amongst their posterityes. Of which sort (they say) be most of the surnames which end in an, as Hernan, Shinan, Mungan, &c. the which now account themselves naturall Irish. Other great houses there bee of the English in Ireland, which thorough licentious conversing with the Irish, or marrying, or fostering with them, or lacke of meete nurture, or other such un-happy occasions, have degendred from their auncient dignities, and are now growne as Irish, as O-hanlans breech, as the proverbe there is.

Eudox.   In truth this which you tell is a most shamefull hearing, and to be reformed with most sharpe censures, in so great personages to the terrour of the meaner: for if the lords and cheife men degenerate, what shall be hoped of the peasants, and baser people? And hereby sure you have made a faire way unto your selfe to lay open the abuses of their evill customes, which you have now next to declare, the which, no doubt, but are very bad, being borrowed from the Irish, as their apparell, their language, their riding, and many other the like.

Iren.   You cannot but hold them sure to be very uncivill; for were they at the best that they were of old, when they were brought in, they should in so long an alteration of time seeme very uncouth and strange. For it is to be thought, that the use of all England was in the raigne of Henry the Second, when Ireland was planted with English, very rude and barbarous, so as if the same should be now used in England by any, it would seeme worthy of sharpe correction, and of new lawes for reformation, for it is but even the other day since England grew civill: Therefore in counting the evill customes of the English there, I will not have regard, whether the beginning thereof were English or Irish, but will have respect onely to the inconvenience thereof. And first I have to finde fault with the abuse of language, that is, for the speaking of Irish among the English, which as it is unnaturall that any people should love anothers language more then their owne, so it is very inconvenient, and the cause of many other evills.

Eudox.   It seemeth strange to me that the English should take more delight to speake that language, then their owne, whereas they should (mee thinkes) rather take scorne to acquaint their tongues thereto. For it hath ever beene the use of the conquerour, to despise the lan-guage of the conquered, and to force him by all meanes to learne his. So did the Romans alwayes use, insomuch that there is almost no nation in the world, but is sprinckled with their language. It were good therefore (me seemes) to search out the originall cause of this evill; for, the same being discovered, a redresse thereof will the more easily be provided: For I thinke it very strange, that the English being so many, and the Irish so few, as they then were left, the fewer should draw the more unto their use.

Iren.   I suppose that the chiefe cause of bringing in the Irish language, amongst them, was specially their fostering, and marrying with the Irish, the which are two most dangerous infections; for first the childe that sucketh the milke of the nurse, must of necessity learne his first speach of her, the which being the first inured to his tongue, is ever after most pleasing unto him, insomuch as though hee afterwards be taught English, yet the smacke of the first will allwayes abide with him; and not onely of the speach, but also of the manners and conditions. For besides that young children be like apes, which will affect and imitate what they see done before them, especially by their nurses, whom they love so well, they moreover drawe into themselves, together with their sucke, even the nature and disposition of their nurses: for the minde followeth much the temperature of the body: and also the words are the image of the minde, so as they proceeding from the minde, the minde must needes be affected with the words. So that the speach being Irish, the heart must needes bee Irish: for out of the abundance of the heart, the tongue speaketh. The next is the marrying with the Irish, which how dangerous a thing it is in all commonwealthes, appeareth to every simplest sence, and though some great ones have perhaps used such matches with their vassals, and have of them neverthelesse raised worthy issue, as Telamon did with Teemessa, Alexander the Great with Roxana, and Iulius Cæsar with Cleopatra, yet the example is so perillous, as it is not to be adventured: for in stead of those few good, I could count unto them infinite many evill. And indeed how can such matching succeede well, seeing that commonly the childe taketh most of his nature of the mother, besides speach, manners, and inclynation, which are (for the most part) agreeable to the conditions of their mothers: for by them they are first framed and fashioned, so as what they receive once from them, they will hardly ever after forgoe. Therefore are these evill customes of fostering and marrying with the Irish, most carefully to be restrayned: for of them two, the third evill that is the custome of language, (which I spake of,) chiefly proceedeth.

Eudox.　But are there not lawes already provided, for avoyding of this evill?

Iren.　Yes, I thinke there be, but as good never a whit as never the better. For what doe statutes availe without penalties, or lawes without charge of execution? for so there is another like law enacted against wearing of the Irish apparell,[49] but neverthemore is it observed by any, or executed by them that have the charge: for they in their private discretions thinke it not fit to bee forced upon the poore wretches of that country, which are not worth the price of English apparell, nor expedient to be practised against the abler sort, by reason that the country (say they) doth yeeld no better, and were there better to be had, yet these were fitter to be used, as namely, the mantle in travalling, because there be no Innes where meete bedding may be had, so that his mantle serves him then for a bed; the leather quilted iacke in iourneying and in camping, for that is fittest to be under his shirt of mayle, and for any occasion of suddaine service, as there happen may, to cover his trouse on horsebacke; the great linnen roll, which the women weare, to keepe their heads warme, after cutting their haire, which they use in sicknesse; besides their thicke folded linnen shirts, their long-sleived smocks, their halfe-sleived coates, their silken fillets, and all the rest; they will devise some colour for, either of necessity, or of antiquity, or of comelynesse.

Eudox.　But what colour soever they alledge, mee thinkes it is not expedient, that the execution of a law once ordayned should be left to the discretion of the iudge, or officer, but that, without partialitie or regard, it should be fulfilled as well on English, as Irish.

Iren.　But they thinke this precisenes in reformation of apparell not to be so materiall, or greatly pertinent.

Eudox.　Yes surely but it is: for mens apparell is commonly made according to their conditions, and their conditions are oftentimes governed by their garments: for the person that is gowned, is by his gowne put in minde of gravitie, and also restrained from lightnes, by the very unaptnesse of his weed. Therefore it is written by Aristotle, that when Cyrus had overcome the Lydians that were a warlike nation, and devised to bring them to a more peaceable life, hee changed their apparell and musick, and, in stead of their short warlike coat, cloathed them in

49　There were laws against the English wearing Irish clothes as early as 1297.

long garments like women, and, in stead of their warlike musick, appointed to them certaine lascivious layes, and loose jiggs, by which in short space their mindes were so mollified and abated, that they forgot their former fiercenesse, and became most tender and effeminate; whereby it appeareth, that there is not a little in the garment to the fashioning of the minde and conditions. But be these, which you have described, the fashions of the Irish weedes?

Iren. No: all these which I have rehearsed to you, be not Irish garments, but English; for the quilted leather iack is old English: for it was the proper weed of the horseman, as you may read in Chaucer, when he describeth Sir Thopas apparell and armour, as hee went to fight against the gyant, in his robe of shecklaton, which is that kind of guilded leather with which they use to imbroyder their Irish iackets. And there likewise by all that description, you may see the very fashion and manner of the Irish horseman most truely set forth, in his long hose, his ryding shooes of costly cordwaine, his hacqueton, and his haberjeon, with all the rest thereunto belonging.

Eudox. I surely thought that the manner had beene Irish, for it is farre differing from that we have now, as also all the furniture of his horse, his strong brasse bit, his slyding reynes, his shanke pillion without stirruppes, his manner of mounting, his fashion of ryding, his charging of his speare aloft above head, the forme of his speare.

Iren. No sure; they be native English, and brought in by the Englishmen first into Ireland: neither is the same accounted an uncomely manner of ryding; for I have heard some great warriours say, that, in all the services which they had seene abroad in forraigne countreyes, they never saw a more comely man then the Irish man, nor that commeth on more bravely in his charge; neither is his manner of mounting unseemely, though hee lacke stirruppes, but more ready then with stirruppes; for, in his getting up, his horse is still going, whereby hee gayneth way. And therefore the stirrup was called so in scorne, as it were a stay to get up, being derived of the old English word sty, which, is, to get up, or mounte.

Eudox. It seemeth then that you finde no fault with this manner of ryding? why then would you have the quilted iacke laid away?

Iren. I doe not wish it to be laide away, but the abuse thereof to be put away; for being used to the end that it was framed, that is, to be worne in warre under a shirt of mayle, it is allowable, as also the shirt of mayle, and all his other furniture: but to be worne daylie at home, and in townes and civile places, is a rude habite and most uncomely seeming like a players painted coate.

Eudox. But it is worne (they say) likewise of Irish footmen; how doe you allow of that? for I should thinke it very unseemely.

Iren. No, not as it is used in warre, for it is worne then likewise of footmen under their shirts of mayle, the which footmen they call Galloglasses, the which name doth discover them also to be auncient English: for *Gall-ogla* signifies an English servitour or yeoman. And he being so armed in a long shirt of mayle downe to the calfe of his leg, with a long broad axe in his hand, was then *pedes gravis armaturæ*, and was insteed of the armed footeman that now weareth a corslet, before the corslet was used, or almost invented.

Eudox. Then him belike you likewise allow in your straite reformation of old customes.

Iren. Both him and the kerne also, (whom onely I take to bee the proper Irish souldier,) can I allow, so that they use that habite and custome of theirs in the warres onely, when they are led forth to the service of their Prince, and not usually at home, and in civile places, and besides doe laye aside the evill and wilde uses which the galloglasse and kerne do use in their common trade of life.

Eudox. What be those?

Iren. Marrie those bee the most barbarous and loathly conditions of any people (I thinke) under heaven: for, from the time that they enter into that course, they doe use all the beastly behaviour that may bee; they oppresse all men, they spoile aswell the subject, as the enemy; they steale, they are cruell and bloodie, full of revenge and delighting in deadly execution, licentious, swearers, and blasphemers, common ravishers of woemen, and murtherers of children.

Eudox. These bee most villainous conditions; I marvaile then that they be ever used or imployed, or almost suffered to live; what good can there then be in them?

Iren. Yet sure they are very valiaunt, and hardie, for the most part great indurers of colde, labour, hunger, and all hardnesse, very active and strong of hand, very swift of foot, very vigilant and circumspect in their enterprises, very present in perils, very great scorners of death.

Eudox. Truely by this that you say, it seemes that the Irishman is a very brave souldier.

Iren. Yea surely, in that rude kinde of service, hee beareth himselfe very couragiously. But when hee commeth to experience of service abroad, or is put to a peece, or a pike, hee maketh as worthie a souldiour as any nation hee meeteth with. But let us (I pray you) turne againe to our discourse of evill customes among the Irish.

Eudox. Me thinkes, all this which you speake of, concerneth the customes of the Irish very materially, for their uses in warre are of no small importance to bee considered, aswell to reforme those which are evill as to confirme and continue those which are good. But follow you your owne course, and shew what other their customes you have to dislike of.

Iren. There is amongst the Irish a certaine kind of people, called Bardes, which are to them instead of poets, whose profession is to set foorth the praises or dispraises of men in their poems or rymes, the which are had in so high regard and estimation amongst them, that none dare displease them for feare to runne into reproach thorough their offence, and to be made infamous in the mouthes of all men. For their verses are taken up with a generall applause, and usually sung at all feasts and meetings, by certaine other persons, whose proper function that is, who also receive for the same great rewards and reputation amongst them.

Eudox. Doe you blame this in them which I would otherwise have thought to have beene worthy of good accompt, and rather to have beene maintained and augmented amongst them, then to have been disliked? for I have reade that in all ages Poets have beene had in speciall reputation, and that (me thinkes) not without great cause; for besides their sweete inventions, and most wittie layes, they have alwayes used to set foorth the praises of the good and vertuous, and to beate downe and disgrace the bad and vitious. So that many brave yong mindes, have oftentimes thorough hearing the praises and famous eulogies of worthie men sung and reported unto them, beene stirred up to affect the like commendations, and so to strive to the like deserts. So they say that the Lacedemonians were more excited to desire of honour, with the excellent verses of the Poet Tirtæus, then with all the exhortations of their Captaines, or authority of their Rulers and Magistrates.

Iren. It is most true, that such Poets as in their writings doe labour to better the manners of men, and thorough the sweete baite of their numbers, to steale into the young spirits a desire of honour and vertue, are worthy to bee had in great respect. But these Irish Bardes are for the most part of another minde, and so farre from instructing yong men in morall discipline, that they themselves doe more deserve to bee sharpely disciplined; for they seldome use to choose unto themselves the doings of good men for the arguments of their poems, but whomsoever they finde to be most licentious of life, most bolde and lawlesse in his doings, most dangerous and desperate in all parts of disobedience and rebellious disposition, him they set up and glorifie in their rithmes, him they praise to the people, and to yong men make an example to follow.

Eudox. I marvaile what kinde of speeches they can finde, or what face they can put on, to praise such bad persons as live so lawleslie and licentiouslie upon stealthes and spoyles, as most of them doe, or how can they thinke that any good mind will applaude or approve the same.

Iren. There is none so bad, Eudoxus, but shall finde some to favour his doings; but such licentious partes as these, tending for the most part to the hurt of the English, or maintenance of their owne lewde libertie, they themselves being most desirous therof, doe most allow. Besides this, evill things being decked and attired with the gay attire of goodly words, may easily deceive and carry away the affection of a young mind, that is not well stayed, but desirous by some bolde adventures to make proofe of himselfe; for being (as they all be brought up idely) without awe of parents, without precepts of masters, and without feare of offence, not being directed, nor imployed in any course of life, which may carry them to vertue, will easily be drawne to follow such as any shall set before them; for a yong minde cannot rest; if he be not still busied in some goodnesse, he will finde himselfe such businesse, as shall soone busie all about him. In which if he shall finde any to praise him, and to give him encouragement, as those Bardes and rythmers doe for little reward, or a share of a stolne cow, then waxeth he most insolent and halfe madde with the love of himselfe, and his owne lewd deeds. And as for words to set forth such lewdnes, it is not hard for them to give a goodly and painted shew thereunto, borrowed even from the praises which are proper to vertue it selfe. As of a most notorious thiefe and wicked out-law, which had lived all his life-time of spoyles and robberies, one of their Bardes in his praise will say, That he was none of the idle milke-sops that was brought up by the fire side, but that most of his dayes he spent in armes and valiant enterprises, that he did never eat his meat, before he had won it with his sword, that he lay not all night slugging in a cabbin under his mantle, but used commonly to keepe others waking to defend their lives, and did light his candle at the flames of their houses, to leade him in the darknesse; that the day was his night, and the night his day; that he loved not to be long wooing of wenches to yeeld to him, but where he came he tooke by force the spoyle of other mens love, and left but lamentation to their lovers; that his musick was not the harpe, nor layes of love, but the cryes of people, and clashing of armor; and finally, that he died not bewayled of many, but made many waile when he died, that dearly bought his death. Doe you not thinke (Eudoxus) that many of these praises might be applyed to men of best deserts? yet are they all yeelded to a most notable traytor, and amongst some of the Irish not smally accounted of. For the song, when it was first made and sung to a person of high degree there, was bought (as their manner is) for fourty crownes.

Eudox. And well worthy sure. But tell me (I pray you) have they any art in their compostions? or bee they any thing wittie or well savoured, as poemes should be?

Iren. Yea truely, I have caused divers of them to be translated unto me, that I might understand them, and surely they savoured of sweet wit and good invention, but skilled not of the goodly ornaments of poetry; yet were they sprinkled with some pretty flowers of their naturall device, which gave good grace and comlinesse unto them, the which it is great pitty to see abused, to the gracing of wickednes and vice, which with good usage would serve to adorne and beautifie vertue.[50] This evill custome therefore needeth reformation. And now next after the Irish Kerne, me thinks the Irish Hors-boyes would come well in order, the use of which, though necessity (as times now be) do enforce, yet in the thorough reformation of that realme they should be cut off. For the cause why they are now to be permitted, is want of convenient innes for lodging of travailers on horsback, and of hostlers to tend their horses by the way. But when things shalbe reduced to a better passe, this needeth specially to be reformed. For out of the fry

---

50 Further evidence that Spenser was interested in Irish culture.

of these rakehell horse-boyes, growing up in knavery and villainy, are their kerne continually supplyed and maintained. For having been once brought up an idle horse-boy, he will never after fall to labour, but is only made fit for the halter. And these also (the which is one foule over-sight) are for the most part bred up amongst the Englishmen, of whom learning to shoote in a piece, and being made acquainted with all the trades of the English, they are afterwards when they become kerne, made more fit to cut their throats. Next to this, there is another much like, but much more lewde and dishonest, and that is, of their Carrows, which is a kinde of people that wander up and downe to Gentle-mens houses, living onely upon cardes and dice, the which, though they have little or nothing of their owne, yet will they play for much money, which if they winne, they waste most lightly, and if they lose, they pay as slenderly, but make recompence with one stealth or another, whose onely hurt is not, that they themselves are idle lossells, but that thorough gaming they draw others to like lewdnesse and idlenesse. And to these may be added another sort of like loose fellowes, which doe passe up and downe amongst gentlemen by the name of Iesters, but are (indeed) notable rogues, and partakers not onely of many stealthes, by setting forth other mens goods to be stolne, but also privy to many traitrous practices, and common carryers of newes, with desire whereof you would wonder how much the Irish are fed; for they use commonly to send up and downe to knowe newes, and if any meet with another, his second word is, What news? Insomuch that hereof is tolde a prettie jest of a French-man, who having beene sometimes in Ireland, where he marked their great inquirie for newes, and meeting afterwards in France an Irishman, whom hee knew in Ireland, first saluted him, and afterwards said thus merrily: O Sir, I pray you tell me of curtesie, have you heard any thing of the news, that you so much inquired for in your countrey?

Eudox. This argueth sure in them a great desire of innovation, and therefore these occasions which nourish the same must be taken away, as namely, those Iesters, Carrowes, Mona-shules, and all such straglers, for whom (me thinkes) the short riddance of a Marshall were meeter then an ordinance or prohibition to restrain them. Therefore (I pray you) leave all this rabblement of runnagates, and passe to other customes.

Iren. There is a great use amongst the Irish, to make great assemblies together upon a rath or hill, there to parlie (as they say) about matters and wrongs betweene township and township, or one privat person and another. But well I wot, and true it hath beene oftentimes proved, that in their meetings many mischiefes have beene both practised and wrought; for to them doe commonly resort all the scumme of the people, where they may meete and conferre of what they list, which else they could not doe without suspition or knowledge of others. Besides at these meetings I have knowne divers times, that many Englishmen, and good Irish subjects, have bin villanously murdered by moving one quarrell or another against them. For the Irish never come to those raths but armed, whether on horse or on foot, which the English nothing suspecting, are then commonly taken at advantage like sheep in the pin-folde.

Eudox. It may be (Iræneus) that abuse may be in those meetings. But these round hills and square bawnes, which you see so strongly trenched and throwne up, were (they say) at first ordained for the same purpose, that people might assemble themselves therein, and therefore aunciently they were called Folkmotes, that is, a place of people, to meete or talke of any thing that concerned any difference betweene parties and towneships, which seemeth yet to me very requisite.

Iren. You say very true, Eudoxus, the first making of these high hils, were at first indeed to very good purpose for people to meet; but howsoever the times when they were first made, might well serve to good occasions, as perhaps they did then in England, yet things being since altered, and now Ireland much differing from the state of England, the good use that then was of them, is now turned to abuse; for those hills whereof you speak, were (as you may gather by reading) appointed for 2 special uses, and built by 2 several nations. The one is that which you call Folk-motes, which were built by the Saxons, as the word bewraieth, for it signifieth in Saxon, a meeting of folk, and these are for the most part in forme foure square, well intrenched; the others that were round, were cast up by the Danes, as the name of them doth betoken, for they are called Danesraths, that is, hills of the Danes, the which were by them devised, not for treaties and parlies, but appointed as fortes for them to gather unto, in troublesome time, when any trouble arose; for the Danes being but a few in comparison

of the Saxons* (in England) used this for their safety; they made those
small round hills, so strongly fenced, in every quarter of the hundred,
to the end that if in the night, or any other time, any troublous cry or
uproare should happen, they might repaire with all speed unto their
owne fort, which was appointed for their quarter, and there remaine
safe, till they could assemble themselves in greater strength; for they
were made so strong with one small entrance, that whosoever came
thither first, were he one or two, or like few, he or they might there
rest safe, and defend themselves against many, till more succour came
unto them: and when they were gathered to a sufficient number, they
marched to the next fort, and so forward till they met with the perill,
or knew the occasions thereof. But besides these two sorts of hills,
there were anciently divers others; for some were raised, where there
had been a great battle fought, as a memory or trophie thereof; others, as monuments of burialls, of the carcasses of all those that were
slaine in any field, upon whom they did throwe such round mounts,
as memorialls of them, and sometimes did cast up great heapes of
stones, (as you may read the like in many places of the Scripture,) and
other whiles they did throw up many round heapes of earth in a cir-
cle, like a garland, or pitch many long stones on end in compasse,
every of which (they say) betokened some person of note there slaine
and buried; for this was their auncient custome, before Christianity
came in amongst them, that Church-yards were inclosed.

Eudox.   You have very well declared the originall of their mounts and
great stones incompassed, which some vainely terme the ould Giants
Trevetts, and thinke that those huge stones would not else be brought
into order or reared up, without the strength of gyants. And others
vainely thinke that they were never placed there by mans hand or art,
but onely remained there so since the beginning, and were afterwards
discovered by the deluge, and laide open as then by the washing of
the waters, or other like casualty. But let them dreame their owne
imaginations to please themselves, you have satisfied me much better,
both for that I see some confirmation thereof in the Holy Writt, and
also remember that I have read, in many Historyes and Chronicles,
the like mounts and stones oftentimes mentioned.

---

* The like person may be given for the making of such rathes in Ireland, by the Danes
or Norwegians. Vid. Gir. Cambr. topog. Hib. distinct. 3. cap. 37.

Iren.   There be many great authorities (I assure you) to prove the same, but as for these meetings on hills, whereof we were speaking, it is very inconvenient that any such should be permitted.

Eudox.   But yet it is very needefull (me thinkes) for many other purposes, as for the countryes to gather together, when there is any imposition to be laide upon them, to the which they then may all agree at such meetings to devide upon themselves, according to their holdings and abilities. So as if at these assemblies, there be any officers, as Constables, Bayliffes, or such like amongst them, there can be no perill, or doubt of such bad practises.

Iren.   Neverthelesse, dangerous are such assemblies, whether for cesse or ought else, the Constables and Officers being also of the Irish; and if any of the English happen to be there, even to them they may prove perillous. Therefore for avoyding of all such evill occasions, they were best to be abolished.

Eudox.   But what is that which you call cesse? it is a word sure unused among us here, therefore (I pray you) expound the same.

Iren.   Cesse is none other then that which your selfe called imposition, but it is in a kinde unacquainted perhaps unto you. For there are cesses of sundry sorts; one is, the cessing of souldiours upon the countrey: For Ireland being a countrey of warre (as it is handled) and alwayes full of souldiours, they which have the government, whether they finde it the most ease to the Queenes purse, or the most ready meanes at hand for victualing of the souldiour, or that necessity inforceth them thereunto, do scatter the army abroad in the countrey, and place them in villages to take their victuals of them, at such vacant times as they lye not in campe, nor are otherwise imployed in service. Another kinde of cesse, is the imposing of provision for the Governors house-keeping, which though it be most necessary, and be also (for avoyding of all the evills formerly therein used) lately brought to a composition, yet it is not without great inconveniences, no lesse then here in England, or rather much more. The like cesse is also charged upon the countrey sometimes for victualling of the souldiours, when they lye in garrison, at such times as there is none remayning in the Queenes store, or that the same cannot be conveniently conveyed to their place of garrison. But these two are not easily to be redressed when necessity thereto compelleth; but as for the former, as it is not necessary, so it is most hurtfull and offensive to the poore country,

and nothing convenient for the souldiers themselves, who, during
their lying at cesse, use all kinde of outragious disorder and villany,
both towards the poore men, which victuall and lodge them, as also
to all the country round about them, whom they abuse, oppresse,
spoyle, and afflict by all the meanes they can invent, for they will not
onely not content themselves with such victuals as their hostes nor yet
as the place perhaps affords, but they will have other meate provided
for them, and *aqua vita* sent for, yea and money besides laide at their
trenchers, which if they want, then about the house they walk with
the wretched poore man and his silly wife, who are glad to purchase
their peace with any thing. By which vile manner of abuse, the countrey
people, yea and the very English which dwell abroad and see, and
sometimes feele this outrage, growe into great detestation of the
souldiours, and thereby into hatred of the very government, which
draweth upon them such evills: And therefore this you may also ioyne
unto the former evill customes, which we have to reprove in Ireland.

Eudox.   Truly this is one not the least, and though the persons, by
whom it is used, be of better note then the former roguish sort, which
you reckoned, yet the fault (me thinkes) is no lesse worthy of a Marshall.

Iren.   That were a harder course, Eudoxus, to redresse every abuse by
a Marshall: it would seeme to you very evill surgery to cut off every
unsound or sicke part of the body, which, being by other due meanes
recovered, might afterwards doe very good service to the body againe,
and haply helpe to save the whole: Therefore I thinke better that
some good salve for the redresse of the evill bee sought forth, then
the least part suffered to perish: but hereof wee have to speake in
another place. Now we will proceede to other like defects, amongst
which there is one generall inconvenience, which raigneth almost
throughout all Ireland: that is, the Lords of land and Free-holders,
doe not there use to set out their land in farme, or for tearme of
yeares, to their tennants, but onely from yeare to yeare, and some
during pleasure, neither indeede will the Irish tennant or husbandman
otherwise take his land, then so long as he list himselfe. The reason
hereof in the tennant is, for that the land-lords there use most shame-
fully to racke their tennants, laying upon them coigny and livery at
pleasure, and exacting of them (besides his covenants) what he pleaseth.
So that the poore husbandman either dare not binde himselfe to him
for longer tearme, or thinketh, by his continuall liberty of change, to

keepe his land-lord the rather in awe from wronging of him. And the reason why the land-lord will no longer covenant with him, is, for that he dayly looketh after change and alteration, and hovereth in expectation of new worlds.

Eudox.   But what evill commeth hereby to the common-wealth, or what reason is it that any landlord should not set nor any tennant take his land, as himselfe list?

Iren.   Marry, the evils which commeth hereby are great, for by this meanes both the land-lord thinketh that he hath his tennant more at commaund, to follow him into what action soever hee shall enter, and also the tennant being left at his liberty is fit for every occasion of change that shall be offered by time: and so much also the more ready and willing is he to runne into the same, for that hee hath no such state in any his houlding, no such building upon any farme, no such coste imployed in fensing or husbanding the same, as might with-hold him from any such wilfull course, as his lords cause, or his owne lewde disposition may carry him unto. All which hee hath forborne, and spared so much expence, for that he had no firme estate in his tenement, but was onely a tennant at will or little more, and so at will may leave it. And this inconvenience may be reason enough to ground any ordinance for the good of the common-wealth, against the private behoofe or will of any landlord that shall refuse to graunt any such terme or estate unto his tennant, as may tende to the good of the whole realme.

Eudox.   Indeede (me thinkes) it is a great willfullnes in any such land-lord to refuse to make any longer farmes unto their tennants, as may, besides the generall good of the realme, be also greatly for their owne profit and availe: For what reasonable man will not thinke that the tenement shal be made much better for the lords behoofe, if the tennant may by such good meanes bee drawne to build himselfe some handsome habitation thereon, to ditch and inclose his ground, to manure and husband it as good farmours use? For when his tennants terme shal be expired, it will yeeld him, in the renewing his lease, both a good fine, and also a better rent. And also it shall be for the good of the tennant likewise, who by such buildings and inclosures shall receive many benefits: first, by the handsomenesse of his house, he shall take more comfort of his life, more safe dwelling, and a delight to keepe his said house neate and cleanely, which now being, as they commonly are, rather swyne-styes then houses, is the cheifest cause of his so beastly manner of life, and savage condition, lying and living together with his beast in one house, in one roome, in one bed, that is, cleane strawe, or rather a foul dunghill. And to all these other commodities hee shall in short time find a greater added, that is his owne wealth and riches increased, and wonderfully inlarged, by keeping his cattle in inclosures, where they shall alwayes have fresh pasture, that now is all trampled and over-runne; warme covert, that now lyeth open to all weather; safe being, that now are continually filched and stolne.

Iren. You have, Eudoxus, well accompted the commodities of this one good ordinance, amongst which, this that you named last is not the least; for, all the other being most beneficiall to the land-lord and tennant, this cheifly redoundeth to the good of the common-wealth, to have the land thus inclosed, and well fenced. For it is both a principall barre and impeachment unto theeves from stealing of cattle in the night, and also a gaule against all rebels, and outlawes, that shall rise up in any numbers against the government; for the theife thereby shall have much adoe, first to bring forth and afterwards to drive away his stolne prey, but thorough the common high wayes, where he shall soone bee descryed and met withall: And the rebell or open enemy, if any such shall happen, either at home, or from abroad, shall easily be found when he commeth forth, and also be well incountered withall by a few, in so straight passages and strong inclosures. This therefore, when we come to the reforming of all those evill customes before mentioned, is needefull to be remembred. But now by this time me thinkes that I have well run thorough the evill uses which I have observed in Ireland. Neverthelesse I well wote that there be many more, and infinitely many more in the private abuses of men. But these that are most generall, and tending to the hurt of the common-weale, (as they have come to my remembrance) I have as breifly as I could rehearsed unto you. And therefore now I thinke best that we passe unto our third part, in which we noted inconveniences that are in religion.

Eudox. Surely you have very well handled these two former, and if yee shall as well goe thorough the third likewise, you shall merit a very good meed.

Iren. Little have I to say of religion, both because the parts thereof be not many, (it selfe being but one,) and my selfe have not much beene conversant, in that calling: but as lightly passing by I have seene or heard: Therefore the fault which I finde in religion is but one, but the same is universall, thoroughout all that country, that is, that they be all Papists by their profession, but in the same so blindly and brutishly informed, (for the most part) that not one amongst a hundred knoweth any ground of religion, or any article of his faith, but can perhaps say his Pater noster, or his Ave Maria, without any knowledge or under-standing what one word thereof meaneth.

Eudox. Is it not then a little blot to them that now hold the place of government, that they which now are in the light themselves, suffer a people under their charge to wallow in such deadly darkenesse?

Iren. That which you blame, Eudox. is not (I suppose) any fault of will in those godly fathers which have charge thereof, but the inconven-ience of the time and troublous occasions, wherewith that wretched realme hath continually beene turmoyled; for instruction in religion needeth quiet times, and ere we seeke to settle a sound discipline in the clergy, we must purchase peace unto the laity, for it is ill time to preach among swords, and most hard or rather impossible it is to settle a good opinion in the mindes of men for matters of religion doubtfull, which have doubtlesse an evill opinion of us. For ere a new be brought in, the old must be removed.

Eudox. Then belike it is meete that some fitter time be attended, that God send peace and quietnesse there in civill matters, before it be attempted in ecclesiasticall. I would rather have thought that (as it is said) correction must first begin at the house of God, and that the care of the soule should have beene preferred before the care of the body.

Iren. Most true, Eudoxus, the care of the soule and soule matters is to be preferred before the care of the body, in consideration of the worthynesse thereof, but not till the time of reformation; for if you should know a wicked person dangerously sicke, having now both soule and body greatly diseased, yet both recoverable, would you not thinke it evill advertizement to bring the preacher before the phisitian? for if his body were neglected, it is like that his languishing soule being disquieted by his diseasefull body, would utterly refuse and loath all spirituall comfort; but if his body were first recured, and broght to good frame, should there not then be found best time, to recover the soule also? So it is in the state of a realme: Therefore (as I said) it is expedient, first to settle such a course of government there, as thereby both civill disorders and ecclesiasticall abuses may be reformed and amended, whereto needeth not any such great distance of times, as (you suppose) I require, but one joynt resolution for both, that each might second and confirm the other.

Eudox.   That we shall see when we come thereunto; in the meane time I conceive thus much, as you have delivered, touching the generall fault, which you suppose in religion, to wit, that it is popish; but doe you finde no particular abuses therein, nor in the ministers thereof?

Iren.   Yes verily; for what ever disorders you see in the Church of England, yee may finde there, and many more: Namely, grosse simony, greedy covetousnesse, fleshly incontinency, carelesse sloath, and generally all disordered life in the common clergyman: And besides all these, they have their particular enormityes; for all Irish priests, which now injoy the church livings, they are in a manner meere laymen, saving that they have taken holy orders, but otherwise they doe goe and live like lay men, follow all kinde of husbandry, and other worldly affaires, as other Irish men doe. They neither read scriptures, nor preach to the people, nor administer the communion, but baptisme they doe, for they christen yet after the popish fashion, onely they take the tithes and offerings, and gather what fruite else they may of their livings, the which they convert as badly and some of them (they say) pay as due tributes and shares of their livings to their Bishops, (I speake of those which are Irish,) as they receive them duely.

Eudox.   But is that suffered amongst them? It is wonder but that the governours doe redresse such shamefull abuses.

Iren.   How can they, since they know them not? for the Irish bishops have their clergy in such awe and subjection under them, that they dare not complaine of them, so as they may doe to them what they please, for they knowing their owne unworthynesse and incapacity, and that they are therefore still removeable at their bishops will, yeeld what pleaseth him, and he taketh what he listeth: yea, and some of them whose diocesses are in remote parts, somewhat out of the worlds eye, doe not at all bestow the benefices, which are in their owne donation, upon any, but keep them in their owne hands, and set their owne servants and horse-boyes to take up the tithes and fruites of them, with the which some of them purchase great lands, and build faire castles upon the same. Of which abuse if any question be moved they have a very seemely colour and excuse, that they have no worthy ministers to bestow them upon, but keepe them so bestowed for any such sufficient person as any shall bring unto them.

Eudox.   But is there no law nor ordinance to meet with this mischiefe? nor hath it never before beene looked into?

Iren.   Yes, it seemes it hath, for there is a statute there enacted in Ireland, which seemes to have beene grounded upon a good meaning, That whatsoever Englishman of good conversation and sufficiencie, shall bee brought unto any of the bishoppes, and nominated unto any living, within their diocesse that is presently voyde, that he shall (without contradiction) be admitted thereunto before any Irish.

Eudox.   This is surely a very good law, and well provided for this evill, whereof you speake; but why is not the same observed?

Iren.   I thinke it is well observed, and that none of the bishops transgresse the same, but yet it worketh no reformation thereof for many defects. First there are no such sufficient English ministers sent over as might be presented to any bishop for any living, but the most part of such English as come over thither of themselves, are either unlearned, or men of some bad note, for which they have forsaken England. So as the bishop, to whom they shal be presented, may justly reject them as incapable and insufficient. Secondly, the bishop himselfe is perhappes an Irish man, who being made iudge, by that law, of the sufficiencie of the ministers, may at his owne will, dislike of the Englishman, as unworthy in his opinion, and admit of any Irish, whom hee shall thinke more for his turne. And if hee shall at the instance of any Englishman of countenance there, whom hee will not displease, accept of any such English minister as shall bee tendred unto him, yet hee will under hand carry such a hard hand over him, or by his officers wring him so sore, that hee will soone make him weary of his poore living. Lastly, the benefices themselves are so meane, and of so small profite in those Irish countreyes, thorough the ill husbandrie of the Irish people which doe inhabit them, that they will not yeelde any competent maintenance for any honest minister to live upon, scarcely to buy him a gowne. And were all this redressed (as haply it might bee) yet what good should any English minister doe amongst them, by teaching or preaching to them, which either cannot understand him, or will not heare him? Or what comfort of life shall he have, where his parishioners are so insatiable, so intractable, so ill-affected to him, as they usuall bee to all the English; or finally, how dare almost any honest minister, that are peaceable civill men, commit his safetie to the handes of such neighbours, as the boldest captaines dare scarcely dwell by?

Eudox. Little good then (I see) was by that statute wrought, how ever well intended; but the reformation thereof must grow higher, and be brought from a stronger ordinance, then the commaundement, or penaltie of a law, which none dare informe or complain of when it is broken; but have you any more of those abuses in the clergy?

Iren. I could perhappes reckon more, but I perceive my speech to grow too long, and these may suffise to judge of the generall disorders which raigne amongst them; as for the particulars, they are too many to be reckoned. For the clergy there (excepting the grave fathers which are in high place about the state, and some few others which are lately planted in their new Colledge,*) are generally bad, licentious, and most disordered.

Eudox. You have then (as I suppose) gone thorough those three first parts which you proposed unto your selfe, to wit, The inconveniencies which you observed in the lawes, in the customes, and in the religion of that land. The which (me thinkes) you have so thoroughly touched, as that nothing more remaineth to be spoken thereof.

Iren. Not so thoroughly as you suppose, that nothing can remaine, but so generally as I purposed, that is, to lay open the generall evills of that realme, which doe hinder the good reformation thereof; for, to count the particular faults of private men, should be a worke too infinite; yet some there be of that nature, that though they be in private men, yet their evill reacheth to a generall hurt, as the extortion of sheriffs, and their sub-sheriffs, and bayliffes, the corruption of victuallers, cessors, and purveyors, the disorders of seneschalls, captaines, and their souldiers, and many such like: All which I will onely name here, that their reformation may bee mended in place where it most concerneth. But there is one very foule abuse, which by the way I may not omit, and that is in captaines, who notwithstanding that they are specially imployed to make peace thorough strong execution of warre,

---

* Trinity Colledge by Dublin, which was founded by Queene Eliz. 3 Martij 1591. The 13. of the same moneth, its first stone was laide by Thomas Smyth, then Mayor of Dublin, and the 9. of Jan 1593. it first admitted students.

yet they doe so dandle their doings, and dallie in the service to them committed, as if they would not have the enemy subdued, or utterly beaten downe, for feare lest afterwardes they should need imployment, and so be discharged of pay: for which cause some of them that are layde in garrison, doe so handle the matter, that they will doe no great hurt to the enemyes, yet for colour sake some men they will kill, even halfe with the consent of the enemy, being persons either of base regard, or enemies to the enemy, whose heads eftsoones they send to the governor for a commendation of their great endevour, telling how weighty a service they performed, by cutting off such and such dangerous rebells.

Eudox. Truely this is a prettie mockerie, and not to be permitted by the governours.

Iren. But how can the governour know readily what persons those were, and what the purpose of their killing was? yea and what will you say, if the captaines do iustifie this their course by ensample of some of their governours, which (under Benedicite, I doe tell it to you,) doe practise the like sleight in their governments?

Eudox. Is it possible? Take heed what you say, Irenaeus.

Iren. To you onely, Eudoxus, I doe tell it, and that even with great hearts griefe, and inward trouble of mind to see her Majestie so much abused by some who are put in speciall trust of those great affaires: of which, some being martiall men, will not doe alwayes what they may for quieting of things, but will rather winke at some faults, and will suffer them unpunished, lest that (having put all things in that assurance of peace that they might) they should seeme afterwards not to be needed, nor continued in their governments with so great a charge to her Maiestie. And therefore they doe cunningly carry their course of government, and from one hand to another doe bandie the service like a tennis-ball, which they will never strike quite away, for feare lest afterwards they should want.

Eudox. Doe you speake of under magistrates, Iræneus, or principall governours?

Iren. I doe speake of no particulars, but the truth may be found out by triall and reasonable insight into some of their doings. And if I should say, there is some blame thereof in the principall governours, I thinke I might also shew some reasonable proofe of my speech. As for example, some of them seeing the end of their government to draw nigh, and some mischiefes and troublous practice growing up, which afterwardes may worke trouble to the next succeeding governour, will not attempt the redresse or cutting off thereof, either for feare they should leave the realme unquiet at the end of their government, or that the next that commeth, should receive the same too quiet, and so happily winne more prayse thereof then they before. And therefore they will not (as I said) seeke at all to represse that evill, but will either by graunting protection for a time, or holding some emparlance with the rebell, or by treatie of commissioners, or by other like devices, onely smother and keepe downe the flame of the mischiefe, so as it may not breake out in their time of government: what comes afterwards, they care not, or rather wish the worst. This course hath beene noted in some governors.

Eudox. Surely (Irenæus) this, if it were true, should bee worthy of an heavy iudgment: but it is hardly to bee thought, that any governour should so much either envie the good of that realme which is put into his hand, or defraude her Maiestie who trusteth him so much, or maligne his successour which shall possesse his place, as to suffer an evill to grow up, which he might timely have kept under, or perhaps to nourish it with coloured countenance, or such sinister meanes.

Iren. I doe not certainely avouch so much, (Eudoxus) but the sequele of things doth in a manner proove, and plainly speake so much, that the governours usually are envious one of anothers greater glory, which if they would seeke to excell by better governing, it should be a most laudable emulation. But they doe quite otherwise. For this (as you may marke) is the common order of them, that who commeth next in place, will not follow that course of government, how ever good, which his predecessors held, either for disdaine of himselfe, or doubt to have his doings drowned in another mans praise, but will straight take a way quite contrary to the former: as if the former thought (by keeping under the Irish) to reforme them: the next, by discountenancing the English, will curry favour with the Irish, and so make his government seeme plausible, as having all the Irish at his commaund: but he that comes after, will perhappes follow neither the one nor the other, but will dandle the one and the other in such sort, as hee will sucke sweete out of them both, and leave bitternesse to the poore countrey, which if he that comes after shall seeke to redresse, he shall perhappes find such crosses, as hee shall hardly bee able to beare, or doe any good that might worke the disgrace of his predecessors. Examples you may see hereof in the governours of late times sufficiently, and in others of former times more manifestly, when the government of that realme was committed sometimes to the Geraldines, as when the House of Yorke had the Crowne of England; sometimes to the Butlers, as when the House of Lancaster got the same. And other whiles, when an English governour was appointed, hee perhappes found enemies of both.

Eudox. I am sorry to heare so much as you report, and now I begin to conceive somewhat more of the cause of her continuall wretchedness then heeretofore I found, and wish that this inconvenience were well looked into; for sure (me thinkes) it is more weightie then all the former, and more hardly to be redressed in the governor then in the governed; as a malady in a vitall part is more incurable then in an externall.

Iren. You say very true; but now that we have thus ended all the abuses and inconveniences of that government which was our first part. It followeth now, that we passe unto the second part, which was of the meanes to cure and redresse the same, which wee must labour to reduce to the first beginning thereof.

Eudox. Right so, Irenæus: for by that which I have noted in all this your discourse, you suppose, that the whole ordinance and institution of that realmes government, was both at first, when it was placed, evill plotted, and also sithence, thorough other over-sights, came more out of square to that disorder which it is now come unto, like as two indirect lines, the further that they are drawne out, the further they goe asunder.

Iren. I doe see, Eudoxus, and as you say, so thinke, that the longer that government thus continueth, in the worse course will the realme be; for it is all in vaine that they now strive and endeavour by faire meanes and peaceable plotts to redresse the same, without first remmoving all those inconveniences, and new framing (as it were) in the forge, all that is worne out of fashion: For all other meanes will be but as lost labour, by patching up one hole to make many; for the Irish doe strongly hate and abhorre all reformation and subjection to the English, by reason that having beene once subdued by them, they were thrust out of all their possessions. So as now they feare, that if they were againe brought under, they should be likewise expelled out of all, which is the cause that they hate the English government, according to the saying, "Quem metuunt oderunt:"[51] Therefore the reformation must now bee the strength of a greater power.

Eudox.   But me thinkes that might be by making of good lawes, and establishing of new statues, with sharpe penalties and punishments, for amending of all that is presently amisse, and not (as you suppose) to beginne all as it were anew, and to alter the whole forme of the government, which how dangerous a thing it is to attempt, you your selfe must needes confesse, and they which have the managing of the realmes whole policy, cannot, without great cause, feare and refraine; for all innovation is perillous, inso much as though it bee meant for the better, yet so many accidents and fearefull events may come betweene, as that it may hazard the losse of the whole.

Iren.   Very true, Eudoxus; all change is to be shunned, where the affaires stand in such sort, as that they may continue in quietnes, or be assured at all to abide as they are. But that in the realme of Ireland we see much otherwise, for every day wee perceive the troubles growing more upon us, and one evill growing upon another, insomuch as there is no part now sound or ascertained, but all have their eares upright, wayting when the watch-word shall come, that they should all arise generally into rebellion, and cast away the English subjection. To which there now little wanteth; for I thinke the word be already given, and there wanteth nothing but opportunitie, which truely is the death of one noble person,[52] who being himselfe most stedfast to his soveraigne Queene, and his countrey, coasting upon the South-Sea, stoppeth the ingate of all that evill which is looked for, and holdeth in all those which are at his becke, with the terrour of his greatnesse, and the assurance of his most immoveable loyaltie: And therefore where you thinke, that good and sound lawes might amend, and reforme things there amisse, you think surely amisse. For it is vaine to prescribe lawes, where no man careth for keeping of them, nor feareth the daunger for breaking of them. But all the realme is first to be reformed, and lawes are afterwards to bee made for keeping and continuing it in that reformed estate.

---

51   'Whom they fear, they hate' (Variorum translation).
52   It has been suggested that the person referred to is the Earl of Essex or (less plausibly) the Earl of Ormond.

Eudox. How then doe you think is the reformation thereof to be begunne, if not by lawes and ordinances?

Iren. Even by the sword; for all these evills must first be cut away by a strong hand, before any good can bee planted, like as the corrupt braunches and unwholesome boughs are first to bee pruned, and the foule mosse cleansed and scraped away, before the tree can bring forth any good fruite.

Eudox. Did you blame me even now, for wishing of Kerne, Horse-boyes, and Carrowes to be cleane cut off, as too violent a meanes, and doe you your selfe now prescribe the same medicine? Is not the sword the most violent redresse that may bee used for any evill?

Iren. It is so; but where no other remedie may bee devised, nor hope of recovery had, there must needes this violent meanes bee used. As for the loose kinde of people which you would have cut off, I blamed it, for that they might otherwise perhaps bee brought to good, as namely by this way which I set before you.

Eudox. Is not your way all one with the former in effect, which you found fault with, save onely this odds, that I said by the halter, and you say by the sword? what difference is there?

Iren. There is surely great, when you shall understand it; for by the sword which I named, I did not meane the cutting off all that nation with the sword, which farre bee it from mee, that I should ever thinke so desperately, or wish so uncharitably, but by the sword I meane the royall power of the Prince, which ought to stretch it selfe forth in the chiefest strength to the redressing and cutting off. Those evills, which I before blamed, and not of the people which are evill. For evill people, by good ordinances and government, may be made good; but the evill that is of it selfe evill, will never become good.

Eudox. I pray you then declare your minde at large, how you would wish that sword, which you mean, to be used in the reformation of all those evills.

Iren. The first thing must be to send over into that realme, such a strong power of men, as should perforce bring in all that rebellious route and loose people, which either doe now stand out in open armes, or in wandring companies doe keepe the woods, spoyling the good subjects.

Eudox. You speake now, Irenæus, of an infinite charge to her Majestie, to send over such an army, as should tread downe all that standeth

before them on foot, and lay on the ground all the stiff-necked people of that land, for there is now but one out-law of any great reckoning, to wit, the Earle of Tyrone, abroad in armes, against whom, you
see what huge charges shee hath beene at this last yeare, in sending of
men, providing of victualls, and making head against him; yet there is
little or nothing at all done, but the Queenes treasure spent, her people wasted, the poor countrey troubled, and the enemy neverthelesse
brought into no more subjection then he was, or list outwardly to
shew, which in effect is none, but rather a scorne of her power, and
emboldening of a proud rebell, and an incouragement to all like lewdlie
disposed traytors, that shall dare to lift up their heele against their
Soveraigne Lady. Therefore it were hard counsell to drawe such an
exceeding great charge upon her, whose event should be so uncertaine.

Iren.   True indeede, if the event should be uncertaine, but the certainty of the effect hereof shall be so infallible, as that no reason can
gainesay it, neither shall the charge of all this army (the which I
demaund) be much greater, then so much as in these last two yeares
warres, have vainely been expended. For I dare undertake, that it hath
coste the Queene about 200000 pounds already, and for the present
charge, that she is now at there, amounteth to very neere 12000 pounds
a moneth, whereof cast you the accompt; yet nothing is done. The
which summe, had it beene employed as it should bee, would have
effected all this which now I goe about.[53]

Eudox.   How meane you to have it imployed, but to bee spent in the
pay of souldiours, and provision of victualls?

Iren.   Right so, but it is now not disbursed at once, as it might be, but
drawne out into a long length, by sending over now 20000 pounds,
and next halfe yeare 10000 pounds; so as the souldiour in the meane
time for want of due provision of victual, and good payment of his
due, is starved and consumed; that of a 1000 which came over lusty
able men, in halfe a yeare there are not left 500. And yet is the Queenes
charge never a whit the lesse, but what is not payd in present mony, is
accounted in debt, which will not be long unpayd; for the Captaine,

53   Irenius' estimates are not inaccurate, nor his reasoning false. In September, 1595 Sir
     Henry Wallop estimated that army costs ran at £12,000 per month. The eventual
     cost of defeating Tyrone was in the region of £2,000,000, the most significant ex-
     penditure of Elizabeth's later years. Revenues from Ireland were approximately
     £30,000 per annum.

halfe of whose souldiours are dead, and the other quarter never mustered, nor seene, comes shortly to demand payment of his whole accompt, where by good meanes of some great ones, and privy shareings with the officers and servants of other some, hee receiveth his debt, much lesse perhaps then was due, yet much more indeede then he justly deserved.

Eudox. I take this sure to be no good husbandry; for what must needes be spent, as good spend it at once, where is enough, as to have it drawne out into long delayes, seeing that thereby both the service is much hindred, and yet nothing saved: but it may be, Irenæus, that the Queenes treasure in so great occasions of disbursements (as it is well knowne she hath beene at lately) is not alwayes so ready, nor so plentifull, as it can sparre so great a summe together, but being payed as it is, now some, and then some, it is no great burthen unto her, nor any great impoverishment to her coffers, seeing by such delay of time, it dailie cometh in, as fast as she parteth it out.

Iren. It may be as you say, but for the going thorough of so honorable a course I doubt not but if the Queenes coffers be not so well stored, (which we are not to looke into) but that the whole realme which now, as things are used, doe feele a continuall burthen of that wretched realme hanging upon their backes, would, for a small riddance of all that trouble, be once troubled for all; and put to all their shoulders, and helping hands and hearts also, to the defraying of that charge, most gladfully and willingly; and surely the charge in effect, is nothing to the infinite great good, which should come thereby, both to the Queene, and all this realme generally, as when time serveth shall be shewed.

Eudox. How many men would you require to the furnishing of this which yee take in hand? and how long space would you have them entertained?

Iren. Verily not above 10000. footemen, and a 1000. horse, and all these not above the space of a yeare and a halfe, for I would still, as the heate of the service abateth, abate the number in pay, and make other provision for them as I will shew.

Eudox. Surely it seemeth not much which you require, nor no long time; but how would you have them used? would you leade forth your army against the enemy, and seeke him where he is to fight?

Iren. No, Eudoxus; that would not be, for it is well knowne that he is a flying enemie, hiding himselfe in woodes and bogges, from whence he will not drawe forth, but into some straight passage or perillous foord, where he knowes the army must needes passe;[54] there will he lye in waite, and, if hee finde advantage fit, will dangerously hazard the troubled souldiour. Therefore to seeke him out that still flitteth, and follow him that can hardly bee found, were vaine and bootlesse; but I would devide my men in garrison upon his countrey, in such places as I should thinke might most annoy him.

Eudox. But how can that be, Irenæus, with so few men? for the enemie, as you now see, is not all in one countrey, but some in Ulster, some in Connaught, and others in Leinster. So as to plant strong garrisons in all those places should need manye more men then you speake of, or to plant all in one, and to leave the rest naked, should be but to leave them to the spoyle.

Iren. I would wish the cheife power of the army to be garrisoned in one countrey that is strongest, and the other upon the rest that is weakest: As for example, the Earle of Tyrone is now accompted the strongest, upon him would I lay 8000 men in garrison, 1000 upon Pheagh Mac-Hugh and the Cavanaghes, and 1000 upon some parts of Connaght, to be at the direction of the Governour.

Eudox. I see now all your men bestowed, but what places would you set their garrison that they might rise out most conveniently to service? and though perhaps I am ignorant of the places, yet I will take the mappe of Ireland, and lay it before me, and make mine eyes (in the meane time) my schoole-masters, to guide my understanding to judge of your plot.[55]

Iren. Those eight thousand in Ulster I would devide likewise into foure parts, so as there should be 2000 footemen in every garrison; the

---

54 Perhaps a recollection of the defeat of Grey by O'Byrne at Glenmalure on 25 August 1580 or Tyrone's victory at Clontibret (13 June 1595). Tyrone was to win an even more significant victory at the Yellow Ford (14 August 1598).

55 The production of the map signals the increasingly technical and tactical significance of the military discussion, as well as being a demonstration of the power invested in the practice of early modern map-making. Without the map, Irenius' proposals would not be viable. Yet it is Eudoxus who produces the map to help the reader, perhaps an attempt to disguise the link between mapping and military conquest (see the section on 'Mapping' in the Guide to Further Reading).

which I would thus place. Upon the Blacke water,[56] in some convenient place, as high upon the river as might be, I would lay one garrison. Another would I put at Castle-liffer, or there-abouts, so as they should have all the passages upon the river to Logh-foyle. The third I would place about Fermanagh or Bundroise, so as they might lye betweene Connaght and Ulster, to serve upon both sides, as occasion shall be offered, and this therefore would I have stronger than any of the rest, because it should be most inforced, and most imployed, and that they might put wardes at Balls-shanon and Belick, and all those passages. The last would I set about Monaghan or Balturbut, so as it should fronte both upon the enemie that way, and also keepe the countreys of Cavan and Meath in awe, from passage of straglers from those parts, whence they use to come forth, and oftentimes use to worke much mischeife. And to every of these garrisons of 2000. footemen, I would have 200. horsemen added, for the one without the other can doe but little service. The 4 garrisons, thus being placed, I would have to bee victualled before hand for halfe a yeare, which you will say to be hard, considering the corruption and usuall waste of victualls.[57] But why should not they be aswell victualled for so long time, as the ships are usually for a yeare, and sometimes two, seeing it is easier to keepe victual on land then water? Their bread I would have in flower, so as it might be baked still to serve their necessary want. Their beere there also brewed within them, from time to time, and their beefe before hand barrelled, the which may bee used but as it is needed: For I make no doubt but fresh victualls they will sometimes purvay for themselves, amongst their enemies. Hereunto likewise would I have them have a store of hose and shooes, with such other necessaries as may be needefull for souldiours, so as they shall have no occasion to looke for releife from abroad, or occasion of such trouble, for their continuall supply, as I see and have often proved in Ireland to bee more cumberous to the Deputy, and dangerous to them that releive them, then halfe the leading of an army; for the enemy, knowing the

---

56 Spenser may have visited the Blackwater Fort during Grey's campaign in Ulster in August 1581. Irenius' suggestion that garrisons would be the means of winning the war against the Irish was borne out by Mountjoy's campaign and victory over Hugh O'Neill, culminating in O'Neill's formal surrender (30 March 1603).

57 Feeding troops was a perpetual problem in Elizabethan Ireland, which no one solved adequately.

ordinary wayes thorough the which their releife must be brought them, useth commonly to draw himselfe into the straight passages thitherward, and oftentimes doth dangerously distresse them; besides the pay of such force as should be sent for their convoy, the charge of the carriages, the exactions of the countrey shall be spared. But onely every halfe yeare the supply brought by the Deputy himselfe, and his power, who shall then visite and overlooke all those garrisons, to see what is needefull to change, what is expedient, and to direct what hee shall best advise. And those 4 garrisons issuing forth, at such convenient times as they shall have intelligence or espiall upon the enemy, will so drive him from one side to another, and tennis him amongst them, that he shall finde no where safe to keepe his creete in, nor hide himselfe, but flying from the fire shall fall into the water, and out of one danger into another, that in short space his creete, which is his cheife sustenence, shall be wasted with preying, or killed with driving, or starved for want of pasture in the woods, and he himselfe brought so lowe, that he shall have no heart nor ability to indure his wretchednesse, the which will surely come to passe in very short time; for one winter well followed upon him will so plucke him on his knees, that he will never be able to stand up againe.[58]

Eudox. Doe you then thinke the winter time fittest for the services of Ireland? how falls it then that our most imployments bee in summer, and the armies then led commonly forth?

Iren. It is surely misconceived; for it is not with Ireland as it is with other countryes, where the warres flame most in summer, and the helmets glister brightest in the fairest sunshine: But in Ireland the winter yeeldeth best services, for then the trees are bare and naked, which use both to cloath and house the kerne; the ground is cold and wet, which useth to be his bedding; the aire is sharpe and bitter, to blowe thorough his naked sides and legges; the kyne are barren and without milke, which useth to be his onely foode, neither if he kill them, will they yeeld him flesh, nor if he keepe them, will they give him food, besides being all with calfe (for the most part) they will, thorough much chasing and driving, cast all their calves, and lose

---

58 The recommendation of military tactics which will drive the Irish to surrender through starvation implies that Irenius' description of the terrible effects of the Munster famine should not be read too sentimentally (see below, pp. 101–2; 'Introduction', p. xx).

their milke, which should releive him the next summer.

Eudox. I doe well understand your reason; but by your leave, I have heard it otherwise said, of some that were outlawes: That in summer they kept themselves quiet, but in winter they would play their parts, and when the nights were longest, then burne and spoyle most, so that they might safely returne before day.

Iren. I have likewise heard, and also seene proofe thereof true: But that was of such outlawes as were either abiding in well inhabited countryes, as in Mounster, or bordering on the English pale, as Feagh Mac Hugh, the Cavanaghes, the Moors, the Dempsies, or such like: For, for them the winter indeede is the fittest time for spoyling and robbing, because the nights are then (as you said) longest and darkest, and also the countryes round about are then most full of corne, and good provision to be gotten every where by them, but it is farre otherwise with a strong peopled enemy, that possesse a whole countrey; for the other being but a few, and indeede privily lodged, and kept in out villages, and corners nigh to the woodes and mountaines, by some of their privy friends, to whom they bring their spoyles and stealthes, and of whom they continually receive secret releife; but the open enemy having all his countrey wasted, what by himselfe, and what by the souldiours, findeth them succour in no place: Townes there are none, of which he may get spoyle, they are all burnt: bread he hath none, he ploweth not in summer: Flesh he hath, but if he kill it in winter, he shall want milke in summer, and shortly want life. Therefore if they bee well followed but one winter, you shall have little worke with them the next summer.

Eudox. I doe now well perceive the difference, and doe verily thinke that the winter time is there fittest for service; withall I conceive the manner of your handling of the service, by drawing suddaine draughts upon the enemy, when he looketh not for you, and to watch advantages upon him, as hee doth upon you. By which straight keeping of them in, and not suffering them at any time long to rest, I must needes thinke that they will soone be brought lowe, and driven to great extreamities. All which when you have: performed, and brought them to the very last cast, suppose that they will offer, either to come to you and submit themselves, or that some of them will seeke to withdraw themselves, what is your advice to doe? will you have them received?

Iren. No, but at the beginning of those warres, and when the garrisons are well planted, and fortified, I would wish a proclamation were made generally, to come to their knowledge: That what persons soever would within twenty dayes absolutely submit themselves, (excepting onely the very principalls and ringleaders,) should finde grace: I doubt not, but upon the settling of these garrisons, such a terrour and neere consideration of their perillous state, would be strucken into most of them, that they will covet to drawe away from their leaders. And againe I well know that the rebells themselves (as I saw by proofe in Desmonds warre)[59] will turne away all their rascall people, whom they thinke unserviceable, as old men, women, children, and hyndes, (which they call churles,) which would onely waste their victualls, and yeeld them no ayde; but their cattle they will surely keepe away: These therefore, though policy would turne them backe againe, that they might the rather consume and afflict the other rebells, yet in a pittyfull commisseration I would wish them to be received; the rather for that this sort of base people doth not for the most part rebell of themselves, having no heart thereunto, but are by force drawne by the grand rebells into their action, and carryed away with the violence of the streame, else they should be sure to loose all that they have, and perhaps their lives too: The which they now carry unto them, in hope to enjoy them there, but they are there by the strong rebells themselves, soone turned out of all, so that the constraint hereof may in them deserve pardon. Likewise if any of their able men or gentlemen shall then offer to come away, and to bring their cattle with them, as some no doubt may steale them away privily, I wish them also to be received, for the disabling of the enemy, but withall, that good assurance may be taken for their true behaviour and absolute submission, and that then they be not suffered to remaine any longer in those parts, no nor about the garrisons, but sent away into the inner parts of the realme, and dispersed in such sort as they may not come together, nor easily returne if they would: For if they might bee suffered to remaine about the garrisons, and there inhabite, as they will offer to till the ground, and yeeld a great part of the profit thereof, and of their cattle, to the Coronell, wherewith they have heretofore tempted many, they would (as I have by experience knowne) bee ever after

---

59 A further suggestion that Irenius is an *alter ego* of the author.

such a gaule and inconvenience to them, as that their profit shall not recompence their hurt; for they will privily releive their friends that are forth; they will send the enemy secret advertizements of all their purposes and journeyes, which they meane to make upon them; they will not also sticke to drawe the enemy privily upon them, yea and to betray the forte it selfe, by discovery of all her defects and disadvantages (if any be) to the cutting of all their throates. For avoiding whereof and many other inconveniencies, I wish that they should be carried farre from hence into some other parts, so that (as I say) they come in and submit themselves, upon the first summons: But afterwards I would have none received, but left to their fortune and miserable end: my reason is, for that those which will afterwards remaine without, are stout and obstinate rebells, such as will never be made dutifull and obedient, nor brought to labour or civill conversation, having once tasted that licentious life, and being acquainted with spoyle and out-rages, will ever after be ready for the like occasions, so as there is no hope of their amendment or recovery, and therefore needefull to be cut off.

Eudox.   Surely of such desperate persons, as will follow the course of their owne folly, there is no compassion to bee had, and for others you have proposed a mercifull meanes, much more then they have deserved, but what then shall be the conclusion of this warre? for you have prefixed a short time of its continuance.

Iren.   The end will (I assure me) bee very short and much sooner then can be in so great a trouble, as it seemeth hoped for, although there should none of them fall by the sword, nor bee slaine by the souldiour, yet thus being kept from manurance, and their cattle from running abroad, by this hard restraint they would quickly consume themselves, and devoure one another. The proofe whereof, I saw sufficiently exampled in these late warres of Mounster; for not withstanding that the same was a most rich and plentifull countrey, full of corne and cattle, that you would have thought they should have beene able to stand long, yet ere one yeare and a halfe they were brought to such wretchednesse, as that any stony heart would. have rued the same. Out of every corner of the woods and glynnes they came creeping forth upon their hands, for their legges could not beare them; they looked like anatomies of death, they spake like ghosts crying out of their graves; they did eate the dead carrions, happy where they could finde them, yea, and one another soone after, insomuch as the very carcasses they spared not to scrape out of their graves; and, if they found a plot of water-cresses or shamrocks, there they flocked as to a feast for the time, yet not able long to continue therewithall; that in short space there were none almost left, and a most populous and plentifull countrey suddainely left voyde of man and beast; yet sure in all that warre, there perished not many by the sword, but all by the extremitie of famine, which they themselves had wrought.

Eudox.   It is a wonder that you tell, and more to bee wondred how it should so shortly come to passe.

Iren.   It is most true, and the reason also very ready; for you must conceive that the strength of all that nation, is the Kerne, Galloglasse, Stocah, Horseman, and Horseboy, the which having beene never used to have any thing of their owne, and now being upon spoyle of others, make no spare of any thing, but havocke and confusion of all they meet with, whether it bee their owne friends goods, or their foes. And if they happen to get never so great spoyle at any time, the same they waste and consume in a tryce, as naturally delighting in spoyle, though it doe themselves no good. On the other side, whatsoever they leave unspent, the souldier when hee commeth there, spoyleth and havocketh likewise, so that betweene both nothing is very shortly left. And yet this is very necessary to bee done for the soone finishing of the warre, and not only this in this wise, but also those subiects which doe border upon those parts, are either to bee removed and drawne away, or likewise to bee spoyled, that the enemy may find no succour thereby. For what the souldier spares, the rebell will surely spoyle.

Eudox.   I doe now well understand you. But now when all things are brought to this passe, and all filled with these ruefull spectacles of so many wretched carcases starving, goodly countreys wasted, so huge desolation and confusion, that even I that doe but heare it from you, and do picture it in my minde, doe greatly pittie and commisserate it. If it shall happen, that the state of this miserie and lamentable image of things shall bee tolde, and feelingly presented to her Sacred Maiestie, being by nature full of mercy and clemency, who is most inclinable to such pittifull complaints, and will not endure to heare such tragedies made of her poore people and subiects, as some about her may insinuate; then she perhappes, for very compassion of such calamities, will not onely stoppe the streame of such violences, and returne to her wonted mildnesse, but also conne them little thankes which have beene the authours and counsellours of such bloodie platformes. So I remember that in the late govevernment of that good Lord Grey, when after long travell, and many perillous assayes, he had brought things almost to this passe that you speake of, that it was even made ready for reformation, and might have beene brought to what her Maiestie would, like complaint was made against him, that he was a bloodie man, and regarded not the life of her subiects no more than dogges, but had wasted and consumed all, so as now she had nothing almost left, but to raigne in their ashes; eare was soon lent therunto, and all suddenly turned topside-turvy; the noble Lord eft-soones was blamed; the wretched people pittied; and new counsells plotted, in which it was concluded that a general pardon should be sent over to all that would accept of it, upon which all former purposes were blancked, the Governour at a bay, and not only all that great and long charge which shee had before beene at quite lost and cancelled, but also that hope of good which was even at the doore put back, and cleane frustrated. All which, whether it be true, or no, your selfe can well tell.

Iren. Too true, Eudoxus, the more the pitty, for I may not forget so memorable a thing: neither can I bee ignorant of that perillous device, and of the whole meanes by which it was compassed, and very cunningly contrived by sowing first dissention betweene him, and an other Noble Personage;[60] wherein they both at length found how notably they had beene abused, and how thereby under hand this universall alteration of things was brought about, but then too late to stay the same; for in the meane time all that was formerly done with long labor, and great toyle, was (as you say) in a moment undone, and that good Lord blotted with the name of a bloody man, whom, who that well knew, knew to be most gentle, affable, loving, and temperate; but that the necessitie of that present state of things inforced him to that violence, and almost changed his naturall disposition. But otherwise he was so farre from delighting in blood, that oftentimes he suffered not just vengeance to fall where it was deserved: and even

---

60 This is probably a reference to Ormond, who was perceived by most New English writers as the main critic of Grey at court and instrumental in having him removed from the Deputyship.

some of them which were afterwardes his accusers, had tasted too much of his mercy, and were from the gallowes brought to bee his accusers. But his course indeede was this, that hee spared not the heades and principalls of any mischievous practises or rebellion, but shewed sharpe iudgement on them, chiefly for ensamples sake, that all the meaner sort, which also were generally then infected with that evill, might by terrour thereof bee reclaymed, and saved, if it were possible. For in the last conspiracy of some of the English Pale,*[61] thinke you not that there were many more guiltie then they that felt the punishment? yet hee touched only a few of speciall note; and in the tryall of them also even to prevent the blame of cruelty and partiall proceeding, and seeking their blood, which he, as in his great wisedome (as it seemeth) did fore-see would bee objected against him; hee, for the avoyding thereof, did use a singular discretion and regard. For the Iury that went upon their tryall, hee made to bee chosen out of their nearest kinsmen, and their Iudges he made of some of their owne fathers, of others their uncles and dearest friends, who when they could not but justly condemne them, yet hee uttered their judgement in aboundance of teares, and yet hee even herein was called bloody and cruell.

Eudox. Indeed so have I heard it heere often spoken, but I perceive (as I alwayes verily thought) that it was most unjustly, for hee was alwayes knowne to bee a most iust, sincere, godly, and right noble man, farre from such sternenesse, farre from such unrighteousnesse. But in that sharpe execution of the Spaniards, at the Fort of Smerwicke, I heard it specially noted, and if it were true as a some reported, surely it was a great touch to him in honour, for some say that he promised them life; others at least hee did put them in hope thereof.

Iren. Both the one and the other is most untrue; for this I can assure you, my selfe being as neare them as any, that hee was so farre either from promising, or putting them in hope, that when first their Secretarie (called, as I remember) Signior Ieffrey an Italian, being

---

* Consulas (si placet) Camden. annal. rerum Anglic. & Hiber. ad an. 1580.

61 Irenius is referring to the conspiracy apparently inaugurated by Nicholas Nugent in 1581. Nugent was executed on 6 April 1582. Grey refused to halt the course of the law even after the English Privy Council demanded that he stay the proceedings of the trial; the Queen was rumoured to be highly displeased by Grey's actions.

sent to treat with the Lord Deputie for grace, was flatly refused; and afterwards their Coronell named Don Sebastian, came forth to intreate that they might part with their armes like souldiers, at least with their lives according to the custome of warre, and law of nations; it was strongly denyed him, and tolde him by the Lord Deputie himselfe, that they could not iustly pleade either custome of warre, or law of nations, for that they were not any lawfull enemies, and if they were, hee willed them to shew by what commission they came thither into another Princes dominions to warre, whether from the Pope or the King of Spaine, or any other; the which when they said they had not, but were onely adventurers that came to seeke fortune abroad, and to serve in warre amongst the Irish, who desired to entertaine them; it was then tolde them, that the Irish themselves, as the Earle and John of Desmond, with the rest, were no lawfull enemies; but rebells and traytours; and therefore they that came to succour them, no better then rogues and runnagates, specially comming with no licence, nor commission from their owne King: So as it should bee dishonourable for him in the name of his Queene, to condition or make any tearmes with such rascalls, but left them to their choyce, to yeeld and submit themselves, or no: Whereupon the said Colonell did absolutely yeeld himselfe and the fort, with all therein, and craved onely mercy, which it being not thought good to shew them, for daunger of them, if, being saved, they should afterwardes ioyne with the Irish; and also for terrour to the Irish, who are much imboldened by those forraigne succours, and also put in hope of more ere long: there was no other way but to make that short end of them as was made. Therefore most untruely and maliciously doe these evill tongues backbite and slander the sacred ashes of that most iust and honourable personage, whose least virtue of many most excellent that abounded in his heroicke spirit, they were never able to aspire unto.

Eudox. Truely, Irenæus, I am right glad to be thus satisfied by you, in that I have often heard questioned, and yet was never able till now, to choake the mouth of such detractours, with the certaine knowledge of their slanderous untruthes, neither is the knowledge hereof imper-tinent to that which wee formerly had in hand, I meane for the thor-ough prosecuting of that sharpe course which you have set downe for the bringing under of those rebells of Ulster and Connaght, and pre-paring a way for their perpetuall reformation, least haply, by any such sinister suggestions of crueltie and too much blood-shed, all the plot might be overthrowne, and all the coste and labour therein imployed bee utterly lost and cast away.[62]

Iren. You say most true; for, after that Lords calling away from thence, the two Lords Iustices continued but a while: of which the one was of minde (as it seemed) to have continued in the footing of his predecessors, but that he was curbed and restrayned. But the other was more mildly disposed, as was meete for his profession, and willing to have all the wounds of that common-wealth healed and recured, but not with that heede as they should bee. After, when Sir Iohn Perrot succeeding (as it were) into another mans harvest, found an open way to what course hee list, the which hee bent not to that point which the former governours intended, but rather quite contrary, as it were in scorne of the former, and in vaine vaunt of his owne councells, with the which hee was too wilfully carryed; for hee did treade downe and disgrace all the English, and set up and countenance the Irish all that hee could, whether thinking thereby to make them more tractable and buxome to his government, (where in hee thought much amisse,) or privily plotting some other purposes of his owne, as it partly afterwards appeared; but surely his manner of governement could not be sound nor wholesome for that realme, it being so contrary to the former. For it was even as two physicians should take one sicke body in hand, at two sundry times: of which the former would minister all things meete to purge and keepe under the bodie, the other to pamper and strengthen it suddenly againe, whereof what is to bee looked for but a most daungerous relapse? That which wee now see thorough his rule, and the next after him, happened thereunto, being now more daungerously sicke then ever before. Therefore by all meanes it must be fore-seene and assured, that after once entering into this course of reformation, there bee afterwards no remorse nor drawing backe for the sight of any such ruefull objects, as must thereupon followe, nor for compassion of their calamities, seeing that by no other meanes it is possible to cure them, and that these are not of will, but of very urgent necessitie.

Eudox. Thus farre then you have now proceeded to plant your garri-

---

62 These were Adam Loftus, Archbishop of Dublin, and the Lord Chancellor, Sir Henry Wallop, who assumed the Deputyship from 25 August 1582 until 7 January 1584, when Sir John Perrot took over.

sons, and to direct their services, of the which neverthelesse I must needes conceive that there cannot be any certaine direction set downe, so that they must follow the occasions which shall bee daylie offered, and diligently awayted. But by your leave (Irenæus) notwithstanding all this your carefull fore-sight and provision (mee thinkes) I see an evill lurke unespyed, and that may chance to hazard all the hope of this great service, if it bee not very well looked into, and that is, the corruption of their captaines; for though they be placed never so carefully, and their companies filled never so sufficiently, yet may they, if they list, discarde whom they please, and send away such as will perhappes willingly bee ridde of that dangerous and hard service, the which (well I wote) is their common custome to doe, when they are layde in garrison, for then they may better hide their defaults, then when they are in campe, where they are continually eyed and noted of all men. Besides, when their pay commeth, they will (as they say) detaine the greatest portions thereof at their pleasure, by a hundred shifts that need not here be named, through which they oftentimes deceive the souldier, and abuse the Queene, and greatly hinder the service. So that let the Queene pay never so fully, let the muster-master view them never so diligently, let the deputy or generall looke to them never so exactly, yet they can cozen them all. Therefore me-thinkes it were good, if it be possible, to make provision for this inconvenience.

Iren.   It will surely be very hard; but the chiefest helpe for prevention hereof must be the care of the coronell that hath the government of all his garrison, to have an eye to their alterations, to know the numbers and names of their sick souldiers, and the slaine, to marke and observe their rankes in their daylie rising forth to service, by which he cannot easily bee abused, so that hee himselfe bee a man of speciall assurance and integritie. And therefore great regard is to bee had in the choosing and appointing of them. Besides, I would not by any meanes, that the captaines should have the paying of their souldiers, but that there should bee a pay-master appointed, of speciall trust, which should pay every man according to his captaines ticket, and the accompt of the clerke of his band, for by this meanes the captaine will never seeke to falsifie his alterations, nor to diminish his company, nor to deceive his souldiers, when nothing thereof shalbe sure to come unto himselfe, but what is his owne bare pay. And this is the manner of the Spaniards captaine, who never hath to meddle with his souldiers pay, and indeed scorneth the name as base, to be counted his souldiers pagadore; whereas the contrary amongst us hath brought things to so bad a passe, that there is no captaine, but thinkes his band very sufficient, if hee can muster 60: and stickes not to say openly, that he is unworthy to have a captainship, that cannot make it worth 500 *l.* by the yeare, the which they right well verifie by the proofe.

Eudox.　Truely I thinke this is a very good meanes to avoid that inconvenience of captaines abuses. But what say you to the coronell? What authority thinke you meete to be given him? whether will you allow him to protect or safe conduct, and to have martiall lawes as they are accustomed?

Iren.　Yea verily, but all these to bee limited with very straite instructions. As first for protections, that hee shall have authority after the first proclamation, for the space of twentie dayes, to protect all that shall come in, and them to send to the Lord Deputy, with their safe conduct or passe, to bee at his disposition, but so as none of them returne backe againe, being once come in, but be presently sent away out of the countrey, to the next sheriffe, and so conveyed in safetie. And likewise for martiall lawe, that to the souldier it be not extended, but by tryall formerly of his cryme, by a iury of his fellow souldiers as it ought to bee, and not rashly, at the will or displeasure of the coronell, as I have sometimes seene too lightly. And as for other of the rebells that shall light into their handes, that they bee well aware of what condition they bee, and what holding they have. For, in the last generall warres there, I knew many good free-holders executed by martiall law, whose landes were thereby saved to their heires, which should have otherwise escheated to her Majestie. In all which, the great discretion and uprightnesse of the coronell himselfe is to bee the cheifest stay both for all those doubts, and for many other difficulties that may in the service happen.

Eudox.　Your caution is very good; but now touching the arch-rebell himselfe, I meane the Earle of Tyrone, if he, in all the time of these warres, shonld offer to come in and submit himselfe to her Majestie, would you not have him received, giving good hostages, and sufficient assurance of himselfe?

Iren.　No, marrie; for there is no doubt, but hee will offer to come in, as hee hath done divers times already, but it is without any intent of true submission, as the effect hath well shewed, neither indeed can hee now, if hee would, come in at all, nor give that assurance of himselfe that should bee meete: for being as hee is very subtle headed, seeing himselfe now so farre engaged in this bad action, can you thinke that by his submission, hee can purchase to himselfe any safetie, but that heereafter, when things shall bee quieted, these his villanies will be ever remembered? and whensoever hee shall treade awry, (as needes the most righteous must sometimes) advantage will bee taken thereof, as a breach of his pardon, and hee brought to a reckoning for all former matters; besides, how hard it is now for him to frame himselfe to subjection, that having once set before his eyes the hope of a kingdome, hath therunto not onely found incouragement from the greatest King in Christendome, but also found great faintnes in her Maiesties withstanding him, whereby he is animated to think that his power is able to defend him, and offend further then he hath done, whensoever he please, let every reasonable man iudge. But if hee himselfe should come and leave all other, his accomplices without, as O Donel, Mac Mahone, Maguire, and the rest, he must needs thinke that then even they will ere long cut his throate, which having drawne them all into this occasion, now in the midst of their trouble giveth them the slip; whereby hee must needes perceive how impossible it is for him to submit himselfe. But yet if hee would so doe, can he give any good assurance of his obedience? For how weake hould is there by hostages, hath too often beene proved, and that which is spoken of taking Shane O-Neales[63] sonnes from him, and setting them up against him as a very perillous counsaile, and not by any meanes to be put in proofe; for were they let forth and could overthrowe him, who should afterwards overthrow them, or what assurance can be had of them? It will be like the tale in Æsop, of the wild horse, who, having enmity with the stagg, came to a man to desire his ayde against his foe, who yeelding thereunto mounted upon his backe, and so following the stagge, ere long slew him, but then when the horse would have him alight he refused, but ever after kept him in his subjection and service. Such I doubt would bee the

---

63   Shane O'Neill, who had usurped the position of tanist of the O'Neills, had been murdered, probably on the orders of Sir Henry Sidney, the Lord Deputy, by the Antrim Scots on 2 June 1567. Tyrone was reported to have his sons captive in 1594. Setting Irish chiefs against each other had been a traditional policy of the English. Ironically enough, it had led to the rise of Hugh O'Neill as a major threat to the government which had sponsored him against rivals within his family, as Irenius notes.

proofe of Shane O-Neales sonnes. Therefore it is most dangerous to attempt any such plot; for even that very manner of plot, was the meanes by which this trayterous Earle is now made great: For when the last O-Neale, called Terlagh Leinagh, began to stand upon some tickle termes, this fellow then, called Baron of Dungannon, was set up as it were to beard him, and countenanced and strengthened by the Queene so far, as that he is now able to keepe her selfe play: much like unto a gamester that having lost all, borroweth of his next fellow-gamester somewhat to maintaine play, which he setting unto him againe, shortly thereby winneth all from the winner.

Eudox. Was this rebell then set up at first by the Queene (as you say) and now become so undutifull?

Iren. He was (I assure you) the most outcast of all the O-Neales then, and lifted up by her Majesty out of the dust, to that he hath now wrought himselfe unto, and now hee playeth like the frozen snake, who being for compassion releived by the husbandman, soone after he was warme began to hisse, and threaten danger even to him and his.

Eudox. He surely then deserveth the punishment of that snake, and should worthily be hewed to peeces. But if you like not the letting forth of Shane O-Neales sonnes against him, what say you then of that advice which (I heard) was given by some, to draw in Scotts, to serve against him? how like you that advice?

Iren. Much worse then the former; for who that is experienced in those parts knoweth not that the O-Neales are neearely allyed unto the Mac-Neiles of Scotland, and to the Earle of Argyle, from whence they use to have all succours of those Scottes and Redshankes: Besides all these Scottes are, through long continuance, intermingled and allyed to all the inhabitants of the North? so as there is no hope that they will ever be wrought to serve faithfully against their old friends and kinsmen:* And though they would, how when they have overthrowne him, and the warres are finished, shall they themselves be put out? Doe we not all know, that the Scottes were the first inhabitants of all the North, and that those which now are called the North Irish, are indeed very Scottes,† which challenge the ancient inheritance and

---

* The causes of these feares have been amputated, since the happy union of England and Scotland, established by his late Majesty.

† Vide Bed, Eccles. Hist. lib. 1. cap. 1.

dominion of that countrey, to be their owne aunciently: This then were but to leap out of the pan into the fire: For the cheifest caveat and provision in reformation of the North, must be to keep out those Scottes.

Eudox. Indeede I remember, that in your discourse of the first peopling of Ireland, you shewed that the Scythians or Scottes were the first that sate downe in the North, whereby it seemes that they may challenge some right therein. How comes it then that O-Neale claimes the dominion thereof, and this Earle of Tyrone saith that the right is in him? I pray you resolve me herein? for it is very needefull to be knowne, and maketh unto the right of the warre against him, whose successe useth commonly to be according to the justnes of the cause, for which it is made: For if Tyrone have any right in that seigniory (me thinkes) it should be wrong to thrust him out: Or if (as I remember) you said in the beginning, that O-Neale, when he acknowledged the King of England for his leige Lord and Soveraigne, did (as he alleadgeth) reserve in the same submission his seigniories and rights unto himselfe, what should it be accounted to thrust him out of the same?

Iren. For the right of O-Neale in the seigniory of the North, it is surely none at all: For besides that the Kings of England conquered all the realme, and thereby assumed and invested all the right of that land to themselves and their heires and successours for ever, so as nothing was left in O-Neale but what he received backe from them, O-Neale himselfe never had any ancient seigniory over that country, but what by usurpation and incroachment after the death of the Duke of Clarence, he got upon the English, whose lands and possessions being formerly wasted by the Scottes, under the leading of Edward le Bruce, (as I formerly declared unto you) he eft-soones entred into, and sithence hath wrongfully detained, through the other occupations and great affaires which the Kings of England (soone after) fell into here at home, so as they could not intend to the recovery of that countrey of the North, nor restraine the insolency of O-Neale; who, finding none now to withstand him, raigned in that desolation, and made himselfe Lord of those few people that remained there, upon whom ever sithence he hath continued his first usurped power, and now exacteth and extorteth upon all men what he list; so that now to subdue or expell an usurper, should bee no unjust enterprise or wrongfull warre, but a restitution of auncient right unto the crowne of England, from whence they were most unjustly expelled and long kept out.

Eudox. I am very glad herein to be thus satisfied by you, that I may the better satisfie them, whom I have often heard to object these doubts, and slaunderously to barke at the courses which are held against that trayterous Earle and his adherents. But now that you have thus settled your service for Ulster and Connaght, I would bee glad to heare your opinion for the prosecuting of Feagh Mac Hugh, who being but a base villaine, and of himselfe of no power, yet so continually troubleth the state, notwithstanding that he lyeth under their nose, that I disdaine his bold arrogancy, and thinke it to be the greatest indignity to the Queene that may be, to suffer such a caytiffe to play such *Rex*, and by his ensample not onely to give heart and incoragement to all such bad rebells, but also to yeeld them succour and refuge against her Majesty, whensoever they fly unto his Comericke, where of I would first wish before you enter into your plot of service against him, that you should lay open by what meanes he, being so base, first lifted himselfe up to this dangerous greatnes, and how he maintaineth his part against the Queene and her power, notwithstanding all that hath beene done and attempted against him. And whether also hee have any pretence of right in the lands which he houldeth, or in the warres that he maketh for the same?

Iren. I will so, at your pleasure, and will further declare, not only the first beginning of his private house, but also the originall of the Sept of the Birnes and Tooles, so farre as I have learned the same from some of themselves, and gathered the rest by reading: The people of the Birnes and Tooles (as before I shewed unto you my conjecture) descended from the auncient Brittaines, which first inhabited all those easterne parts of Ireland, as their names doe betoken; for Brin in the Brittish language signifieth wooddy,* and Toole hilly, which names it seemes they tooke of the countryes which they inhabited, which is all very mountainous and woody. In the which it seemeth that ever since

---

* In Richard Creagh's booke De Lingua Hibernica, there is a very plentiful collection of Irish words, derived from the Brittish or Welch tongue, which doth much strengthen the authors opinion, in houlding that the Birnes, Tooles, and Cavenaghs, with other the ancient inhabitants of the easterne parts, were originally British colonyes.

the comming in of the English with Dermot ni-Gall,* they have continued: Whether that their countrey being so rude and mountainous
was of them despised, and thought unworthy the inhabiting, or that
they were received to grace by them, and suffered to enjoy their lands,
as unfit for any other, yet it seemeth, that in some places of the same
they have put foote, and fortified with sundry castles, of which the
ruines onely doe there now remaine, since which time they are growne
to that strength, that they are able to lift up hand against all that state;
and now lately through the boldnes and late good successe of this
Feagh Mac Hugh,[64] they are so farre imboldened, that they threaten
perill even to Dublin, over whose necke they continually hang. But
touching your demand of this Feaghes right unto that countrey which
he claimes, or the seigniory therein, it is most vaine and arrogant. For
this you cannot be ignorant, that it was part of that which was given
in inheritance by Dermot Mac Morrough, King of Leinster, unto
Strongbowe with his daughter, and which Strongbowe gave over unto
the King and his heires, so as the right is absolutely now in her Majesty, and if it were not, yet could it not be in this Feagh, but in O
Brin, which is the ancient Lord of all that countrey; for he and his
auncestours were but followers unto O Brin; and his grandfather Shane
Mac Terlagh, was a man of meanest regard amongst them, neither
having wealth nor power. But his sonne Hugh Mac Shane, the father
of this Feagh, first began to lift up his head, and through the strength
and great fastnes of Glan-Malor, which adjoyneth unto his house of
Ballinecor, drew unto him many theeves and out-lawes, which fled
unto the succour of that glynne, as to a sanctuary, and brought unto
him part of the spoyle of all the countrey, through which he grew
strong, and in short space got unto himselfe a great name thereby
amongst the Irish, in whose footing this his sonne continuing, hath,
through many unhappy occasions, increased his said name, and the
opinion of his greatnes, insomuch that now he is become a dangerous
enemy to deale withall.

---

* 　Dermot Mac Morrogh, King of Leinster, who was surnamed ni-Gall, as being a friend
　　to the English, and chiefe instrument in inciting them to the conquest of Ireland.
64　Feagh MacHugh, a prominent rebel in the 1570s and 1580s. Lord Grey led three
　　expeditions against him (including the defeat at Glenmalure: (see above, note 54)),
　　so Spenser would have been well acquainted with his actions.

Eudox. Surely I can commend him, that being of himselfe of so meane condition, hath through his owne hardinesse lifted himselfe up to the height, that he dare now front princes, and make tearmes with great potentates; the which as it is to him honourable, so it is to them most disgracefull, to be bearded of such a base varlet, that being but of late growne out of the dunghill, beginneth now to overcrow so high mountaines, and make himselfe great protectour of all outlawes and rebells that will repaire unto him. But doe you thinke he is now so dangerous an enemy as he is counted, or that it is so hard to take him downe as some suppose?

Iren. No verily, there is no great reckoning to bee made of him; for had he ever beene taken in hand, when the rest of the realme (or at least the parts adjoyning) had ben quiet, as the honourable gent. that now governeth there (I meane Sir William Russell)[65] gave a notable attempt thereunto,* and had worthily performed it, if his course had not beene crossed unhappily, he could not have stood 3. moneths, nor ever have looked up against a very meane power: but now all the parts about him being up in a madding moode, as the Moores in Leix, the Cavenaghes in the county of Wexford, and some of the Butlers in the county of Kilkenny, they all flocke unto him, and drawe into his countrey, as to a strong hould, where they thinke to be safe from all that prosecute them: And from thence they doe at their pleasures breake out into all the borders adjoyning, which are well peopled countryes, as the counties of Dublin, of Kildare, of Catherlagh, of Kilkenny, of Wexford, with the spoiles whereof they victuall and strengthen themselves, which otherwise should in short time be starved, and sore pined; so that what he is of himselfe, you may hereby perceive.

Eudox. Then by so much as I gather out of your speech, the next way to end the warres with him, and to roote him out quite, should be to keepe him from invading of those countryes adjoyning, which (as I suppose) is to be done, either by drawing all the inhabitants of those next borders away, and leaving them utterly waste, or by planting garrisons upon all those frontiers about him, that, when he shall breake forth, may set upon him and shorten his returne.

---

*   Vide Camdeni annales, sub finem anni 1594.

65   Sir William Russell, Lord Deputy (1594–7).

Iren. You conceive very rightly, Eudoxus, but for that the dispeopling and driving away all the inhabitants from the countrey about him, which you speake of, should bee a great confusion and trouble aswell for the unwillingnesse of them to leave their possessions, as also for placing and providing for them in other countryes, (me thinkes) the better course should be by planting of garrisons about him, which whensoever he shall looke forth, or be drawne out with the desire of the spoyle of those borders, or for necessity of victuall, shall be alwayes ready to intercept his going or comming.

Eudox. Where then doe you wish those garrisons to be planted that they may serve best against him, and how many in every garrison?

Iren. I my selfe, by reason that (as I told you) I am no martiall man, will not take upon me to direct so dangerous affaires, but onely as I understood by the purposes and plots, which the Lord Gray who was well experienced in that service, against him did lay downe: To the performance whereof he onely required 1000. men to be laid in 6. garrisons, that is, at Ballinecor 200. footemen and 50. horsemen, which should shut him out of his great glynne, whereto he so much trusteth; at Knockelough 200. footemen and 50. horsemen, to answere the county of Caterlagh; at Arclo or Wicklow 200. footemen and 50. horsemen to defend all that side towards the sea. In Shillelagh 100. footemen which should cut him from the Cavanaghes, and the county of Wexford; and about the three castles 50. horsemen, which should defend all the county of Dublin; and 100. footemen at Talbots Towne, which should keepe him from breaking out into the county of Kildare, and be alwayes on his necke on that side: The which garrisons so laide, will so busie him, that he shall never rest at home, nor stirre forth abroad but he shall be had; as for his creete they cannot be above ground, but they must needes fall into their hands or starve, for he hath no fastnes nor refuge for them. And as for his partakers of the Moores, Butlers, and Cavanaghes, they will soone leave him, when they see his fastnes and strong places thus taken from him.

Eudox. Surely this seemeth a plot of great reason, and small difficulty, which promiseth hope of a short end. But what speciall directions will you set downe for the services and risings out of these garrisons?

Iren. None other then the present occasions shall minister unto them, and as by good espialls, whereof there they cannot want store, they shall be drawne continually upon him, so as one of them shall be still upon him, and sometimes all at one instant, bayting him. And this (I assure my selfe) will demaund no long time, but will be all finished in the space of one yeare, which how small a thing it is, unto the eternall quietnesse which shall thereby be purchased to that realme, and the great good which should growe to her Majesty, should (me thinkes) readily drawe on her Highnesse to the undertaking of the enterprise.

Eudox.　You have very well (me thinkes), Irenæus, plotted a course for the atchieving of those warres now in Ireland, which seemes to ask no long time, nor great charge, so as the effecting thereof bee committed to men of sure trust, and sound experience, aswell in that country, as in the manner of those services; for if it bee left in the hands of such rawe captaines, as are usually sent out of England, being thereunto onely preferred by friendship, and not chosen by sufficiency, it will soone fall to the ground.

Iren.　Therefore it were meete (me thinkes) that such captaines onely were thereunto employed, as have formerly served in that country, and been at least lieutenants unto other captaines there. For otherwise being brought and transferred from other services abroad, as in France, in Spain, and in the Low-countryes, though they be of good experience in those, and have never so well deserved, yet in these they will be new to seeke, and, before they have gathered experience, they shall buy it with great losse to her Majesty, either by hazarding of their companies, through ignorance of the places, and manner of the Irish services, or by losing a great part of the time which is required hereunto, being but short, in which it might be finished, almost before they have taken out a new lesson, or can tell what is to be done.

Eudox.　You are no good friend to new captaines; it seemes Iren. that you barre them from the credit of this service: but (to say truth) me thinkes it were meete, that any one before he came to be a captaine, should have beene a souldiour; for, "Parere qui nescit, nescit imperare."[66] And besides there is great wrong done to the old souldiour, from whom all meanes of advancement which is due unto him, is cut off, by shuffling in these new cutting captaines, into the place for which he hath long served, and perhaps better deserved. But now that you have thus (as I suppose) finished all the warre, and brought all things to that low ebbe which you speake of, what course

66　'He who cannot obey, cannot command.'

will you take for the bringing in of that reformation which you intend, and recovering all things from this desolate estate, in which (mee thinkes) I behold them now left, unto that perfect establishment and new commonwealth which you have conceived of, by which so great good may redound unto her Majesty, and an assured peace bee confirmed? for that is it whereunto wee are now to looke, and doe greatly long for, being long sithence made weary with the huge charge which you have laide upon us, and with the strong indurance of so many complaints, so many delayes, so many doubts and dangers, as will hereof (I know well) arise; unto the which before wee come, it were meete (me thinkes) that you should take some order for the souldiour, which is now first to bee discharged and disposed of, some way: the which if you doe not well fore-see, may growe to as great inconvenience as all this that I suppose you have quit us from, by the loose leaving of so many thousand souldiours, which from thence forth will be unfit for any labour or other trade, but must either seeke service and imployment abroad, which may be dangerous, or else imploy themselves heere at home, as may bee discommodious.

Iren. You say very true, and it is a thing much mislyked in this our common-wealth, that no better course is taken for such as have been imployed in service. but that returning, whether maymed, and so unable to labour, or otherwise whole and sound, yet afterwards unwilling to worke, or rather willing to set the hang-man on work. But that needeth another consideration; but to this which wee have now in hand, it is farre from my meaning to leave the souldiour so at randome, or to leave that waste realme so weake and destitute of strength, which may both defend it against others that might seeke then to set upon it, and also keepe it from that relapse which I before did fore-cast. For it is one speciall good of this plot, which I would devise, that 6000. souldiers of these whom I have now imployed in this service, and made throughly acquainted both with the state of the countrey, and manners of the people, should henceforth bee still continued, and for ever maintayned of the countrey, without any charge to her Majestie;[67] and the rest that are either olde, and unable to serve

---

67 Irenius is suggesting the creation of a standing army, something which was traditionally feared in England.

any longer, or willing to fall to thrift, as I have seene many souldiers after the service to prove very good husbands, should bee placed in part of the landes by them wonne, at such rate, or rather better then others, to whome the same shall be set out.

Eudox.   Is it possible, Irenæus? can there be any such meanes devised, that so many men should be kept still in her Majesties service, without any charge to her at all? Surely this were an exceeding great good, both to her Highnes to have so many olde souldiers alwayes ready at call, to what purpose soever she list to imploy them, and also to have that land thereby so strengthned, that it shall neither feare any forraine invasion, nor practise, which the Irish shall ever attempt, but shall keepe them under in continuall awe and firme obedience

Iren.   It is so indeed. And yet this truely I doe not take to be any matter of great difficultie, as I thinke it will also soone appeare unto you. And first we will speake of the North part, for that the same is of more weight and importance. So soone as it shall appeare that the enemy is brought downe, and the stout rebell either cut off, or driven to that wretchednesse, that hee is no longer able to holde up his head, but will come in to any conditions, which I assure my selfe will bee before the end of the second Winter, I wish that there bee a generall proclamation made, that whatsoever out-lawes will freely come in, and submit themselves to her Majesties mercy, shall have liberty so to doe, where they shall either finde that grace they desire, or have leave to returne againe in safety; upon which it is likely that so many as survive, will come in to sue for grace, of which who so are thought meet for subjection, and fit to be brought to good, may be received, or else all of them; (for I thinke that all wilbe but a very few;) upon condition and assurance that they will submit themselves absolutely to her Maiesties ordinance for them, by which they shall be assured of life and libertie, and be onely tyed to such conditions as shall bee thought by her meet for containing them ever after in due obedience. To the which conditions I nothing doubt, but they will all most readily, and upon their knees submit themselves, by the proofe of that which I have seene in Mounster. For upon the like proclamation there, they all came in both tagg and ragg, and when as afterwardes many of them were denyed to be received, they bade them doe with them what they would, for they would not by any meanes returne againe, nor goe forth. For in that case who will not accept almost of any conditions, rather than dye of hunger and miserie?

Eudox. It is very likely so. But what then is the ordinance, and what bee the conditions which you will propose unto them, which shall reserve unto them an assurance of life and liberty?

Iren. So soone then as they have given the best assurance of themselves which may be required, which must be (I suppose) some of their principall men to remaine in hostage one for another, and some other for the rest, for other surety I reckon of none that may binde them, neither of wife, nor of children, since then perhappes they would gladly be ridde of both from the famine; I would have them first unarmed utterly, and stripped quite of all their warrelike weapons, and then, these conditions set downe and made knowne unto them, that they shall bee placed in Leinster, and have land given to them to occupy and to live upon, in such sort as shall become good subjects, to labour thenceforth for their living, and to apply themselves to honest trades of civility, as they shall every one be found meete and able for.

Eudox. Where then a Gods name will you place them in Leinster? or will you finde out any new land there for them that is yet unknowne?

Iren. No, I will place them all in the countrey of the Birnes and Tooles, which Pheagh Mac Hugh hath, and in all the lands of the Cavanaghes, which are now in rebellion, and all the lands which will fall to her Maiestie there-abouts, which I know to be very spacious and large enough to containe them, being very neere twenty or thirty miles wyde.*

Eudox. But then what will you doe with all the Birnes, the Tooles, and the Cavanaghes, and all those that now are joyned with them?

Iren. At the same very time, and in the same very manner that I make that proclamation to them of Ulster, will I have it also made to these, and upon their submission thereunto, I will take like assurance of them as of the other. After which, I will translate all that remaine of them unto the places of the other in Ulster, with all their creete, and what else they have left them, the which I will cause to be divided amongst them in some meete sort, as each may thereby have some-

---

* This carrieth no fit proportion for the transplantation intended by the author, considering the large extent of Ulster, and the narrow bounds heere limited.

what to sustaine himselfe a while withall, untill, by his further travaile and labour of the earth, he shalbe able to provide himselfe better.[68]

Eudox. But will you give the land then freely unto them, and make them heires of the former rebells? so may you perhaps make them also heires of all their former villainies and disorders; or how else will you dispose of them?

Iren. Not so: but all the lands will I give unto Englishmen, whom I will have drawne thither, who shall have the same with such estates as shall bee thought meete, and for such rent as shall eft-soones bee rated; under every of those Englishmen will I place some of those Irish to bee tennants for a certaine rent, according to the quantity of such land, as every man shall have allotted unto him, and shalbe found able to wield, wherein this speciall regard shall be had, that in no place under any land-lord there shall bee many of them placed together, but dispersed wide from their acquaintance, and scattered farre abroad thorough all the country: For that is the evill which now I finde in all Ireland, that the Irish dwell altogether by their septs, and severall nations, so as they may practise or conspire what they will; whereas if there were English well placed among them, they should not bee able once to stirre or to murmure, but that it should be knowne, and they shortened according to their demerites.

Eudox. You have good reason; but what rating of rents meane you? to what end doe you purpose the same?

Iren. My purpose is to rate the rent of all those lands of her Maiestie, in such sort unto those Englishmen which shall take them, as they shall be well able to live thereupon, to yeeld her Maiesty reasonable chiefrie, and also give a competent maintenance unto the garrisons, which shall be there left amongst them; for those souldiours (as I tolde you) remaining of the former garrisons, I cast to maintaine upon the rent of those landes, which shall bee escheated, and to have them divided thorough all Ireland, in such places as shalbe thought most convenient, and occasion may require. And this was the course which the Romanes observed in the conquest of England, for they planted some of their legions in all places convenient, the which they caused

---

68   Irenius's plans for transplanting the Irish were commonly advocated in English trea-
     tises in the 1590s, and they were to be realised after Cromwell's reconquest when
     many were transplanted west of the River Shannon to Connaught (1655–9).

the countrey to maintaine, cutting upon every portion of land a reasonable rent, which they called Romescot, the which might not surcharge the tennant or free-holder, and might defray the pay of the garrison: and this hath beene alwayes observed by all princes in all countries to them newly subdued, to set garrisons amongt them, to containe them in dutie whose burthen they made them to beare; and the want of this ordinance in the first conquest of Ireland by Henry the Second, was the cause of the so short decay of that government, and the quicke recovery againe of the Irish. Therefore by all meanes it is to bee provided for. And this is that I would blame, if it should not misbecome mee, in the late planting of Mounster, that no care was had of this ordinance nor any strength of garrison provided for, by a certaine allowance out of all the saide landes, but onely the present profite looked into, and the safe continuance thereof for ever hereafter neglected.

Eudox.   But there is a band of souldiours layde in Mounster, to the maintenance of which, what oddes is there whether the Queene, receiving the rent of the countrey, doe give pay at her pleasure, or that there be a setled allowance appointed unto them out of her lands there?

Iren.   There is great oddes: for now that said rent of the countrey is not appointed to the pay of the souldiers, but it is, by every other occasion comming betweene, converted to other uses, and the souldiours in time of peace discharged and neglected as unnecessary; whereas if the said rent were appointed and ordained by an establishment to this end onely, it should not bee turned to any other; nor in troublous times, upon every occasion, her Majestie bee so troubled with sending over new souldiours as shee is now, nor the countrie ever should dare to mutinie, having still the souldiour in their neck, nor any forraine enemy dare to invade knowing there so strong and great a garrison, allwayes ready to receive them.

Eudox.   Sith then you thinke that this Romescot of the pay of the souldiours upon the land, to be both the readiest way to the souldiours, and least troublesome to her Majestie; tell us (I pray you) how would you have the said lands rated, that both a rent may rise thereout unto the Queene, and also the souldiours receive pay, which (me thinkes) wilbe hard?

Iren.   First we are to consider, how much land there is in all Ulster, that according to the quantity thereof we may cesse the said rent and allowance issuing thereout. Ulster (as the ancient records of that realme doe testifie) doth containe 9000. plow-lands, every of which plow-lands containeth 120. acres, after the rate of 21. foote to every perch of the acre, every of which plow-lands I will rate at 40s. by the yeare; the which yearely rent amounteth in the whole to 18000l. besides 6s. 8d. chiefrie out of every plow-land. But because the countie of Louth, being a part of Ulster, and containing in it 712. plow-lands is not wholly to escheate to her Majestie, as the rest, they having in all their warres continued for the most part dutifull, though otherwise a great part thereof is now under the rebells, there is an abatement to be made thereout of 400. or 500. plow-lands, as I estimate the same, the which are not to pay the whole yearly rent of 40s. out of every plow-land, like as the escheated lands doe, but yet shall pay for their composition of cesse towards the keeping of soldiers, 20s. out of every plow-land, so as there is to bee deducted out of the former summe 200 or 300l. yearly, the which may neverthelesse be supplied by the rent of the fishings, which are exceeding great in Ulster, and also by an increase of rent in the best lands, and those that lye in the best places neere the sea-coast. The which eighteene thousand pounds will defray the entertainment of 1500. souldiers, with some over-plus towardes the pay of the victuallers, which are to bee imployed in the victualling of these garrisons.

Eudox.   So then belike you meane to leave 1500. souldiers in garrison for Ulster, to bee payde principally out of the rent of those lands, which shall be there escheated unto her Majestie. The which, where (I pray you) will you have them garrisoned?

Iren.   I will have them divided into three parts, that is, 500. in every garrison, the which I will have to remaine in three of the same places, where they were before appointed, to wit, 500. at Strabane and about Loughfoile, so as they may holde all the passages of that part of the countrey, and some of them bee put in wardes, upon all the straights thereabouts, which I know to be such, as may stoppe all passages into the countrey on that side; and some of them also upon the Ban, up towardes Lough-Sidney, as I formerly directed. Also other 500, at the fort upon Lough-Earne, and wardes taken out of them, which shall bee layde at Fermannagh, at Bealick, at Ballyshannon, and all the streights towardes Connaght, the which I know doe so strongly command all the passages that way, as that none can passe from Ulster into Connaght, without their leave. The last 500. shall also remaine in their fort at Monoghan, and some of them bee drawne into wardes, to keepe the kaies of all that countrey, both downwards, and also towards O Relies countrie, and the pale; and some at Eniskillin, some at Belturbut, some at the Blacke Fort, and so along that river, as I formerly shewed in the first planting of them. And moreover at every of these forts, I would have the seate of a towne layde forth and incompassed, in the which I would wish that there should inhabitants of all sortes, as merchants, artificers, and husbandmen, bee placed, to whom there should charters and fraunchises be graunted to incorporate them. The which, as it wilbe no matter of difficultie to draw out of England persons which would very gladly be so placed, so would it in short space turne those parts to great commodity, and bring ere long to her Majestie much profit; for those places are fit for trade and trafficke, having most convenient out-gates by divers to the sea, and in-gates to the richest parts of the land, that they would soone be enriched, and mightily enlarged, for the very seating of the garrisons by them; besides the safetie and assurance which they shall worke unto them, will also draw thither store of people and trade, as I have seene ensample at Mariborogh and Philipstowne in Leinster, where by reason of these two fortes, though there be but small wardes left in them, there are two good townes now growne, which are the greatest stay of both those two countries.

Eudox. Indeed (me thinkes) three such townes as you say, would do very well in those places with the garrisons, and in short space would be so augmented, as they would bee able with little to in-wall themselves strongly; but, for the planting of all the rest of the countrey, what order would you take?

Iren. What other then (as I said) to bring people out of England, which should inhabite the same; whereunto though I doubt not but great troopes would be readie to runne, yet for that in such cases, the worst and most decayed men are most ready to remove, I would wish them rather to bee chosen out of all partes of this realme, either by discretion of wise men thereunto appointed, or by lot, or by the drumme, as was the old use in sending forth of Colonies, or such other good meanes as shall in their wisedome bee thought meetest. Amongst the chiefe of which, I would have the land sett into seigniories, in such sort as it is now in Mounster, and divided into hundreds and parishes, or wardes, as it is in England, and layde out into shires, as it was aunciently, *viz.* The countie of Downe, the countie of Antrim, the countie of Louth, the countie of Armaghe, the countie of Cavan, the countie of Colerane,* the countie of Monoghan, the countie of Tyrone, the countie of Fermannagh, the countie of Donnegall, being in all tenne. Over all which I wish a Lord President and a Councell to bee placed, which may keepe them afterwards in awe and obedience, and minister unto them iustice and equity.

Eudox.   Thus I see the whole purpose of your plot for Ulster, and now I desire to heare your like opinion for Connaght.

Iren.   By that which I have already said of Ulster, you may gather my opinion for Connaght, being very answereable to the former. But for that the lands, which shal therein escheat unto her Maiesty, are not so intirely together, as that they can be accompted in one summe, it needeth that they be considered severally. The province of Connaght in the whole containeth (as appeareth by the Records of Dublin) 7200 plow-lands of the former measure, and is of late divided into six shires or counties: The countie of Clare,† the countie of Leytrim, the countie of Roscoman, the countie of Galway, the countie of Maio, and the countie of Sligo. Of the which all the countie of Sligo, all the countie of Maio, the most part of the countie of Roscoman, the most part of the countie of Leitrim, a great part of the countie of Galway, and some of the countie of Clare, is like to escheat to her Maiestie for the rebellion of their present possessors. The which two counties of Sligo and Maio are supposed to containe almost 3000, plow-lands, the rent whereof rateably to the former, I valew almost at 6000l. *per annum.* The countie of Roscoman, saving that which pertaineth to the house of Roscoman, and some few other English there lately seated, is all one, and therefore it is wholly likewise to escheate to her Majesty, saving those portions of English inhabitants, and even those English doe (as I understand by them) pay as much rent to her Majesty, as is set upon those in Ulster, counting their composition money

---

* This is now part of the countie of London-derry.

† The county of Clare was anciently accounted part of the province of Mounster, whence it hath the name of Tucðmuan, or Thomond, which signifieth North Mounster, and hath at this day its peculiar governour, as being exempted from the presidences of Mounster and Connaght.

therewithall, so as it may all run into one reckoning with the former two counties: So that this county of Roscoman containing 1200. plow-lands, as it is accompted, amounteth to 2400 li. by the yeare, which with the former two counties rent, maketh about 8300 l. for the former wanted somewhat. But what the escheated lands of the county of Gallway and Leitrim will rise unto, is yet uncertaine to define, till survey thereof be made, for that those lands are intermingled with the Earle of Clanricardes, and other lands, but it is thought they be the one halfe of both those counties, so as they may be counted to the value of one whole county, which containeth above 1000. plough-land; for so many the least county of them all comprehendeth, which maketh 2000 li. more, that is in all ten or eleven thousand pounds. The other 2 counties must remaine till their escheates appears, the which letting passe yet, as unknowne, yet this much is knowne to be accompted for certaine, that the composition of these two counties, being rated at 20. shil. every plow-land, will amount to above 2000 pounds more, all which being laide together to the former, may be reasonably estimated to rise unto 13000 pounds, the which summe, together with the rent of the escheated lands in the two last countyes, which cannot yet be valued, being, as I doubt not, no lesse then a thousand pounds more, will yeeld pay largely unto 1000 men and their victuallers, and 1000 pounds over towards the Governour.

Eudox.   You have (me thinkes) made but an estimate of those lands of Connaght, even at a very venture, so as it should be hard to build any certainty of charge to be raised upon the same.

Iren.   Not altogether upon uncertainties; for this much may easily appeare unto you to be certaine, as the composition money of every plowland amounteth unto; for this I would have you principally to understand, that my purpose is to rate all the lands in Ireland at 20 shil: every plowland, for their composition towards the garrison. The which I know, in regard of being freed from all other charges whatsoever, will be readily and most gladly yeelded unto. So that there being in all Ireland (as appeareth by their old Records) 43920 plowlands, the same shall amount to the summe likewise of 43920 pounds, and the rest to be reared of the escheated lands which fall to her Majesty in the said provinces of Ulster, Connaght, and that part of Leinster un-der the rebells; for Mounster wee deale not yet withall.

Eudox.   But tell me this, by the way, doe you then lay composition upon the escheated lands as you doe upon the rest? for so (mee thinkes) you reckon alltogether. And that sure were too much to pay 7. nobles out of every plow land, and composition money besides, that is 20 shill: out of every plow land.

Iren. No, you mistake me; I doe put onely 7 nobles rent and composition both upon every plow land escheated, that is 40. shil: for composition, and 6. shil: 8. pence for cheifrie to her Majestie.

Eudox. I doe now conceive you; proceede then (I pray you) to the appointing of your garrisons in Connaght, and show us both how many and where you would have them placed.

Iren. I would have 1000 laide in Connaght, in 2 garrisons; namely, 500 in the county of Maio, about Clan Mac Costilagh, which shall keepe all Mayo and the Bourkes of Mac William Eighter: The other 500. in the county of Galway, about Garrandough, that they may containe the Conhors and the Bourkes there, the Kellies and Murries, with all them there-abouts; for that garrison which I formerly placed at Lough-earne will serve for all occasions in the county of Sligo, being neere adjoyning thereunto, so as in one nights march they maye be almost in any place thereof, when neede shall require them. And like as in the former places of garrisons in Ulster, I wished three corporate townes to be planted, which under the safeguard of that strength should dwell and trade safely with all the countrey about them; so would I also wish to be in this of Connaght: and that besides, there were another established at Athlone, with a convenient ward in the castle there for their defence.

Eudox. What should that neede, seeing the Governour of Connaght useth to lye there alwayes, whose presence will bee a defence to all that towneship?

Iren. I know he doth so, but that is much to be disliked, that the Governour should lye so farre of, in the remotest place of all the province, whereas it were meeter that he should be continually abiding in the middest of the charge, that he might bothe looke out alike unto all places of his government, and also be soone at hand in any place, where occasion shall demand him; for the presence of the Governour is (as you sayd) a great stay and bridle unto those that are ill disposed: like as I see it is well observed in Mounster, where the dayly good thereof is continually apparant: and, for this cause also, doe I greatly mislike the Lord Deputies seating at Dublin, being the outest corner of the realme, and least needing the awe of his presence; whereas (me thinkes) it were fitter, since his proper care is of Leinster, though he have care of all besides generally, that he should seate himselfe at Athie, or there-abouts, upon the skirt of that unquiet countrey, so that he might sit as it were at the very maine maste of his ship, whence he might easily over looke and sometimes over-reach the Moores, the Dempsies, the Connors, O-Carroll, O-Molloy, and all that heape of Irish nations which there lye hudled together, without any to over-awe them, or containe them in dutie.[69] For the Irishman (I assure you) feares the Government no longer then he is within sight or reach.

Eudox. Surely (me thinkes) herein you observe a matter of much importance more then I have heard ever noted, but sure that seemes so expedient, as that I wonder that heretofore it hath beene overseene or omitted; but I suppose the instance of the citizens of Dublin is the greatest lett thereof.

Iren. Truely then it ought not so to be; for no cause have they to feare that it will be any hinderance to them; for Dublin will be still, as it is the key of all passages and transportations out of England thitherto, no lesse profit of those citizens then it now is, and besides other places will hereby receive some benefit: But let us now (I pray you) come to Leinster, in the which I would wish the same course to be observed, that was in Ulster.

Eudox. You meane for the leaving of the garrisons in their forts, and for planting of English in all those countryes, betweene the county of Dublin and the county of Wexford; but those waste wilde places I thinke when they are won unto her Majesty, that there is none which will be hasty to seeke to inhabite.

Iren. Yes enough, (I warrant you;) for though the whole tracke of the countrey be mountanous and woody, yet there are many goodly valleyes amongst them, fit for faire habitations, to which those mountaines adjoyned will be a great increase of pasturage; for that countrey is a great soyle of cattle, and very fit for breed: as for corne it is nothing naturall, save onely for barly and oates, and some places for rye, and

---

69 Irenius' stress on the importance of provincial governors in Leinster, Ulster, Connaught and Munster follows on from Sir Henry Sidney's establishment of the positions in the 1560s. The demand that the Lord Deputy be more mobile and venture 'beyond the Pale' was also an old complaint. Usually it was suggested that he reside at Athlone rather than Athy (in Kildare, the centre of Leinster).

therefore the larger penny-worthes may be allowed to them, though otherwise the wildnes of the mountaine pasturage doe recompence the badnes of the soyle, so as I doubt not but it will find inhabitants and undertakers enough.

Eudox.   How much doe you thinke that all those lands, which Feagh Mac Hugh houldeth under him, may amount unto, and what rent may be reared thereout, to the maintenance of the garrisons that shall be laide there?

Iren.   Truely it is impossible by ayme to tell it, and for experience and knowledge thereof, I doe not thinke that there was every any of the particulars thereof, but yet I will (if it please you) guesse thereat, upon ground onely of their judgement which have formerly devided all that country into 2 sheires or countyes, namely the countie of Wicklow, and the county of Fernes; the which 2 I see no cause but that they should wholly escheate to her Majesty, all save the barony of Arclo which is the Earle of Ormond's auncient inheritance, and hath ever been in his possession; for all the whole land is the Queenes, unlesse there be some grant of any part thereof, to bee shewed from her Majesty: as I thinke there is onely of New Castle to Sir Henry Harrington, and of the castle of Fernes to Sir Thomas Masterson,[70] the rest, being almost 30 miles over, I doe suppose, can containe no lesse then 2000 plowlands, which I will estimate at 4000. pounds rent, by the yeare. The rest of Leinster being 7. counties, to wit, the county of Dublin, Kildare, Caterlagh, Wexford, Kilkenny, the Kings and the Queenes county, doe contain in them 7400. plow-lands, which amounteth to so many pounds for composition to the garrison, that makes in the whole 11400. pounds, which summe will yeeld pay unto 1000 souldiours, little wanting, which may be supplied out of other lands of the Cavenaghes, which are to be escheated to her Majesty for the rebellion of their possessors, though otherwise indeede they bee of her owne ancient demesne.

Eudox.   It is great reason. But tell us now where you will wish those garrisons to be laide, whether altogether, or to bee dispersed in sundry places of the country?

---

70   Sir Henry Harrington and Sir Thomas Masterson were well-established English settlers, both praised by Sir Henry Sidney in 1580. Sir Henry was the brother of Sir John Harrington, the Queen's godson and translator of Ariosto (an important source for *The Faerie Queene*), who met Hugh O'Neill during Essex's campaign in 1599.

Iren.   Marry, in sundry places, *viz.* in this sort, or much the like as may be better advised, for 200. in a place I doe thinke to bee enough for the safeguard of that country, and keeping under all suddaine up-starts, that shall seeke to trouble the peace thereof; therefore I wish 200. to be laide at Ballinecor for the keeping of all bad persons from Glan-malor, and all the fastnes there-abouts, and also to containe all that shall be planted in those lands thenceforth. Another 200. at Knockelough in their former place of garrison, to keepe the Bracknagh and all those mountaines of the Cavenaghes; 200. more to lie at Fernes and upwards, inward upon the Slane; 200. to be placed at the fort of Leix, to restraine the Moores, Upper-Ossory, and O-Carrol; other 200. at the fort of Ofaly, to curbe the O-Connors, O-Molloyes, Mac-Coghlan, Mageoghegan, and all those Irish nations bordering there-abouts.

Eudox.   Thus I see all your men bestowed in Leinster; what say you then of Meath?

Iren.   Meath which containeth both East Meath and West Meath, and of late the Annaly, now called the country of Longford, is counted therunto: But Meath it selfe according to the old Records, containeth 4320. plowlands, and the country of Longford 947. which in the whole makes 5267 plowlands, of which the composition money will amount likewise to 5267 pounds to the maintenance of the garrison: But because all Meath, lying in the bosome of that kingdome is alwayes quiet enough, it is needelesse to put any garrison there, so as all that charge may be spared. But in the country of Longford I wish 200. footmen and 50. horsemen to bee placed in some convenient seate, betweene the Annaly and the Breny, as about Lough Sillon, or some like place of that river, so as they might keepe both the O-Relies, and also the O-Ferrals, and all that out-skirt of Meath, in awe, the which use upon every light occasion to be stirring, and, having continuall enmity amongst themselves, doe thereby oftentimes trouble all those parts, the charge whereof being 3400. and odde pounds is to be cut out of that composition money for Meath and Longford, the over-plus being almost 2000. pounds by the yeare, will come in clearly to her Majesty.

Eudox.   It is worth the hearkening unto: But now that you have done with Meath, proceede (I pray you) to Mounster, that wee may see how it will rise there for the maintenance of the garrison.

Iren.　Mounster containeth by Record at Dublin 16000. plow-lands, the composition whereof, as the rest, will make 16000. pounds by the yeare, out of the which I would have 1000. souldiours to be maintained for the defence of that province, the charge whereof with the victuallers wages, will amount to 1200. pounds by the yeare; the other 4000. pounds will defray the charge of the Presidency and the Councel of that province.

Eudox.　The reckoning is easie, but in this accompt, by your leave, (me thinkes) you are deceived; for, in this summe of the composition money, you accompt the lands of the undertakers of that province, who are, by their graunt from the Queene, to be free from all such impositions whatsoever, excepting their onlie rent, which is surely enough.

Iren.　You say true, I did so, but the same 20. shil. for every plowland, I meant to have deducted out of that rent due upon them to her Majesty, which is no hinderance, nor charge at all more to her Majesty then it now is; for all that rent which she receives of them, shee putteth forth againe to the maintenance of the Presidency there, the charge whereof it doth scarcely defray; whereas in this accompt both that charge of the Presidency, and also of a thousand souldiours more, shall be maintained.

Eudox.　It should be well if it could be brought to that: But now where will you have your thousand men garrisoned?

Iren.　I would have a hundred of them placed at the Bantry where is a most fit place, not onely to defend all that side of the west part from forraine invasion, but also to answere all occasions of troubles, to which that countrey being so remote is very subject. And surely there also would be planted a good towne, having both a good haven and a plentifull fishing, and the land being already escheated to her Majesty, but being forcibly kept from her, by one that proclaimes himselfe the bastard son of the Earle of Clancar, being called Donell Mac Carty, whom it is meete to foresee to: For whensoever the Earle shall die, all those lands (after him) are to come unto her Majesty, he is like to make a foule stirre there, though of himselfe no power, yet through supportance of some others who lye in the wind, and looke after the fall of that inheritance. Another hundred I would have placed at Castle Mayne, which should keepe all Desmond and Kerry; for it answereth them both most conveniently: Also about Kilmore in the county of

Corke would I have 2. hundred placed, the which should breake that nest of thieves there, and answere equally both to the county of Limericke, and also the county of Corke: Another hundred would I have lye at Corke, aswell to command the towne, as also to be ready for any forraine occasion: Likewise at Waterford, would I place 2. hundred, for the same reasons, and also for other privy causes, that are no lesse important: Moreover on this side of Arlo, near the Muskery Quirke, which is the countrey of the Burkes, about Kill-Patricke, I would have two hundred more to be garrisond, which should skoure both the White Knights country and Arlo, and Muskery Quirk, by which places all the passages of theives doe lye, which convey their stealth from all Mounster downewards towards Tipperary, and the English Pale, and from the English Pale also up unto Mounster, whereof they use to make a common trade: Besides that, ere long I doubt that the county of Tipperary it selfe will neede such a strength in it, which were good to be there ready before the evill fall, that is dayly of some expected: And thus you see all your garrisons placed.

Eudox. I see it right well, but let me (I pray you) by the way aske you the reason, why in those citties of Mounster, namely Waterford and Corke, you rather placed garrisons, then in all others in Ireland? For they may thinke themselves to have great wrong to bee so charged above all the rest.

Iren. I will tell you; those two cities above all the rest, do offer an ingate to the Spaniard most fitly: But yet because they shall not take exceptions to this, that they are charged above all the rest, I will also lay a charge upon the others likewise; for indeed it is no reason that the corporate towness enjoying great franchizes and privileges from her Majesty, and living thereby not onely safe, but drawing to them the wealth of all the land, should live so free, as not to be partakers of the burthen of this garrison for their owne safety, specially in this time of trouble, and seeing all the rest burthened; (and therefore) I will thus charge them all ratably, according to their abilities, towards their maintenance, the which her Majesty may (if she please) spare out of the charge of the rest, and reserve towards her other costes, or else adde to the charge of the Presidency in the North.

Waterford	C.	Clonmell	X.	Dundalke	X.
Corke	L.	Cashell	X.	Mollingare	X.
Limericke	L.	Fedard	X.	Newrie	X.
Galway	L.	Kilkenny	XXV.	Trim	X.
Dinglecush	X.	Wexford	XXV.	Ardee	X.
Kinsale	X.	Tredah	XXV.	Kells	X.
Yoghall	X.	Ross	XXV.	Dublin	C.
Kilmallock	X.				

In all 580.

Eudox. It is easie, Irenaeus, to lay a charge upon any towne, but to foresee how the same may be answered and defrayed, is the cheife part of good advisement.

Iren. Surely this charge which I put upon them, I know to bee so reasonable, as that it will not much be felt; for the port townes that have benefit of shipping may cut it easily off their trading, and inland townes of their corne and cattle; neither do I see, but since to them especially the benefit of peace doth redound, that they especially should beare the burthen of their safeguard and defence, as wee see all the townes of the Low-Countryes,[71] doe cut upon themselves an excise of all things towards the maintenance of the warre that is made in their behalfe, to which though these are not to be compared in richesse, yet are they to bee charged according to their povertie.

Eudox. But now that you have thus set up these forces of soldiers, and provided well (as you suppose) for their pay, yet there remaineth to fore-cast how they may bee victualled, and where purveyance thereof may bee made; for, in Ireland it selfe, I cannot see almost how any thing is to bee had for them, being already so pittifully wasted, as it is with this short time of warre.

Iren. For the first two yeares, it is needefull indeede that they bee victualled out of England thoroughly, from halfe yeare to halfe yeare, afore-hand.[72] All which time the English Pale shall not bee burdened

71 Critics of the English assumption of rights to Ireland usually cited the Spanish dominance over the Netherlands as a parallel case and hence the hypocrisy of the English defence of the Protestant Dutch and Belgians against the Catholic Spanish at the same time that they were fighting a war to maintain control of Ireland. Irenius slyly equates both Protestant causes.

72 Victualling vast sections of the English population in Ireland from England had often occurred because of the frequency of famine in Elizabeth's later years.

at all, but shall have time to recover themselves; and Mounster also, being reasonably well stored, will by that time, (if God send season-able weather,) bee thoroughly well furnished to supply a great part of that charge, for I knowe there is a great plenty of corne sent over sea from thence, the which if they might have sale for at home, they would bee glad to have money so neere hand, specially if they were streightly restrayned from transporting of it. Thereunto also there will bee a great helpe and furtherance given, in the putting forward of husbandrie in all meete places, as heereafter shall in due place appeare. But heereafter when things shall growe unto a better strength, and the countrey be replenished with corne, as in short space it will, if it bee well followed, for the countrey people themselves are great plowers, and small spenders of corne, then would I wish that there should bee good store of houses and magazins erected in all those great places of garrison, and in all great townes, as well for the victualling of souldiers, and shippes, as for all occasions of suddaine services, as also for pre-venting of all times of dearth and scarcitie; and this want is much to bee complained of in England, above all other countreys, who, trust-ing too much to the usuall blessing of the earth, doe never fore-cast any such hard seasons, nor any such suddaine occasions as these troublous times may every day bring foorth, when it will bee too late to gather provision from abroad, and to bringe it perhappes from farre for the furnishing of shippes or souldiers, which peradventure may neede to bee presently imployed and whose want may (which God forbid) hap to hazard a kingdome.

Eudox.   Indeede the want of those magazins of victualls, I have oftentimes complayned of in England, and wondered at in other countreyes, but that is nothing now to our purpose; but as for these garrisons which you have now so strongly planted throghout all Ire-land, and every place swarming with souldiers, shall there bee no end of them? For now thus being (me thinkes) I doe see rather a countrey of warre, then of peace and quiet, which you earst pretended to worke in Ireland; for if you bring all things to that quietnesse that you said, what then needeth to maintaine so great forces, as you have charged upon it?

Iren.   I will unto you Eudox. in privitie discover the drift of my pur-pose: I meane (as I tolde you) and doe well hope thereby both to settle an eternall peace in that countrey, and also to make it very profitable to her Majestie,[73] the which I see must bee brought in with a strong hand, and so continued, till it runne in a steadfast course of governement, which in this sort will neither bee difficult nor dangerous; for the souldier being once brought in for the service into Ulster, and having subdued it and Connaght, I will not have him to lay downe his armes any more, till hee have effected that which I purpose, that is, first to have this generall composition for maintenance of these thoroughout all the realme, in regard of the troublous times, and daylie danger which is threatned to this realme by the King of Spaine: And thereupon to bestow all my souldiers in such sort as I have done, that no part of all that realme shall be able to dare to quinch: Then will I eftsoones bring in my reformation, and thereupon establish such a forme of governement, as I may thinke meetest for the good of that realme, which being once settled, and all things put into a right way, I doubt not but they will runne on fairely. And though they would ever seeke to swerve aside, yet shall they not bee able without forreine violence, once to remoove, as you your selfe shall soone (I hope) in your own reason readily conceive; which if it shall ever appeare, then may her Majestie at pleasure with-draw some of the garrisons, and turne their pay into her purse, or if shee will never please so to doe (which I would rather wish) then shall shee have a number of brave olde souldiers alwayes ready for any occasion that shee will imploy them unto, supplying their garrisons with fresh ones in their steed; the maintenance of whome, shall bee no more charge to her Majestie then now that realme is for all the revenue thereof; and much more shee spendeth, even in the most peaceable times, that are there, as things now stand. And in time of warre, which is now surely every seventh yeare, shee spendeth infinite treasure besides, to small purpose.

Eudox. I perceive your purpose; but now that you have thus strongly made way unto your reformation, and that I see the people so humbled and prepared, that they will and must yeeld to any ordinance that shall bee given them, I doe much desire to understand the same; for in the beginning you promised to shewe a meanes how to redresse all those inconveniences and abuses, which you shewed to bee in that state of government, which now stands there, as in the lawes, cus-

---

73   The dream of Tudor politicians from the region of Henry VIII onwards.

toms, and religion, wherein I would gladly know first, whether, in steed of those lawes, you would have new lawes made; for now, for ought that I see, you may doe what you please.

Iren. I see Eudox. that you well remember our first purpose, and doe rightly continue the course thereof. First therefore to speake of lawes, since wee first beganne with them, I doe not thinke it now convenient, though it bee in the power of the Prince to change all the lawes and make new; for that should breede a great trouble and confusion, aswell in the English there dwelling, and to be planted, as also in the Irish. For the English having beene alwayes trayned up in the English governement, will hardly bee inured to any other, and the Irish will better be drawne to the English then the English to the Irish government. Therefore sithence wee cannot now apply lawes fit to the people, as in the first institutions of common-wealths it ought to bee, wee will apply the people, and fit them unto the lawes, as it most conveniently may bee. The lawes therefore wee resolve shall abide in the same sort that they doe, both Common Law and Statutes, onely such defects in the Common-law, and inconveniences in the Statutes, as in the beginning wee noted, and as men of deeper insight shall advise, may be changed by some other new acts and ordinances to bee by Parliament there confirmed: As those for tryalls of Pleas of the Crowne, and private rights betweene parties, colourable conveyances, and accessaries.

Eudox. But how will those be redressed by Parlament, when as the Irish which sway most in Parlament (as you said) shall oppose themselves against them?

Iren. That may well now be avoyded: For now that so many Free-holders of English shall bee established, they together with Burgesses of townes, and such other loyal Irish-men, as may bee preferred to bee Knights of the shire, and such like, will bee able to beard and to counter-poise the rest, who also, being now more brought in awe, will the more easily submit to any such ordinances as shall bee for the good of themselves, and that realme generally.

Eudox. You say well, for by the increase of Free-holders their numbers hereby will be greatly augmented; but how should it passe through the higher house, which still must consiste all of Irish?

Iren. Marry, that also may bee redressed by ensample of that which I have heard was done in the like case by King Edward the Third (as I remember) who being greatly bearded and crossed by the Lords of the Cleargie, they being there by reason of the Lords Abbots, and others, too many and too strong for him, so as hee could not for their frowardnesse order and reforme things as hee desired, was advised to direct out his writts to certaine Gentlemen of the best ability and trust, entitling them therein Barons, to serve and sitt as Barons in the next Parlament. By which meanes hee had so many Barons in his Parlament, as were able to weigh downe the Cleargy and their friends: The which Barons they say, were not afterwardes Lords, but onely Baronets, as sundry of them doe yet retayne the name. And by the like device her Maiestie may now likewise curbe and cut short those Irish and unruly Lords, that hinder all good proceedings.

Eudox.   It seemes no lesse than for reforming of all those inconvenient statutes that you noted in the beginning, and redressing of all those evill customes; and lastly, for settling of sound religion amongst them, me thinkes you shall not neede any more to over-goe those particulars againe, which you mentioned, nor any other which might besides be remembred, but to leave all to the reformation of such a Parlament, in which, by the good care of the Lord Deputie and Councell they may all be amended. Therefore now you may come unto that generall reformation which you spake of, and bringing in of that establishment, by which you said all men should be contained in duty ever after, without the terror of warlike forces, or violent wresting of things by sharpe punishments.

Iren.   I will so at your pleasure, the which (me thinkes) can by no meanes be better plotted then by ensample of such other realmes as have beene annoyed with like evills, that Ireland now is, and useth still to bee. And first in this our realme of England, it is manifest by report of the Chronicles, and auncient writers, that it was greatly infested with robbers and out-lawes, which, lurking in woods and fast places, used often to breake foorth into the highwayes, and sometimes into small villages to rob and spoyle.[74] For redresse whereof it is written, that King Alured, or Aldred, did divide the realme into shires,* and the

---

*   De his qui plura scire avet, consulat D. Hen. Spelmanni eq. aur. Archeologum, in Borsholder & Hundred.

74   A commonly held belief, manifested at various points in *A View*, was that contemporary Ireland was like ancient England under the Saxons. The concomitant fear was

shires into hundreds, and the hundreds into lathes or wapentackes, and the wapentackes into tythings: So that tenne tythings make an hundred, and five made a lathe or wapentake, of which tenne, each one was bound for another, and the eldest or best of them, whom they called the Tythingman or Borsolder, that is, the eldest pledge became surety for all the rest. So that if any one of them did start into any undutiful action, the Borsolder was bound to bring him forth, when, joyning eft-soones with all his tything, would follow that loose person thorough all places, till they brought him in. And if all that tything fayled, then all that lathe was charged for that tything, and if that lathe fayled, then all that hundred was demaunded for them; and if the hundred, then the shire, who, joyning eft-soones together, would not rest till they had found out and delivered in that undutifull fellow, which was not amesnable to law. And herein it seemes, that that good Saxon King followed the Counsell of Iethro to Moyses, who advised him to divide the people into hundreds, and to set Captaines and wise men of trust over them, who should take the charge of them, and ease of that burthen. And so did Romulus (as you may read) divide the Romanes into tribes,* and the tribes into centuries or hundreths. By this ordinance, this King brought this realme of England, (which before was most troublesome,) unto that quiet state, that no one bad person could stirre but he was straight taken holde of by those of his owne tything, and their Borsholder, who being his neighbor or next kinsman were privie to all his wayes, and looked narrowly into his life. The which institution (if it were observed in Ireland) would worke that effect which it did in England, and keep all men within the compasse of dutie and obedience.

Eudox. This is contrary to that you said before; for as I remember, you said, that there was a great disproportion betweene England and Ireland, so as the lawes which were fitting for one, would not fit the

---

* Livie speaking of Romulus hath it thus, Populum in curias 30. divisit, &c. Eodem tempore & centuriæ tres equitum conscriptæ sunt. And so we have it in Sextus Aurel. Victor's booke, de viris illustribus urbis Romæ. Tres equitum centuriae instiutuit (saith he) Plebem in triginta curias distribuit.

---

that the process could be reversed because 'it is but even the other day, since *England* grew civill' (p. 70).

other. How comes it now then that you would transferre a principall
institution from England to Ireland?

Iren.   This law was not made by the Norman Conqueror, but by a
Saxon King, at what time England was very like to Ireland, as now it
stands: for it was (as I tolde you) annoyed greatly with robbers and
out-lawes, which troubled the whole state of the realme, every corner
having a Robin Hood in it, that kept the woods, that spoyled all pas-
sengers and inhabitants, as Ireland now hath; so as, me thinkes, this
ordinance would fit very well, and bring them all into awe.

Eudox.   Then when you have thus tythed the communalty, as you say,
and set Borsolders over them all, what would you doe when you came
to the gentlemen? would you holde the same course?

Iren.   Yea, marry, most especially; for this you must know, that all the
Irish almost boast themselves to be gentlemen, no lesse then the Welsh;
for if he can derive himselfe from the head of any sept, (as most of
them can, they are so expert by their Bardes), then hee holdeth himselfe
a gentleman, and thereupon scorneth to worke, or use any hard labour, which hee saith, is the life of a peasant or churle; but thenceforth becommeth either an horse-boy, or a stocah to some kerne,
inuring himselfe to his weapon, and to the gentlemanly trade of stealing, (as they count it.) So that if a gentleman, or any wealthy man
yeoman of them, have any children, the eldest of them perhaps shall
be kept in some order, but all the rest shall shift for themselves, and
fall to this occupation. And moreover it is a common use amongst
some of their gentlemens sonnes, that so soone as they are able to use
their weapons, they straight gather to themselves three or foure
straglers, or kearne, with whom wandring a while up and downe idely
the countrey, taking onely meate, hee at last falleth unto some bad
occasion that shall be offered, which being once made known, hee is
thenceforth counted a man of worth, in whome there is courage;
whereupon there draw to him many other like loose young men, which,
stirring him up with incouragement, provoke him shortly to flat
rebellion; and this happens not onely sometimes in the sonnes of
their gentle-men, but also of their noble-men, specially of them who
have base sonnes. For they are not onely not ashamed to acknowledge them, but also boaste of them, and use them to such secret
services, as they themselves will not be seene in, as to plague their
enemyes, to spoyle their neighbours, to oppresse and crush some of

their owne too stubburne free-holders, which are not tractable to their wills.

Eudox. Then it seemeth that this ordinance of tithing them by the pole, is not onely fit for the gentlemen, but also for the noble-men, whom I would have thought to be of so honourable a mind, as that they should not neede such a kinde of being bound to their allegiance, who should rather have held in and stayde all the other from undutifulnesse, then neede to bee forced thereunto themselves.

Iren. Yet so it is, Eudoxus; but because that noblemen cannot be tythed, there being not many tythings of them, and also because a Borsolder over them should be not onely a great indignitie, but also a danger to adde more power to them then they have, or to make one the commander of tenne, I holde it meeter that there were onely sureties taken of them, and one bound for another, whereby, if any shall swerve, his sureties shall for safeguard of their bonds either bring him in, or seeke to serve upon him; and besides this, I would wish them all to bee sworne to her Majestie, which they never yet were, but at the first creation; and that oath would sure contayne them greatly, or the breach of it bring them to shorther vengeance, for God useth to punish perjurie sharpely: So I reade, that there was a corporall oath taken in the raignes of Edward the Second,* and of Henry the Seventh,† (when the times were very broken) of all the lords and best gentle-men, of fealtie to the Kings, which now is no lesse needfull, because many of them are suspected to have taken an other oath privily to some bad purposes, and thereupon to have received the Sacrament, and beene sworne to a priest, which they thinke bindeth them more then their alleagiance to their Prince, or love of their countrey.

Eudox. This tything to the common-people, and taking sureties of lords and gentlemen, I like very well, but that it wilbe very troublesome; should it not be as well for to have them all booked, and the lords and gentle-men to take all the meaner sort upon themselves? for they are best able to bring them in, whensoever any of them sarteth out.

Iren. This indeed (Eudoxus) hath beene hitherto, and yet is a com-

---

* Richard the Second.

† The service was performed by Sir Richard Edgecombe, being appointed thereunto by a speciall commission from K. Henry, the Seventh. There is yet extant an exact diary of all his proceedings therein, from his first landing at Kinsale the 27th of June 1488, till his departure from Dublin the 30th of July next.

mon order amongst them, to have all the people booked by the lords
and gentlemen; but yet the worst order that ever was devised; for, by
this booking of men, all the inferiour sort are brought under the command of their lords, and forced to follow them into any action whatsoever. Now this you are to understand, that all the rebellions which
you see from time to time happen in Ireland, are not begun by the
common people, but by the lords and captaines of countries, upon
pride or wilfull obstinacy against the government, which whensoever
they will enter into, they drawe with them all their people and followers, which thinke themselves bound to goe with them, because they
have booked them and undertaken for them. And this is the reason
that in England you have such few bad occasions, by reason that the
noble men, however they should happen to be evill disposed, have no
commaund at all over the communalty, though dwelling under them,
because that every man standeth upon himselfe, and buildeth his for-
tunes upon his owne faith and firme assurance: The which this manner of tything the poles will worke also in Ireland. For by this the
people are broken into small parts like little streames, that they cannot easily come together into one head, which is the principall regard
that is to be had in Ireland, to keepe them from growing unto such a
head, and adhering unto great men.

Eudox. But yet I cannot see how this can bee well brought, without
doing great wrong unto the noble men there; for, at the first conquest of that realme, those great seigniories and lordships were given
them by the King, that they should bee the stronger against the Irish,
by the multitudes of followers and tennants under them: all which
hold their tenements of them by fealty, and such services, whereby
they are (by the first graunt of the King) made bounden unto them,
and tyed to rise out with them into all occasions of service. And this I
have often heard, that when the Lord Deputy hath raised any generall
hostings, the noble men have claimed the leading of them, by graunt
from the Kings of England, under the Greate Seal exhibited; so as the
Deputies could not refuse them to have the leading of them, or, if
they did, they would so worke, as none of their followers should rise
forth to the hostage.

Iren. You say very true; but will you see the fruite of those grants? I
have knowne when those lords have had the leading of their owne
followers under them to the generall hostings, that they have for the

same cut upon every plowland within their country 40. shil. or more, whereby some of them have gathered above seven or eight hundred pounds, and others much more into their purse, in lieu whereof they have gathered unto themselves a number of loose kearne out of all parts, which they have carried forth with them, to whom they never gave any penny of entertainment, allowed by the countrey or forced by them, but let them feede upon the countryes, and extort upon all men where they come; for that people will never aske better entertainement then to have a colour of service or imployment given them, by which they will pole and spoyle so outragiously, as the very enemy cannot doe much worse: and they also sometimes turne to the enemy.

Eudox. It seemes the first intent of those graunts was against the Irish, which now some of them use against the Queene her selfe: But now what remedy is there for this? or how can those graunts of the Kings be avoyded, without wronging of those lords, which had those lands and lordships given them?

Iren. Surely they may be well enough; for most of those lords, since their first graunts from the Kings by which those lands were given them, have sithence bestowed the most part of them amongst their kinsfolke, as every lord perhaps hath given in his time one or other of his principall castles to his younger sonne, and other to others, as largely and as amply as they were given to him, and others they have sold, and others they have bought, which were not in their first graunt, which now neverthelesse they bring within the compasse thereof, and take and exact upon them, as upon their first demeasnes all those kinde of services, yea and the very wild exactions, Coignie, Livery,* Sorehon, and such like, by which they pole and utterly undoe the poore tennants and free-houlders unto them, which either thorough ignorance know not their tenures, or through greatnes of their new lords dare not challenge them; yea, and some lords of countryes also, as great ones as themselves, are now by strong hand brought under them, and made their vassals. As for example Arundell of the Stronde in the County of Corke, who was aunciently a great lord, and was able

---

* What Coigny and Livery doe signifie, has been already expressed. Sorehon was a tax laide upon the free-holders, for certaine dayes in each quarter of a yeare, to finde victualls, and lodging, and to pay certaine stipends to the kerne, galloglasses, and horsemen.

to spend 3500. pounds by the yeare, as appeareth by good recordes, is now become the Lord Barries man, and doth to him all those services, which are due unto her Majesty. For reformation of all which, I wish that there were a commission graunted forth under the Great Seale, as I have seene one recorded in the old counsell booke of Mounster, that was sent forth, in the time of Sir William Drurie,[75] unto persons of speciall trust and judgement to inquire thoroughout all Ireland, beginning with one country first, and so resting a while till the same were settled, by the verdict of a sound and substantiall iury, how every man houldeth his land, of whom, and by what tenure, so that every one should be admitted to shew and exhibite what right he hath, and by what services hee houldeth his land, whether in cheife or in soccage, or by knights service, or how else soever. Thereupon would appeare, first how all those great English lords doe claime those great services, what seigniories they usurpe, what wardships they take from the Queene, what lands of hers they conceale: And then, how those Irish captaines of countryes have incroached upon the Queenes freeholders and tennants, how they have translated the tenures of them from English houlding unto Irish Tanistry, and defeated her Majesty of all her rights and dutyes, which are to acrew to her thereout, as wardships, liveries, marriages, fines of alienations, and many other commodities; which now are kept and concealed from her Majesty, to the value of 4000. pounds *per annum*, I dare undertake in all Ireland, by that which I know in one country.

Eudox.   This, Irenæus, would seeme a dangerous commission, and ready to stirre up all the Irish in rebellion, who knowing that they have nothing to shew for all those lands which they hould, but their swords, would rather drawe them then suffer the lands to bee thus drawne away from them.

Iren.   Neither should their lands be taken away from them, nor the utmost advantages inforced against them: But this by discretion of the commissioners should be made knowne unto them, that it is not her Majesties meaning to use any such extreamity, but onely to reduce things into order of English law, and make them hould their lands of her, and to restore to her her due services, which they detaine

75   Sir William Drury was President of Munster (1576–8) and Lord Justice of Ireland (1578–9).

out of those lands, which were aunciently held of her. And that they should not onely not be thrust out, but also have estates and grants of their lands new made to them from her Majesty, so as they should thence-forth hould them rightfully, which they now usurpe wrongfully; and yet withall I would wish, that in all those Irish countryes there were some land reserved to her Majesties free disposition for the better containing of the rest, and intermingling them with English inhabitants and customes, that knowledge might still be had of them, and of all their doings, so as no manner of practise or conspiracy should be had in hand amongst them, but notice should bee given thereof by one meanes or another, and their practises prevented.

Eudox.   Truely neither can the Irish, nor yet the English lords, thinke themselves wronged, nor hardly dealt withall herein, to have that which is indeede none of their owne at all, but her Majesties absolutely, given to them with such equall conditions, as that both they may be assured thereof, better then they are, and also her Majesty not defrauded of her right utterly; for it is a great grace in a prince, to take that with conditions, which is absolutely her owne. Thus shall the Irish be well satisfied, and as for the great men which had such graunts made to them at first by the Kings of England, it was in regard that they should keepe forth the Irish, and defend the Kings right, and his subjects: but now seeing that, in stead of defending them, they robbe and spoyle them, and, in stead of keeping out the Irish, they doe not onely make the Irish their tennants in those lands, and thrust out the English, but also some of themselves become meere Irish, with marrying with them, with fostering with them, and combyning with them against the Queene; what reason is there but that those graunts and priviledges should bee either revoked, or at least reduced to the first intention for which they were gruanted? for sure in mine opinion they are more sharpely to be chastised and reformed then the rude Irish, which, being very wilde at the first, are now become more civill; when as these, from civillity, are growne to be wilde and meere Irish.

Iren.   Indeede as you say, Eudoxus, these doe neede a sharper reformation then the Irish, for they are more stubborne, and disobedient to law and government, then the Irish be.

Eudox.   In truth, Irenæus, this is more then ever I heard, that any English there should bee worse then the Irish: Lord, how quickely doth that countrey alter mens natures! It is not for nothing (I perceive) which I have heard, that the Councell of England thinke it no good policie to have that realme reformed, or planted with English, least they should grow so undutifull as the Irish, and become much more dangerous: As appeareth by the ensamples of the Lacies in the time of Edward the Second, which you spake of, that shooke off their allegiance to their naturall Prince, and turned to Edward le Bruce, to make him King of Ireland.

Iren.　No times have beene without bad men: But as for that purpose of the Councell of England which you spake of, that they should keepe that realme from reformation, I thinke they are most lewdly abused; for their great carefulnesse, and earnest endeavours, doe witnesse the contrary. Neither is it the nature of the countrey to alter mens manners, but the bad mindes of the men, who having beene brought up at home under a straight rule of duty and obedience, being alwayes restrayned by sharpe penalties from lewde behaviour, so soone as they come thither, where they see lawes more slackely tended, and the hard restraint which they were used unto now slacked, they grow more loose and carelesse of their duty: and as it is the nature of all men to love liberty, so they become flat libertines, and fall to all licentiousnes, more boldly daring to disobey the law, thorough the presumption of favour and friendship, then any Irish dareth.

Eudox.　Then if that be so, (me thinkes) your late advisement was very evill, whereby you wished the Irish to be sowed and sprinckled with English, and in all the Irish countryes to have English planted amongst them, for to bring them to English fashions, since the English sooner drawe to the Irish then the Irish to the English: For as you said before, if they must runne with the streame, the greater number will carry away the lesse: Therefore (me thinkes) by this reason it should bee better to part the Irish and English, then to mingle them together.

Iren.　Not so, Eudoxus; for where there is no good stay of government, and strong ordinances to hould them, there indeede the fewer follow the more, but where there is due order of discipline and good rule, there the better shall goe foremost, and the worst shall follow. And therefore now, since Ireland is full of her owne nation, that ought not to be rooted out, and somewhat stored with English already, and more to be, I thinke it best by an union of manners, and conformity of mindes, to bring them to be one people, and to put away the dislikefull conceipt both of the one, and the other, which will be by no meanes better then by this intermingling of them: For neither all the Irish may dwell together, nor all the English, but by translating of them and scattering them amongst the English, not onely to bring them by dayly conversation unto better liking of each other, but also to make both of them lesse able to hurt. And therefore when I come to the tything of them, I will tithe them one with another, and for the most part will make an Irish man the tything-man, whereby he shall take the lesse exception to partiality, and yet be the more tyed thereby. But when I come to the Head Borough, which is the head of the lathe, him will I make an English man, or an Irish man of speciall assurance: As also when I come to appoint the Alderman, that is the head of the hundreth, him will I surely choose to be an English man of speciall regard, that may be a stay and pillar of all the borough under him.

Eudox.   What doe you meane by your hundred, and what by your borough? By that, that I have read in auncient records of England, an hundred did containe an hundreth villages, or as some say an hundred plough-lands, being the same which the Saxons called Cantred;* the which cantred, as I finde it recorded corded in the blacke booke of [the Exchequer of] Ireland, did contain xxx. Villatas terræ, which some call, quarters of land, and every Villata can maintaine 400 cowes in pasture, and the 400. cowes to be divided into 4. heards, so as none of them shall come neere other: every Villata containing 18. plowlands, as is there set downe: And by that which I have read of a borough it signifieth a free towne, which had a principall officer, called

---

* Cantred is a British word, answering to the Saxon Hunðreð. How much land a cantred containeth, is variously delivered. Some hould that it containes 100 townes. So Gir. Barry or Cambrensis, in his Itinerary of Wales, (lib. 2. cap. 7.) "Dicitur autem cantredus, (saith he) composito vocabulo tam Britannica quam Hibernica lingua, tanta terra portio, quanta 100. villas continere solet." The author here cites a record which makes it containe but 30. towne-lands: and Iohn Clynn, (if my copy therein be not mistaken) hath but 20. But another more auncient MS. sometime belonging to the Friars Minors of Multifernan, hath 30. "Quælibet cantreda (saith Clinne) continet xx. (al. xxx.) villatas terræ, quælibet villata potest sustinere 300 vaccas in pascuis, ita quod vaccæ in X. (al. IIII.) partes divisa, nulla alteri appropinquabit, quælibet villata continet viii, carucatas." We finde also there the provinces of Ireland thus divided into cantreds. Ultonia continet 35. cantredas, Conacia 30. Lagenia 31. Midia 18. & Momonia 70. See more concerning cantreds in Sir Hen. Spelmann's excellent Glossary. As cantreds are diversly estimated, so are also carues or plowlands.

a head-borough, to become ruler, and undertake for all the dwellers under him, having, for the same, franchises and priviledges graunted them by the King, whereof it was called a free borough, and of the lawyers *franci-plegium.*[76]

Iren.   Both that which you said, Eudoxus, is true, and yet that which I say not untrue; for that which you spake of deviding the countrey into hundreds, was a devision of the lands of the realme, but this which I tell, was of the people, which were thus devided by the pole: so that hundreth in this sense signifieth a 100. pledges, which were under the command and assurance of their alderman, the which (as I suppose) was also called a wapentake, so named of touching the weapon or speare of their alderman, and swearing to follow him faithfully, and serve their Prince truly. But others thinke that a wapentake was 10. hundreds or boroughs: Likewise a borough, as I here use it, and as the old lawes still use, is not a borough towne, as they now call it, that is a franchised towne, but a maine pledge of 100. free persons, therefore called a free borough or (as you say) *franciplegium:* For Borh in old Saxon signifieth a pledge or surety, and yet it is so used with us in some speeches, as Chaucer saith; St. John to *borrow*, that is for assurance and warranty.[77]

Eudox.   I conceive the difference: But now that you have thus devided the people into these tythings and hundreths, how will you have them so preserved and continued? for people doe often change their dwelling places, and some must die, whilst other some doe growe up into strength of yeares, and become men.

Iren.   These hundreds I would wish to assemble themselves once every yeare with their pledges, and to present themselves before the iustices of the peace, which shall bee thereunto appointed, to bee surveyed and numbered, to see what change hath happened since the yeare before; and, the defects to supplie, of young plants late growne up, the which are diligently to bee overlooked and viewed of what condition and demeanour they be, so as pledges may bee taken for them, and they put into order of some tything; of all which alterations note is to be taken, and bookes made thereof accordingly.

---

76   Franciplegium. '*frankpledge*, having pledge or surety for the good behaviour of free-man' (Variorum).

77   The source is *The Squire's Tale*, a major source for *The Faerie Queene*, Book IV.

Eudox. Now (mee thinkes) Irenæus, your are to be warned to take heede lest unawares you fall into that inconvenience which you formerly found fault with in others: namely, that by this booking of them, you doe not gather them into a new head, and, having broken their former strength, doe not unite them more strongly againe: For every alderman, his having all these free pledges of his hundred under his command, may (me thinkes) if hee be evill disposed drawne all his companie into an evill action. And likewise, by this assembling of them once a yeare unto their alderman by their weapentakes, take heede lest you also give them occasion and meanes to practise together in any conspiracyes.

Iren. Neither of both is to be doubted; for their aldermen and headboroughs, will not be such men of power and countenance of themselves, being to be chosen thereunto, as neede to be feared: Neither if hee were, is his hundred at his commaund, further then his Princes service; and also every tything man may controll him in such a case. And as for the assembling of the hundred, much lesse is any danger thereof to be doubted, seeing it is before some iustice of the peace, or some high constable to bee thereunto appointed: So as of these tythings there can no perill ensue, but a certaine assurance of peace and great good; for they are thereby withdrawne from their lords, and subjected to the Prince: Moreover for the better breaking of these heads and septs, which (I told you) was one of the greatest strengthes of the Irish, me thinkes it should bee very well to renewe that ould statute, which was made in the raigne of Edward the Fourth* in Ireland, by which it was commaunded, that whereas all men† then used to be called by the name of their septs, according to the severall nations, and had no surnames at all, that from henceforth each one should take upon himselfe a severall surname, either of his trade and facultie, or of some quality of his body or minde, or of the place where he dwelt, so as every one should be distinguished from the other, or from the most part, wherby they shall not onely not depend

---

* An. 5. Edw. 4.
† The statute referres onely to the Irish, dwelling among the English in the counties of Dublin, Moth, Uriel, and Kildare. Uriel, called also Ergallia, did anciently comprehend all that countrey which is now divided into the counties of Louth and Monoghan, although it may be conceived, that Louth was onely intended by the statute, because Monoghan was then (in a manner) wholly possessed by the Irish.

upon the head of their sept, as now they do, but also in time learne quite to forget his Irish nation. And herewithall would I also wish all the O's and the Mac's, which the heads of septs have taken to their names, to bee utterly forbidden and extinguished. For that the same being an ordinance (as some say) first made by O Brien* for the strengthning of the Irish, the abrogating thereof will asmuch infeeble them.[78]

Eudox.   I like this ordinance very well; but now that you have thus divided and distinguished them, what other order will you take for their manner of life?

Iren.   The next thing that I will doe, shalbe to appoint to every one that is not able to live of his free-holde, a certaine trade of life, to which he shall finde himselfe fittest, and shall be thought ablest, the which trade hee shalbe bound to follow, and live onely thereupon. All trades therefore are to be understood to be of three kindes, manuall, intellectuall, and mixed. The first containeth all such as needeth exercise of bodily labour, to the performance of their profession. The second consisting only of the exercise of wit and reason. The third sort, part of bodily labor, and part of the wit, but depending most of industrie and carefulnes. Of the first sort be all handycrafts and husbandry labour. Of the second be all sciences, and those which be called liberall arts. Of the third is merchandize and chafferie, that is, buying and selling; and without all these three, there is no commonwealth can almost consit, or at the least be perfect. But the realme of Ireland wanteth the most principall of them, that is, the intellectuall; therfore in seeking to reforme her state, it is specially to be looked unto. But because by husbandry, which supplyeth unto us all things necessary for food, wherby we chiefly live; therefore it is first to be provided for. The first thing therefore that wee are to draw these new

---

*   The custome of prefixing the vowell O to many of the chiefe Irish surnames, began soon after the yeere M. in the raigne of Brien Bororha (the son of Kennethy) king of Ireland. As for Mac in surnames, it beareth no other signification, then Fitz doth among the French, and (from them) the English; and Ap with the Welsh. And although it were more anciently used then the other, yet it varied according to the fathers name, and became not so soone fully settled in families.

78   It was a common complaint among English writers that the use of the prefixes 'O' and 'Mac' by Irish chiefs helped to subvert English authority by establishing an alternative Irish hierarchy. Attempts were made to integrate the Irish into English hierarchies and so break up the Irish clans.

tythed men into, ought to be husbandry. First, because it is the most easie to be learned, needing onely the labour of the body. Next, because it is most generall and most needful; then because it is most naturall; and lastly, because it is most enemy to warre, and most hateth unquietnes: As the Poet saith,

—— "bella execrata colonis:"[79]

for husbandry being the nurse of thrift, and the daughter of industrie and labour, detesteth all that may worke her scathe, and destroy the travaile of her hands, whose hope is all her lives comfort unto the plough: therefore are those Kearne, Stocaghes, and Horse-boyes, to bee driven and made to imploy that ablenesse of bodie, which they were wont to use to theft and villainy, hencefoorth to labour and industry. In the which, by that time they have spent but a little paine, they will finde such sweetenesse and happy contentment, that they will afterwardes hardly bee haled away from it, or drawne to their wonted lewde life in theeverie and roguerie. And being once thus inured thereunto, they are not onely to bee countenanced and encouraged by all good meanes, but also provided that their children after them may be brought up likewise in the same, and succeede in the roomes of their fathers. To which end there is a Statute in Ireland already well provided,* which commaundeth that all the sonnes of husbandmen shall be trained up in their fathers trades, but it is (God wot) very slenderly executed.

Eudox.   But doe you not count, in this trade of husbandry, pasturing of cattle, and keeping of their cowes? for that is reckoned as a part of husbandrie.

Iren.   I know it is, and needefully to bee used, but I doe not meane to allow any of those able bodies, which are able to use bodily labour, to follow a few cowes grazing. But such impotent persons, as being unable for strong travaile, are yet able to drive cattle to and fro to their pasture; for this keeping of cowes is of it selfe a very idle life, and a fit nurserie for a thiefe. For which cause (you remember) I disliked the Irish manner of keeping Boolies in Summer upon the mountaines, and living after that savage sort. But if they will algates feede many

---

*   Anno 25° Hen. 6.
79   'Wars are cursed by husbandmen'.

cattle, or keepe them on the mountaines, let them make some townes neare to the mountaines side, where they may dwell together with neighbours, and be conversant in the view of the world. And to say truth, though Ireland bee by nature counted a great soyle of pasture, yet had I rather have fewer cowes kept, and men better mannered, then to have such huge increase of cattle, and no increase of good conditions. I would therefore wish that there were some ordinances made amongst them, that whosoever keepeth twentie kine, should keep a plough going; for otherwise all men would fall to pasturage, and none to husbandry, which is a great cause of this dearth now in England, and a cause of the usuall stealthes in Ireland: For looke into all countreyes that live in such sort by keeping of cattle, and you shall finde that they are both very barbarous and uncivill, and also greatly given to warre. The Tartarians, the Muscovites, the Norwegians, the Gothes, the Armenians, and many other doe witnesse the same. And therefore since now wee purpose to draw the Irish, from desire of warre and tumults, to the love of peace and civility, it is expedient to abridge their great custome of hardening, and augment their trade of tillage and husbandrie. As for other occupations and trades, they need not bee inforced to, but every man to be bound onely to follow one that hee thinkes himselfe aptest for. For other trades of artificers will be occupied for very necessitie, and constrayned use of them; and so likewise will merchandize for the gaine thereof; but learning, and bringing up in liberall sciences, will not come of it selfe, but must bee drawne on with streight lawes and ordinances: And therefore it were meete that such an act were ordained, that all the sonnes of lords, gentlemen, and such others as are able to bring them up in learning, should be trayned up therein from their child-hoods. And for that end every parish should be forced to keepe a pettie schoole-master, adjoyning unto the parish church, to bee the more in view, which should bring up their children in the first elements of letters: and that, in every countrey or baronie, they should keepe an other able schoole-master, which should instruct them in grammar, and in the principles of sciences,* to whom they should be compelled to send their youth

---

* How requisite also an universitie is for the further growth in learning, the judicious well know. This happinesse we now enjoy, to the great benefit of this land. And although former attempts have beene made for erecting and establishing universities in Ireland, yet through want of meanes, which should have beene allotted for their

to bee disciplined, whereby they will in short space grow up to that civill conversation, that both the children will loath their former rudenesse in which they were bred, and also their parents will even by the ensample of their young children perceive the foulenesse of their own behaviour, compared to theirs: For learning hath that wonderfull power in it selfe, that it can soften and temper the most sterne and savage nature.

Eudox. Surely I am of your minde, that nothing will bring them from their uncivill life sooner then learning and discipline, next after the knowledge and feare of God. And therefore I doe still expect, that you should come thereunto, and set some order for reformation of religion, which is first to bee respected; according to the saying of CHRIST, "Seeke first the kingdome of heaven, and the righteousnesse thereof."

Iren. I have in minde so to doe; but let me (I pray you) first finish that which I had in hand, whereby all the ordinances which shall afterwardes bee set for religion, may abide the more firmely, and bee observed more diligently. Now that this people is thus tythed and ordered, and every one bound unto some honest trade of life, which shall bee particularly entered and set downe in the tything booke, yet perhappes there will bee some stragglers and runnagates, which will not of themselves come in and yeeld themselves to this order, and yet after the well finishing of the present warre, and establishing of the garrisons in all strong places of the countrey, where there wonted refuge was most, I suppose there will few stand out, or if they doe, they will shortly bee brought in by the eares: But yet afterwardes, lest any one of them should swerve, or any that is tyed to a trade, should afterwardes not

---

maintenance, they have soone faded. So hapned it with that academy which Alexander de Bignor, Archbishop of Dublin, erected (in S. Patricks Church) in Dublin, and procured to be confirmed by Pope Iohn the 12th. And no better succeeded that which was afterwards erected at Tredagh by act of parliament Anno 5. Edw. 4. (as appeares in the roll of that yeare in the Chauncery) whereby all the like priviledges, as the University of Oxford (in England) enjoyed, were conferred upon it. Besides these wee finde mention of others, farre more ancient, as at Armagh, and Ross. Carbry, or Ross. Ailithry, as it is called in the life of S. Faghnan the founder, who lived in the yeare 590. "Ipse Sanctus (saith the author) in australi Hiberniæ plagâ iuxta mare, in suo monasterio quod ipse fundavit, ibi crevit civitas, in quâ semper manens magnum studium scholarium, quod dicitur Rossailithry, habitabat." But a further search were fit to bee made touching those of the elder times.

follow the same, according to this institution, but should straggle up and downe the countrey, or mich in corners amongst their friends idely, as Carrowes, Bardes, Iesters, and such like, I would wishe that a Provost Marshall should bee appointed in every shire, which should continually walke about the countrey, with halfe a dozen, or halfe a score horsemen, to take up such loose persons as they should finde thus wandering, whome hee should punish by his owne authority, with such paines as the person shall seeme to deserve; for if hee be but once so taken idely roguing, hee may punish him more lightly, as with stockes, or such like; but if hee bee found againe so loytering, hee may scourge him with whippes, or rodds, after which if hee bee againe taken, let him have the bitternesse of marshall lawe. Likewise if any reliques of the olde rebellion bee found by any, that either have not come in and submitted themselves to the law, or that having once come in, doe breake forth againe, and walke disorderly, let them taste of the same cuppe in Gods name; for it was due to them for their first guilt, and now being revived by their later loosenesse, let them have their first desert, as now being found unfit to live in the common-wealth.

Eudox. This were a good ordinance: but mee thinkes it is an unnecessary charge, and also unfit to continue the name or forme of any marshall law, when as there is a proper officer already appointed for these turnes, to wit the sheriffe of the shire, whose peculiar office it is to walke up and downe his bayliwicke, as you would have a marshall to snatch up all those runnagates and unprofitable members, and to bring them to his gaole to bee punished for the same. Therefore this may well be spared.

Iren. Not so, me thinkes; for though the sheriffe have this authority of himselfe to take up all such stragglers, and imprison them, yet shall hee not doe so much good, nor worke that terrour in the hearts of them, that a marshall will, whom they shall know to have power of life and death in such cases, and especially to bee appointed for them: Neither doth it hinder that, but that though it pertaine to the sheriffe, the sheriffe may doe therein what hee can, and yet the marshall may walke his course besides; for both of them may doe the more good, and more terrifie the idle rogue, knowing that though he have a watch upon the one, yet hee may light upon the other: But this proviso is needefull to bee had in this case, that the sheriffe may not have the like power of life, as the marshall hath, and as heretofore they have beene accustomed; for it is dangerous to give power of life into the hands of him which may have benefit by the parties death, as, if the said loose liver have any goods of his owne, the Sheriffe is to seize thereupon, whereby it hath come to passe, that some who have not deserved judgement of death, though otherwise perhaps offending, have beene for their goods sake caught up, and carryed straight to the bough; a thing indeed very pittifull and horrible. Therefore by no meanes I would have the Sheriffe have such authority, nor yet to imprison that lozell till the sessions, for so all gaoles might soon be filled; but to send him to the Marshall, who, eftsoones finding him faultie, shall give him meete correction, and ridd him away forthwith.

Eudox. I doe now perceive your reason well: But come wee now to that whereof wee earst spake, I meane, to religion and religious men; what order will you set amongst them?

Iren. For religion little have I to say, my selfe being (as I said) not professed therein, and it selfe being but one, so as there is but one way therein; for that which is true onely is, and the rest is not at all; yet, in planting of religion, thus much is needefull to be observed, that it bee not sought forcibly to bee impressed into them with terrour and sharpe penalties, as now is the manner, but rather delivered and intimated with mildnesse and gentlenesse, so as it may not be hated before it be understood, and their Professors despised and rejected. And therefore it is expedient that some discreete Ministers of their owne countrey-men, bee first sent over amongst them, which by their meeke perswasions and instructions, as also by their sober lives and conversations, may draw them first to understand, and afterwards to imbrace, the doctrine of their salvation; for if that the auncient godly fathers, which first converted them, when they were infidells, to the faith, were able to pull them from idolatry and paganisme to the true beliefe in CHRIST, as S. Patricke, and S. Columb, how much more easily shall godly teachers bring them to the true understanding of that which they already professed? wherein it is great wonder to see the oddes which is betweene the zeale of Popish Priests, and the Ministers of the Gospell; for they spare not to come out of Spaine, from Rome, and from Remes, by long toyle and daungerous travayling hither, where they know perill of death awayteth them, and no reward or richesse is to be found, onely to draw the people unto the

Church of Rome; whereas some of our idle Ministers, having a way for credite and estimation thereby opened unto them, and having the livings of the countrey offered unto them, without paines, and without perill, will neither for the same, nor any love of God, nor zeale of religion, nor for all the good they may doe, by winning soules to God, bee drawne foorth from their warme neastes, to looke out into Gods harvest, which is even ready for the sickle, and all the fields yellow long agoe; doubtlesse those good olde godly Fathers, will (I feare mee) rise up in the day of judgement to condemne them.

Eudox.   Surely, it is great pitty, Iren. that there are none chosen out of the Ministers of England, good, sober, and discreet men, which might be sent over thither to teach and instruct them, and that there is not as much care had of their soules, as of their bodies; for the care of both lyeth upon the Prince.

Iren.   Were there never so many sent over, they should doe smal good till one enormity be taken from them, that is, that both they bee restrayned from sending their youg men abroad to other Universities beyond the sea, as Remes, Doway, Lovaine,[80] and the like, and others from abroad bee restrayned for comming into them; for their lurking secretly in their houses, and in corners of the countrey, doe more hurt and hinderance to religion with their private perswasions then all the others can doe good with their publique instructions; and though for these latter there be a good statute there ordained, yet the same is not executed; and as for the former there is no law nor order for their restraint at all.

Eudox.   I marvaile it is no better looked unto, and not only this, but that also which I remember you mentioned in your abuses concerning the profits and revenewes of the lands of fugitives in Ireland, which by pretence of certaine colourable conveyances are sent continually over unto them, to the comforting of them and others against her Majestie, for which here in England there is good order taken; and why not then aswell in Ireland? For though there be no statute there yet enacted therefore, yet might her Majestie, by her only preroga-

---

80   The main seminaries which trained Jesuit priests who came to Britain and Ireland in order to convert the Protestant population and bolster the underground efforts of Catholics.

tive, seize the fruites and profites of those fugitive lands into her handes, till they come over to testifie their true allegiance.

Iren. Indeede shee might so doe; but the comberous times doe perhappes hinder the regard thereof, and of many other good intentions.

Eudox. But why then did they not mend it in peaceable times?

Iren. Leave we that to their grave considerations; but proceed we forward. Next care in religion is to build up and repayre all the ruined churches, whereof the most part lye even with the ground, and some that have bin lately repayred are so unhandsomely patched, and thatched, that men doe even shunne the places for the uncomelinesse thereof; therefore I would wishe that there were order taken to have them built in some better forme, according to the churches of England; for the outward shew (assure your selfe) doth greatly drawe the rude people to the reverencing and frequenting thereof. What ever some of our late too nice fooles say, there is nothing in the seemely forme, and comely order of the Church.[81] And for the keeping and continuing them, there should likewise Church-wardens of the gravest men in the parish be appointed, as they bee here in England, which should take the yearely charge both hereof, and also of the schoole-houses which I wish to be built neere the said churches; for maintenance of both which, it were meete that some small portion of lands were allotted, sith no more mortmaines are to be looked for.

Eudox. Indeede (me thinkes) it would be so convenient; but when all is done, how will you have your churches served, and your Ministers maintained? since the livings (as you say) are not sufficient scarce to make them gownes, much lesse to yeelde meete maintenance according to the dignity of their degree.

Iren. There is no way to helpe that, but to lay 2. or 3. of them together, untill such time as the countrey grow more rich and better inhabited, at which time the tythes, and other obventions, will also be more augmented and better valued: But now that we have thus gone

---

81 Irenius' stress on the necessity of the 'outward shewe' of religion would appear to sit awkwardly with the assumption of most critics that Spenser occupied a more puritan position in terms of contemporary religious affiliations than this would suggest. Perhaps the point is that such practices were necessary in Ireland and are to be regarded in the same way as the regrettable necessity of using Irish ministers to persuade their fellow countrymen (presumably in Irish, but Irenius does not state this).

through all the 3. sorts of trades, and set a course for their good establishment; let us (if it please you) goe next to some other needefull points of other publicke matters no lesse concerning the good of the commonwealth, though but accidentally depending on the former. And first I wish, that order were taken for the cutting and opening of all places through woods, so that a wide way of the space of 100. yards might be layde open in every of them for the safety of travellers, which use often in such perillous places to be robbed, and sometimes murdered. Next, that bridges were built upon the rivers, and all the fordes marred and spilt, so as none might passe any other way but by those bridges, and every bridge to have a gate and a gate house set thereon, whereof this good will come that no night stealths which are commonly driven in by-wayes, and by blinde fordes unused of any but such like, shall not be conveyed out of one country into another, as they use, but they must passe by those bridges, where they may either be haply encountered, or easily tracked, or not suffered to passe at all, by meanes of those gate-houses thereon: Also that in all straights and narrow passages, as between 2 boggs, or through any deepe foord, or under any mountaine side, there should be some little fortilage, or wooden castle set, which should keepe and command that straight, whereby any rebells that should come into the country might be stopped that way, or passe with great perill. Moreover, that all high wayes should be fenced and shut up on both sides, leaving onely 40. foote bredth for passage, so as none shall be able to passe but through the high wayes, whereby theeves and night robbers might be the more easily pursued and encountred, when there shall be no other way to drive their stolne cattle, but therein, as I formerly declared. Further, that there should bee in sundry convenient places, by the high wayes, townes appointed to bee built, the which should be free Burgesses, and incorporate under Bayliffes, to be by their inhabitants well and strongly intrenched, or otherwise fenced with gates on each side thereof, to be shut nightly, like as there is in many places in the English Pale, and all the wayes about it to be strongly shut up, so as none should passe but through those townes: To some of which it were good that the priviledge of a market were given, the rather to strengthen and inable them to their defence, for there is nothing doth sooner cause civility in any countrie then many market townes, by reason that people repairing often thither for their needes, will dayly see and learne civil manners of the better sort: Besides, there is nothing doth more stay and strengthen the country then such corporate townes, as by proofe in many rebellions hath appeared, in which when all the countryes have swerved, the townes have stood fast, and yeelded good releife to the souldiours in all occasions of services. And lastly there is nothing doth more enrich any country or realme then many townes; for to them will all the people drawe and bring the fruites of their trades, aswell to make money of them, as to supply their needefull uses; and the countrymen will also be more industrious in tillage, and rearing of all husbandry commodities, knowing that they shall have ready sale for them at those townes; and in all those townes should there be convenient innes, erected for the lodging and harbouring of travellers, which are now oftentimes spoyled by lodging abroad in weake thatched houses, for want of such safe places to shroude them in.

Eudox.   But what profit shall your market townes reape of their market? when as each one may sell their corne and cattle abroad in the country, and make their secret bargaines amongst themselves as now I understand they use.

Iren.   Indeede, Eudoxus, they do so, and thereby no small inconvenience doth rise to the commonwealth; for now when any one hath stolne a cowe or a garron, he may secretly sell it in the country without privity of any, whereas if he brought it to a market towne it would perhaps be knowne, and the theife discovered. Therefore it were good that a straight ordinance were made, that none should buy or sell any cattle, but in some open market, (there being now market townes every where at hand,) upon a great penalty, neither should they likewise buy any corne to sell the same againe, unlesse it were to make malt thereof; for by such ingrosing and regrating wee see the dearth, that now commonly raigneth here in England, to have beene caused. Hereunto also is to bee added that good ordinance, which I remember was once, proclaimed throughout all Ireland: That all men should marke their cattle with an open severall marke upon their flanckes or buttockes, so as if they happened to be stolne, they might appeare whose they were, and they, which should buy them, might thereby suspect the owner, and be warned to abstaine from buying them of a suspected person, with such an unknowne marke.

Eudox.   Surely these ordinances seeme very expedient, but specially that of free townes, of which I wonder there is so small store in Ireland, and that, in the first peopling and planting thereof, they were neglected and omitted.

Iren. They were not omitted; for there were, through all places of the country convenient, many good townes seated, which thorough that inundation of the Irish, which I first told you of, were utterly wasted and defaced, of which the ruines are yet in many places to be seene, and of some no signe at all remaining, save only their bare names; but their seats are not to be found.

Eudox. But how then commeth it to passe, that they have never since been recovered, nor their habitations reedified, as of the rest, which have beene no lesse spoyled and wasted?

Iren. The cause thereof was, for that, after their desolation, they were begged by gentlemen of the Kings, under colour to repaire them, and gather the poore reliques of the people againe together, of whom having obtained them, they were so farre from reedifying of them, as that by all meanes they have endeavoured to keepe them waste, least that, being repaired, their charters might be renewed, and their Burgesses restored to their lands, which they had now in their possession; much like as in those old monuments of abbeyes, and religious houses, we see them likewise use to doe: For which cause it is judged that King Henry the Eight bestowed them upon them, conceiving that thereby they should never bee able to rise againe. And even so doe these Lords, in these poore old corporate townes, of which I could name divers, but for kindling of displeasure. Therefore as I wished many corporate townes to be erected, so would I againe wish them to be free, not depending upon the service, nor under the commaund of any but the Governour. And being so, they will both strengthen all the country round about them, which by their meanes will be the better replenished and enriched, and also be as continuall houldes for her Majesty, if the people should revolt or breake out againe; for without such it is easie to forrage and over-run the whole land. Let be for ensample all those free-boroughes, in the low-countreyes, which are now all the strength thereof. These and other liks ordinances might be delivered for the good establishment of the realme, after it is once subdued and reformed, in which it might afterwards be very easily kept and maintained, with small care of the Governours and Councell there appointed, so as it should in short space yeeld a plentifull revenue to the crowne of England; which now doth but sucke and consume the treasure thereof, through those unsound plots and changefull orders, which are dayly devised for her good, yet never effectually prosecuted or performed.

Eudox. But in all this your discourse I have not marked any thing by you spoken touching the appointment of the principall Officer, to whom you wish the charge of the performance of all this to be committed: Onely I observed some fowle abuses by you noted in some of the late Governours, the reformation whereof you left of for this present place.

Iren. I delight not to lay open the blames of great Magistrates to the rebuke of the world, and therefore their reformation I will not meddle with, but leave unto the wisedome of greater heads to be considered; only thus much I will speake generally thereof, to satisfie your desire, that the Government and cheife Magistracy, I wish to continue as it doth, to wit, that it be ruled by a Lord Deputy or Iustice, for that it is a very safe kinde of rule; but there-withall I wish that over him there were placed also a Lord Lieutenant,[82] of some of the greatest personages in England, such a one I could name, upon whom the eye of all England is fixed, and our last hopes now rest; who being intituled with that dignity, and being here alwayes resident, may backe and defend the good course of that government against all maligners, which else will, through their cunning working under hand, deprave and pull back what ever thing shall be begun or intended there, as we commonly see by experience at this day, to the utter ruine and desolation of that poore realme; and this Lieutenancy should be no discountenancing of the Lord Deputy, but rather a strengthening of all his doings; for now the chiefe evill in that government is, that no Governour is suffered to goe on with any one course, but upon the least information here, of this or that, hee is either stopped and crossed, or other courses appointed him from hence which he shall run, which how inconvenient it is, is at this houre too well felt: And therefore this should be one principall in the appointing of the Lord Deputies authority, that it should bee more ample and absolute then it is, and that

---

82 Irenius probably means Essex, who was appointed Lord Lieutenant on 12 March 1599, having been suggested by many as a suitable candidate for the post earlier. Essex was the first Lord Lieutenant, as opposed to Lord Deputy, appointed since 1562.

he should have uncontrouled power to doe any thing, that he with the advisement of the Councell should thinke meete to be done: For it is not possible for the Councell here, to direct a Governour there, who shall be forced oftentimes to follow the necessitie of present actions, and to take the suddaine advantage of time, which being once lost will not bee recovered; whilst, through expecting direction from hence, the delayes whereof are oftentimes through other greater affaires most irkesome, the oportunityes there in the meane time passe away, and great danger often groweth, which by such timely prevention might easily be stopped: And this (I remember) is worthily observed by Machiavel in his discourses upon Livie, where he commendeth the manner of the Romans government, in giving absolute power to all their Councellors and Governours, which if they abused, they should afterwards dearely answere.[83] And the contrary thereof he reprehendeth in the States of Venice, of Florince, and many other principalityes of Italy; who use to limit their chiefe officers so strictly, as that thereby they have oftentimes lost such happy occasions, as they could never come unto againe: The like whereof, who so hath beene conversant in that government of Ireland, hath too often seene to their great hinderance and hurt. Therefore this I could wish to be redressed, and yet not so but that in particular things he should be restrained, though not in the generall government; as namely in this, that no offices should bee should by the Lord Deputy for money, nor no pardons, nor no protections bought for reward, nor no beoves taken for Captainries of countryes, nor no shares of Bishopricks for nominating Bishops, nor no forfeytures, nor dispensations with pœnall Statutes given to their servants or friends, nor no selling of licences for transportation of prohibited wares, and specially of corne and flesh; with many the like; which neede some manner of restrainte, or else very great trust in the honorable disposition of the Lord Deputy.

Thus I have, Eudoxus, as briefly as I could, and as my memorie would serve me, run through the state of that whole country, both to let you see what it now is, and also what it may bee by good care and amendment: Not that I take upon me to change the policy of so great a kingdome, or prescribe rules to such wise men as have the handling

---

83   Ironically, this could be said to have been the fate of Wentworth, to whom Ware's edition was dedicated.

thereof, but onely to shew you the evills, which in my small experience I have observed, to be the chiefe hinderance of the reformation; and by way of conference to declare my simple opinion for the redresse thereof and establishing a good course for government; which I doe not deliver as a perfect plot of mine owne invention to be onely followed, but as I have learned and understood the same by the consultations and actions of very wise Governours and Councellours, whom I have (sometimes) heard treate hereof: So have I thought good to set downe a remembrance of them for my owne good, any your satisfaction, that who so list to overlooke them, although perhaps much wiser then they which have thus advised of that state, yet at least by comparison hereof may perhaps better his owne judgement, and by the light of others fore-going him, may follow after with more ease, and haply finde a fairer way thereunto, then they which have gone before.

Eudox. I thanke you, Irenæus, for this your gentle paines; withall not forgetting, now in the shutting up, to put you in minde of that which you have formerly halfe promised, that hereafter when wee shall meete againe, upon the like good occasion, you will declare unto us those your observations, which you have gathered of the antiquities of Ireland.

Appendix I:
Ware's Annotations

VPon review of that part which was printed, before I began to inferte any notes, thefe few animadverfions are added.

[Page 16]

—*the firft originall of this word Tanift and Taniftry came*. See whether it may not be more fitly derived from *Thane*, which word commonly ufed among the *Danes*, and alfo among the *Saxons* in *England*, for a noble man, and a principall officer.

[Page 24]

—*duke of Clarence, who having married the heire of the Earle of Vlfter, &c*. It was not *George* Duke of *Clarence* here fpoken of by the author, but *Lionell Duke of *Clarence*, third fonne of King, *Edw*. the 3. who married the Earle of *Vlfters* daughter, and by her had the Earledome of *Vlfter*. and although *Edw*. the 4. made his brother the Duke of *Clarence*, Lo. Lieutenant of *Ireland*, yet the place was ftill executed by his Deputyes (which were at feverall times) *Thomas* Earle of *Defmond*, *John* Earle of *Worcefter*, *Tho* Earle of *Kildare*, and *William Shirwood* Bifhop of *Meth*, the Duke himfelf never coming into *Ireland* to governe there in perfon.

[Page 42]

—*Kin is Englifh, and Congifh affinity in Irifh*. I conceive the word to be rather altogether *Irifh*. *Kin* fignifying in *Irifh*, the heads or chiefe of any fepts.

---

*   *De haere vide Camd. Britan, page*. 336 *& annal. Hib. ab re edw. ad an* 1365.

[Page 44]

The difcourfe from the word *Scythians* in the 11.line, unto the end of the parenthefis in the 30.line, is wholly to be croffed out, as being then agreeable to the beft MS.Copie, onely after *Scythians*, add, which.

Touching the *Scythians*† or *Scotts* arrivall in *Ireland,* fee *Nennius* an ancient *Brittifh* author (who lived in the yeare of *Chrift* 858.) where among other things we have the time of their arrivall. *Brittones* (faith he) *venerunt in 3.atate mundi in Britanniam, Scythe antem in 4.obtinuerunt Hiberniam.*

[Page 46]

—*remembrances of Bards.* Of the ancient Bards or Poets, *Lucan* makes this mention in the firft booke of his *Pharfalia.*

> *Vos quoque qui fortes animas, belloque peremptas,*
> *Laudibus in longum vates dimittius avum,*
> *Plurima fecuri fudiftis carmina Bardi.*

Concerning the *Irifh* Bardes fee pag.51. The word fignified among the *Gaules* a finger, as it is noted by Mr *Camden,* and Mr *Selden,* out of *Feftus Pompeius,* and it had the fame fignification among the *Brittifh.* St *John Price* in the defcription of *Wales,* expounds it to bee one that had *knowledge of things to come, and fo* (faith he) *it fignifieth at this day.* taking his ground (amiffe) out of *Lucan's* verfes. Doctor *Powell* in his notes upon *Caradoc* of *Lhancarvan* faith, that in *Wales* they preferved Gentlemens armes and pedegrees. At this time in *Ireland* the *Bard* by common acceptation, is counted a rayling Rimer, and diftinguifhed from the Poet.

[Page 46]

—*an Irifh Scott or Pict by nation. Bede* tells us that the *Picts* were a colony of *Scythians,* who firft comming into *Ireland,* and being denyed refidence there by the *Scots,* were perfwaded by them to inhabit the North part of *Britaine.* But Mr *Camden,* out of *Dio, Heroidan, Tacitus,* &c. and upon confideration of the cuftomes, name and language of the *Picts,* conceives not improbably, that they were naturall *Britons,* although diftinguifhed by name.

† *A regione quondam qua dicitur Scythia; dicitur Scisa, Sciticos, Scoticus, Scotus, Scotia.* Tho. Walsingham *in Mypodigmata Neoflua, ad an* 1185.

[Page 47]

Thofe Bardes indeed Cæsar writeth—— Concerning them I finde no mention in *Cæsar's* commentaryes, but much touching the *Druides*, which were the Priefts and Philofophers, (or *Magi* as *Pliny* calls them) of the Gaules & Britifh. *Illirebus divinis interfunt*, (†faith he) *facrificia publica ac privata procurant, religiones interpretantur. Ad hos magnus adolefcentium numerus difciplin a cauffa concurrit, magnoque ij funt apud eos honore.*&c. The word Οηωι had anciently the fame fignification (as I am informed) among the Irifh.

[Page 48]

—*and Cornelius Tacitus doth alfo ftrongly affirme the fame. Cornelius Tacitus* in the life of *Iulius Agricola* faith thus. *Silurum colorati vultus, & torts plerumque crines, & pofitus contra Hifpaniam, Iberos veteres trajeciffe, eafque fedes occupâffe fidem faciunt.* This he fpeaketh touching the Silures which inhabited that part of South-Wales, which now we call Herefordfhire, Radnorfhire, Brecknockfhire, Monmouth fhire, and Glamorganfhire. And although the like reafon may be given for that part of Ireland which lyeth next unto Spaine, yet in *Tacitus* we find no fuch inference. §*Buchanan* indeed upon the conjecture of *Tacitus* hath thefe words. *Verifimile a. non eft Hifpanos relictâ à tergo Hibernia, terrâ oriouirem & cœli & foli mitioris, in Albium primùm defcendiffe, fed primùvs in Hiberniam appuliffe, atq;inde in Britannia colonos miffos.* Which was obferved unto me by the moft learned Bifhop of Meth, Dʳ *Anth. Martin*, upon conference with his Lordfhip about this point. One paffage in *Tacitus* touching Ireland (in the fame booke) I may not heere omit, although it be *extra oleas. Quinto expedi:ionum anno* (faith he) *nave primâ tranfgreßus, ignotas ad tempus gentes, crebris fimul ac profperis pralijs domuit, camque partem Britannie qua Hibernicum afpicit, copijs inftruxit, in fpem magis quam ob formidinem. Siquidem Hibernia medo inter Britanniam atque Hifpaniam fita, & Gallico queque mari opportuna valentifsimam imperij partem magnu invicem ufibus misfcuerit. Spatium ejus fi Britannia comparaur, anguftius, noftri maris infulas fuperas. Solum cœlumque & ingenia, cultufq; hominum haut muliùm à Britannia differunt, meliùs aditus portufq; per commerica & negotiatores cogniti. Agricola expulfum feditione domefticâ unum ex regulis gentis exceperat, ac fpecie*

*   *Hist. nat. lib.* 16. *cap.* 44.
†   *De bello Galbos lib.* 2.
§   *Her. Scot. lib.* 3.

amicitia in occaſionem retinebat. Sapè ex eo andivi Legionennâ & medicis auixilijs debellari, obtineríque Hiberniam poſſe. idque adverſus Britanniam profuturum, ſi Romana ubique arma, & velut à conſpeĉtu libertas tolleretur.

[Page 49]

——*Slanius, in the end made himſelfe Monarch.* The Iriſh ſtories have a continued ſucceſſion of the Kings of Ireland from this *Slanius*, untill the conqueſt by King *Henry* the ſeccond, but very uncertaine, eſpecially untill the planting of Religion by S.*Patrick*, at which time *Lœgarius*, or *Lagirius* was Monarch.

[Page 52]

Ireland by Diodorus Siculus and by Strabo called Britannia. Iris is by *Diodorus* called a part of *Brittaine:* but *Ireland* by neither of them *Britannia.*

[Page 52]

——*King Arthur, and before him Gurgunt.* Concerning King *Arthur's* conqueſt of Ireland, ſee *Geffry* of Monmouth, and *Matthew* of Weſtminſter, at the yeare 525. where he is ſaid to have landed in Ireland with a great army, and in a battle to have taken King *Gilla-mury* priſoner, and forced the other Princes to ſubjeĉtion. In our Annals it appeares that *Moriertach* (the ſonne of *Erca*) was at that time King of Ireland, of which name ſonne reliques ſeeme to be in *Gilla-Mury, Gilla* being but an addition uſed with many names, as *Gilla-Patrick,* &c. But in the Country writers (which I have ſeene) I find not the leaſt touch of this conqueſt.

[Page 53]

—*amongſt whom he diſtributed the land.* King *Henry* the 2 gave to **Richard Strong-bow* Earle of *Striguil* or *Penbroke*, all Leinſter, excepting the citty of *Dublin*, and the Cantreds adjoyning with the maritime townes and caſtles. Vnto †*Robert fitz Stephen*, and *Miles de Cogan* he granted the Kingdome of *Corke*, excepting the Citty of *Corke*, and the *Oſtmans* Cantred. And unto §*Philp de Bruſe* the Kingdome of Limericke. But in a confirmation of King *John* to *William de Bruſe* (or *Braos*) Nephew to this *Philip*, wee fine that hee

---

*   *Gir. Camb. Hib. expugn. lib. 1. cap. 23.*

†   *Vid. Rog. de Hoveden pag. 567 edit. Franc. & Camd. Brit. pag. 739.*

§   *Rog. de Hoveden ibid.*

gave to him onely **honorem de Limerick, retentu in dominica noſtro* (as the words of the Charter are) *citate de Limerick & donationibus epiſcopatuum & abbatiarum, & retentu in manu noſtrâ cantredo Oſtmannorum & S. infulâ.* Among other large graunts (remembered by *Hoveden*) which this King *Henry* gave to the firſt adventurers, that of Metho to Sʳ *Hugh de Lacy* is of ſpeciall note. The grant was in theſe words.

HEnricus Dei gratiâ Rex Angliæ, & Dux Normandiæ & Aquitaniæ, & Comes Andegauiæ. Archiepiſcopis, Epiſcopis, Abbatibus, Comitibus, Baronibus, Iuſtitiarijs, & omnibus miniſtris & fidelibus ſuis Francis, Anglis & Hibernienſibus totius terræ ſuæ, Salutem. Sciatis me dediſſe & conceſsiſſe, & præſenti chartâ meâ confirmâſſe *Hugoni de Lacy* pro ſervitio ſuo, terram de Midiâ cum omnibus pertinentij ſuis per ſervitium quinquaginta militum ſibi & hæredibus ſuis,t nendú & habendú à me & hæredibus meis, ſicut *Murchardus Hu-melathlin* eam tenuit, vel aliquis alius ante illum vel poſteâ. Et de incremento illi dono omnia feoda quæ præbuit, vel quæ præbebit circa Duveliniam, dum Balivus meus eſt, ad faciendum mihi ſervitium apud civitatem meam Duveliniæ. Quare volo & ſirmiter præcipio, ut ipſe *Hugo* & hæredes ſui poſteum prædiſtam terram habeant, & teneant omnes libertates & liberas conſuetudines quas ibi habeo vel habere poſſum per prænominatum ſervitium, à me & hæredibus meis, benè & in pace, liberè, & quietè, & honorificè, in boſco & plano, in pratis & paſcuis, in aquis & molédinis, in vivarijs & ſtagnis, & piſcationibus & venationibus, in vijs, & ſemitis, & portubus maris, & in omnibus alijs locis, & alijs rebus ad eam pertinentibus cum omnibus libertatibus, quas ibi habeo, vel illi dare poſſum, & hâc meâ chartâ confirmare. *Teſt. counite Ꝛichardo filio Gilberti, VVillielmo de Ꞇraoſa, & c. Apud VVeiſford.*

But above all other graunts made by K. *Henry* the 2. that to his ſonne *Iohn* is moſt memorable. *Deinde* (ſaith †*Hoveden*) *venit rex Oxenford, & in generali concilio ibidem celbrato conſtituit Iohannem filium ſuum Regem in Hiberniâ, conceſſione & confirmatione Alexandri ſummi Pontificis.* By vertue of this graunt both in the life time of his father, and in the raigne of his brother king *Richard,* he was ſtiled in all his charters *Dominus Hibernia,* and direſted them thus, *Ioannes Dominus Hibernia, & comes Morton. Archiepiſcopis, epiſcopis, comitibus, baronibus, Iuſtitiarijs, vicecomitibus, conſtabuarijs, & omnibus ballivis & miniſtris*

---

*   *Chart. an* 2. *Io. in acre* Lond.

†   In Henr. 2 pag. 566.

ſuis totius Hibernia, ſalutem. Thus we have it frequently (although ſometimes with a little variation) in the Regiſters of Saint *Mary* Abbey, and *Thomaſcourt* by *Dublin*. How the Earle in Leinſter, and *Lacy* in Meth, diſtributed their lands, (beſides what they retained in their owne hands,) is delivered by *Maurice Regan*, (interpreter to *Dermot Mac Murrough* King of Leinſter) who wrote the Hiſtorie of thoſe times in *French* verſe. The booke was tranſlated into *Engliſh* by Sir *George Carew* Lo. Preſident of *Mounſter*, afterwards earle of *Totnes*, and communicated to me, by our moſt reverend and excellently learned Primate. There wee finde that the Earle gave to *Reymond le Groſe* in* marriage with *his ſiſter, Fotherd, O-drone, and Glaſcarrig, unto Henry de Mount-mariſh, hee gave Obarthy, unto Maurice de Prindergaſt, Fernegenall,* which was afterwards conferred upon *Robert fitz Godobert* but by what meanes he obtained it (ſaith Regan) *I know not. Vnto Meiler Fitz.Henry he gave Carbry,* unto †*Maurice Fitz Gerald the Naas Oſelin (which had beene poſſeſſed by Mackelan) and Wicklor, unto Walter de Ridclefford he gave the lands of Omorthy, unto Iohn de Clahul the marſhalſhip of Leinſter, and the land betweene Aghabo and Leghlin, unto Robert de Birmingham Oſaly, and unto Adam de Hereford large poſſeſſions.* What theſe poſſeſſions were, are thus noted in the Regiſter of *Thomaſcourt* abbey, where ſpeaking of the Earle, *Poſteâ Lagenâ perquiſitâ, erat quidam juvenis cum co quem multùm dilexit, & dedit eidem pro ſervitio fuo terras & tenementa ſubſcripta, viz. tenementum de ſaltu Salmonis, Cloncoury, Kill, Hounterard, & tenementum de Donning cum omnibus ſuis pertinentijs.* Thus the Regiſter. This *Adam de Hereford* was founder of Saint *Wulſtan's* priory neere *Leixlip* in the county of Kildare. But we proceed with *Regan. Vnto Miles Fitz David who was one of his cheife favorites, he gave Overk in Oſſory, to Thomas le Flemming, Arde, to Gilbert de Borard, Oſelmith, to a knight called Reinand he gave 15. knights fees adioyning to the ſea, and to one Robert (who was afterwards ſlaine in Connaught) the Norragh.* What partition *Lacy* made in *Meth*, he thus delivers. *Vnto his ſpeciall friend Hugh Tirrell he gave Caſtleknock: and unto William Petit Caſtlebreck.* I have ſeene an ancient deede made by Sir *Hugh de Lacy* to this *William Petit* wherein among other things he graunts unto him *Matherethirnam cum omnibus pertinentijs ſuis, exceptis Lacu & villà quæ dicitur*

---

*   *Conſul Gir. Camb. Hib. expugn. lib.* 2 *cap.* 4.

†   This Maurice ſoone after deceſaſing at Wexford, king *John* then earle of *Moreton* confirmed to his ſonne *William FitzMaurice cantredum mera quam Makelanus tenuit, idsum ſc. in qua villa de Naas ſita est, quam comes Richardum dedet Mauriceo patri ipſius.* Thus the charter, *habeant in ros. com. placea an.* 10. Hen. 6. *an ſurri Birminghamiano.*

Differt, &c. Vnto the valiant Meiler fitz Henry (faith Regan) *he gave Magheregay the lands of Rathkenin, and the cantred of Athnotker. Vnto Gilbert de Nangle all Magherigallen, unto Iocelin the fonne of Gilbert de Nangle, the Navan and the land of Ardbraccan: unto Richard de Tuite he gave faire poffeffions, unto Robert de Lacy Rathwer, unto Richard de la Chappell he gave much land, unto Geffry de Conftantine Kilbifky and Rathmarthy: Vnto Adam de Feipo, Gilbert de Nugent, William de Miffet, and Hugh de Hofe, he gave large inheritances.* In *Lacyes* graunt to *Feipo*, we finde that he gave him *Skrine, et praterca* (fayth the *deede) *feodum unius militis circa Duvelinam, ftil. Clantorht & Santref.* &c. In his graunt to *Gilbert de Nugent*, (the originall whereof I have feene, with an impreffion upon the feale, of a knight armed and mounted,) he gave to him *Delvin, Quam in tempore Hibernicorum tenuerunt O-Finelans, cum omnibus pertinentijs & villis, qua infra prædictam Delvin continentur, exceptd quadam villâ Abbatu Foura nomine Torrochelafch pro fervitio 5. militum.* Thus the Charter. To *Miffet* hee gave *Luin*, and to *Huffey* or *Hofe Galtrim. Regan* proceeds. *Vnto Adam Dullard hee gave the lands of Dullenvarthy, unto one Thomas he gave Cramly, Timlath. began northeaft from Kenlu, Lathrashalim, and Sendevonath, and unto Richard le Flemming he gave Crandon at 20. Knightsfees.*

[Page 56]

————*they changed the forme thereof into their cloakes called Pallia.* As the *Romans* had their gowne called *toga*, fo the ancient outward veftiment of the Grecians was called *Pallium*, by fome tranflated a Mantle, although it be now commonly taken for a Cloake, which doth indeed fomewhat refsemble a Mantle. By thefe different kinds of habit, the one was fo certainly diftinguifhed from the other, that the word *Togatus* was often ufed to fignifie a Roman, and *Palliatus* a Grecian, as it is obferved by †Mr *Tho. Godwin* out of §*Sigonius. Togati* (faith he) *pro Romanis dicti, ut Palliati pro Gracis.* But that *the ancient Latines and Romans ufed it,* as the Author alledgeth, (out of I know not what place in *Virgil*) appeareth no way unto mee. That the Gowne was their ufuall outward garment, is moft certaine, and that commonly of wooll, finer or courfer, according to the dignity of the perfon that wore it. Whence *Horace:*

---

*   *Magn. regest. mon., R. Maria iuxta Dublin fol.. 76.*
†   *Romana histor. antholog. lib. 2. sect. 3. cap. 7.*
§   *De ind. l. 3. cap. 19.*

———— *Sit mihi menſa tripes, et*
Concha ſalis puri, et toga quæ defendere frigus
Quam vis craſſa, queſt—*

And from this difference betweene the ancient Roman and Grecian habit, grew the proverbs, *modò palliatus, modò togatus,* and *de togâ ad pallium,* to denote an unconſtant perſon.

[Page 56]

———— *Humi mantilia ſternunt.*

Euanders entertainment of *Æneas,* is ſet out in the 8.booke of *Virgils Æneis,* but there we have no ſuch word as *manti.e.* In his entertainment by *Dido* we have it, but in another ſence.

Iam pater Æneas, *& jam Troiana inventus*
Conveniunt, ſtratoque ſuper diſcumbitur oſtro,
Dant famuli manibus lymphas Cereremque caniſtris
Expediunt, tonſiſq; ferunt mantilia villis.†

[Page 59]
—*as in that battle of Thomyris againſt Cyrus.* Herodotus in the deſcription of that battle hath no ſuch thing.

[Page 63]
—*by the ſword and by the fire.* Lucian hath it, *by the ſword & by the wind.* Somewhat may be gathered to this purpoſe out of the §*Vlſter Annals,* where *Legarius* (or *Lagerius*) a heathen King of Ireland, being taken priſoner by the *Leinſter* men, is ſaid to have bin releaſed upon an oath, which was *per ſolem & ventum.*

---

* *Satyr.* 3. *lib.* 1.
† *Æneid. lib.* 1.
§ An. 458.

Appendix II:
– Passages Omitted from –
Ware's Text

As Ware comments in his preface and in his marginal annotations, he has in places modified the text of *A View* somewhat. Many of these changes are based on his own scholarly knowledge and designed to express what Spenser really meant to say or to correct his errors (see the marginal notes collected in Appendix I). For example, Ware alters Spenser's 'Iriach' to 'Eriach' as the war-cry of the O'Briens; 'Clanriccard' is altered to the more usual name, 'Galway'; and 'Briskelah' has been altered to 'Brackenah' (although, here, Spenser's original usage appears correct).

More significant are the changes Ware appears to have made in order to make the work more acceptable to contemporary readers. Ware laments in his preface that although Spenser's text 'sufficiently testifieth his learning and deep judgement, yet we may wish that in some passages it had bin tempered with more moderation'. He alleges that 'if he [Spenser] had lived to see these times, and the good effects which the last 30 yeares peace have produced in this land . . . he would have omitted those passages which may seeme to lay either any particular aspersion upon some families, or generall upon the Nation.' Accordingly, many passages which are present in virtually all other manuscripts of *A View* (it is not clear which copy Ware consulted, or whether he based his edition on a lost manuscript) are absent from Ware's edition. Most of these either criticize important Irish families or contain harsh descriptions of the Irish. They are reproduced below from the list compiled in the Variorum edition of the work, which compares Ware's edition with the Ellesmere MS 7041 in the Huntington Library.

W	E
W	*E*
that nation (p. 1)	that salvage nacion
they be more unjust (p. 19)	they be muche more vniuste
so many evills as I see more and more to bee layde upon her (p. 27)	soe manye evills, as everye daie I see more and more throwne vppon her
most of the Free-holders of that Realme, are *Irish*, which . . . make no more scruple to passe against an Englishman, and the Queene, though it bee to strayne their oathes, then to drinke milke unstrayned (p. 30)	all the ffrehoulders of that realme are Irishe which . . . make no more scruple to passe againste the Inglishman or the Quene thoughe it be to straine theire oathers then to drinke milke vnstrained
now that the Irish have stepped into very roomes of your English, wee are now to become heedfull and provident in iuryes. (p. 30)	now that the Irishe haue stepped into the romes of the Inglishe whoe are now become soe hedefull and provident to kepe them out from hence forthe that they make no scruple of Conscience to passe againste them it is good reasone that either that course of the lawe for trialls be altered or other provision for Iuryes be made
the evidence being brought in by the baser *Irish* people, will bee as deceiptfull (p. 32)	the evidence beinge broughte in by the base Irishe people wilbe as deceiptefull
they shall lose nothing but themselves, whereof they seeme surely very carelesse (p. 35)	they shall lose nothinge but themselves wheareof they seme surelye verye Careles like as all barbarous people are, as Cesar in his Comentaries saith verye fearlesse of death
having bin in those times without letters (p. 46)	havinge bene allwaies without Lettres

W	E
they are so unlearned still (p. 47)	they are so barbarous still and so vnlearned
they derive themselves (p. 49)	beinge, as they are nowe accounted the moste barbarous nacion in Christendome they to avoide that reproche woulde derive themselves
some of them are degenerated (p. 54)	the moste parte of them are degenerated
they be most to bad intents (p. 58)	they be all to bad intentes
for the Irish glibbes, they are as fit maskes (p. 59)	for the Irishe glibbes I saye that besides theire salvage brutishnes and loathly filthines which is not to be named they are fitt maskes
is meere *Scythian* (p. 62)	is mere salvage and *Scythyan*
the maner of many Nations (p. 64)	the manner of all barbarous nacions
some of them are now much more lawlesse and licentious then the very wilde Irish (p. 67)	the Englishe that weare are now muche more Lawles and Licentious then the verie wilde Irishe
they are almost now growned like the Irish (p. 68)	they are nowe growen to be allmoste as lewde as the Irishe
degenerate (p. 68)	degenerate and growen to be as verye Patchokes as the wilde Irishe
Could they ever conceive any such dislike (p. 68)	Coulde they euer Conceaue anye suche divilishe dislike
Other great houses there bee of the English in Ireland, which thorough licentious conversing (p. 70)	Other great howses theare be of the olde Englishe in Irelande which thoroughe licentious Conuersinge
are now growne as Irish, as O-Hanlons breech, as the proverbe there is. (p. 70)	are now growne as Irishe as Ohanlans breeche, (as the proverbe theare is) of which sorte theare are two moste pittifull ensamples About the reste, to witt the Lo.

W

E

Bremingham, whoe beinge the moste anciente Baron I thinke in Englande is now waxen the moste Salvage Irishe naminge him selfe Irishlike, maccorishe, and the other is the great mortimer whoe forgettinge how greate he was once in Englande or Englishe at all is nowe become the moste barbarous of them all and is Called *macnemarra* and not muche better then he, is the olde *Lò Courcie* whoe havinge lewdlye wasted all the Landes and Seigniories that he had an aliened them vnto the Irishe is himselfe now growen quite Irishe

the Lords and cheife men degener-ate (p. 70)

the Lordes and Chief men wax so barbarous and bastardlike

are very bad (p. 70)

are verye bad and barbarous

very uncivill (p. 70)

verye brute and vncivill

how can such matching succeede well (p. 71)

how cane suche matchinge but bringe forthe an evill race

his trouse (p. 72)

his thinne breche

it is very inconvenient that any such should be permitted. (p. 81)

it is verye inconveniente that anye suche shoule be permitted speciallye in a people so evill minded as they now be an diuerslye shewe themselues

that not one amongst a hundred (p. 85)

as that ye woulde rather thinke them *Atheists* or infidles but not one amongest a hundred

Eudox. Is it not then a little blot to them that now hold the place of government, that they which now

This is trewelie a moste pitifull hearinge . . . But if this Ignorance of the people be suche a burthen

W	E
are in the light themselves, suffer a people under their charge, to wallow in such deadly darknesse. (p. 85)	vnto the Pope is it not a like blott to them that now houlde that place in that they which now are in the lighte them selves suffer a people vnder theire Chardge to wallowe in suche deadlie darkenes? ffor I do not see that the faulte is Chaunged but the faultes master
they christen yet after the popish fashion. (p. 86)	the Christen, yeat after the popische fashion and with the Popishe Latine ministracion.
enemies of both. (p. 91)	enemyes of bothe. And this is the wretchednes of that fatall kingedome which I thinke therefore was in olde time not Called amisse *Banno* or *sacra Insula* takinge *sacra* for accursed
or such like (p. 99)	the ketinges and Kellies, or suche like
in the last conspiracy of some of the English Pale, thinke you not that there were many more guiltie then they that felt the punishment? (p. 104)	in the last conspiracye of the Englishe pale thinke youe not that theare weare manye more guiltye then that felte the punishment? or was theare anie allmoste Cleare from the same?
if they were English well placed among them (p. 120)	if theare weare Englishe shed amongst them and placed ouer them
he might easily overlooke and sometimes over-reach the Moores, the Dempsies, the Connors (p. 127)	he mighte easelye ouerloke and somtimes ouerreache the moores/ the Butlers the dempsies the ketins the Connours
Donnell Mac Carty, whom it is meete to foresee to (p. 130)	donell maccartie whom it is mete to foresee to cutt of

W	E
those two Citties, above all the rest, doe offer an in-gate to the Spaniard most fitly: (p. 131)	those two Citties aboue all the reste doe offer an Ingate to the Spanniarde moste fittlye and allso the inhabitantes of them are moste ill affected to the Englishe gouernment and moste friendes to the Spaniarde
this happens not onely sometimes in the sonnes of their Gentle-men, but also of their Noble-men, specially of them who have base Sonnes (p. 138)	this happens not onelye in the sonns of theire gentlemen but often times allsoe of theire noble men speciallye of theire base sonns as theare are fewe without some of them
free-holders, which are not tractable to their wills (p. 139)	freholders which are not tractable to theire bad wills. Twoe suche Bastardes of the L. *Roches* there are now out in mounster whom he doerthe not onelye Countenance but allso priuilye maynteigne and relieue nightelye amongst his Tenantes., suche another is theare of the Earle of *Clancares* in desmounde and manye other in manye other places/
the rude Irish . . . are now become more civill (p. 143)	the rude Irishe . . . are now become somwhat more Civill
they are more stubborne, and disobedient to law and government, then the Irish be. (p. 143)	they are muche more stubborne and disobedient to lawe and government then the Irishe be, and more malicous againste the Englishe that dailye are sente ouer/ . . . bothe discontente and vndewtifull/
any English there, should bee worse then the Irish (p. 143)	the englishe Irishe theare shoulde be worse then the wilde Irishe
Ireland is full of her owne nation,	Irelande is full of her owne nacion

W	E
that ought not to be rooted out (p. 144)	that maye not be roted out
in time learne quite to forget his Irish Nation (p. 148)	shall in shorte time learne quite to forgett his Irishe nacion
what other order will you take for their manner of life? (p. 148)	what other order will ye take for theire manner of lief for all this thoughe perhaps it maie kepe them from disobedience and disloyaltye yeat will it not bringe them from theire Barabrisme and salvage life/
the realme of Ireland (p. 148)	the wretched Realme of Irelande
their owne behaviour (p. 151)	theire owne brutishe behaviour
And (p. 153)	for this I knowe that the moste of the Irishe are so far from vnderstandinge the Popishe Religion as they are of the Protestantes profession and yeat dothe hate it thoughe vnknowen even for the verye hatred which they haue of the Englishe and theire gouernement
some of our idle Ministers (p. 154)	our Idle ministers
bee drawne foorth from their warme neastes (p. 154)	be drawen forthe from theire warme nestes, and theire swete loues sides

Appendix III: —— Guide to Further —— Reading

The modern reception of Spenser's *View* might usefully be divided into two phases, the first characterized by archival and factual work undertaken by American critics interested in the Irish background to Spenser's work from the 1920s through to the publication of the Variorum edition in 1949, a period of scholarly activity that laid the groundwork for a second phase of more speculative and theoretical engagements. Indeed, the recent flurry of activity that followed on from the appearance of two important essays by Stephen Greenblatt (1980) and Nicholas Canny (1983) would have been unthinkable without the labours of Raymond Jenkins, Ray Heffner, Rudolf Gottfried and Roland Smith. At the same time, the current focus is more analytical than descriptive, and arguably more critical of sources and contexts. Criticism in this century has moved from a narrow historicism concerned with questions of biography, chronology and geography – dating the *View* and plotting out Spenser's career in Ireland – to an exploration of a set of issues around questions of colonialism and cultural identity – censorship, gender, legal imperialism, self-fashioning and representations of the Other. The following list is not intended to be exhaustive, but merely to indicate, under a series of headings, some of the key areas of activity in the field.

Background and Biography

Useful histories of early modern Ireland are Brady and Gillespie (1986), Canny (1987b), Ellis (1985), Lennon (1995) and Quinn (1966). The most important general introductions to Spenser's life and work in an Irish context are Henley (1928) and Judson (1933). The major biography by Judson (1945) provides an overview of Spenser's twin careers of poet and planter. The essential factual information is contained in Carpenter (1923) and Maley (1994). Instructive material on contemporary views of Ireland can be found in Harrington (1991) and Hadfield and McVeagh (1994). Two Irish tracts which have a close bearing upon the *View*, William Herbert's *Croftus sive de Hibernia Liber* and Richard Beacon's *Solon his follie*, have recently appeared in new editions by Keaveney and Madden (1994) and Carroll and Carey (1996) respectively.

Censorship

Baker (1986) argued that the *View* too baldly stated Elizabethan policy in Ireland, hence its suppression. In a provocative essay, Jean Brink (1992), in an exemplary display of textual scholarship, argues forcefully that Spenser may not have written the *View*. Andrew Hadfield (1994a) offers a cautionary note that surveys recent arguments around the suppression of the *View* and leaves an open verdict.

Irish History

Canny's intervention provoked a series of responses from within Irish historiography. Ciarán Brady (1986) claimed that Spenser was unique in his 'pessimistic determinism', and that the *View* was 'a sustained exercise in bad faith'. Both author and text are the products of a particular crisis in Anglo-Irish politics. In his 1988 rejoinder, Brady reinforces his argument of 1986 that Spenser wanted to persuade his contemporaries of the necessity for radical action in Ireland. In 1989 Brady's contention is that Spenser's criticisms of the common law are the key to the radical import of his text, and, by extension, that the reason for its alleged suppression rests upon its claim that English law has failed the colonial enterprise. Bradshaw (1987) argues that the extreme nature of Spenser's proposal for Irish reform 'finds its intellectual source in his protestant world-view'. Canny's own argument developed throughout these various exchanges. In 1987 he expanded the idea that the *View* is a 'synthesis' of New English perceptions. In 1988 he defended his thesis that Spenser is a representative of the New English community, and has to be viewed in that light. In 1989 he argued that Spenser's experience is essentially a Cork one, and that Brady and Bradshaw were too 'value-laden' in their criticisms. Spenser, Canny insisted, is more of a mainstream humanist – 'humanists were not pacifists' – than has been allowed, and the *View* more reform-oriented and conciliatory. David Beers Quinn (1990) is an important contribution that stresses the fundamental ambiguity of Spenser's attitude to the Gaelic Irish.

Dialogue, Form and Narrative

Several critics have drawn attention to the dialogue form of the *View* as a key feature of its composition and reception. Patricia Coughlan (1989) emphasized Spenser's classical precedents and the 'fictive mode of existence of the *View*', and suggested that text and tradition were as important as context and innovation. Anne Fogarty (1989) provides a theoretically informed and historically grounded essay that highlights the problem of reconciling different aspects of Spenser's career. Fogarty sees the *View* as a *bricolage* of discourses holding together a number of conflicting positions, leading in the prose and poetry to impasse and aporia. John Breen (1994–5) sees Spenser's use of dialogue, like allegory, as a deliberate effort to 'complicate the authorial responsibility for what is spoken', and insists on the place of the *View* within the Renaissance dialogue and historiography. See the responses by Hadfield (1994/5) and Maley (1995/6).

Gender

Greenblatt (1980) elaborates upon the relationship between gender and colonialism. Clare Carroll (1990) argues that critics were slow to respond to Greenblatt's claim that *The Faerie Queene* is all about Ireland, and goes on to suggest that Greenblatt's famous reading of the Bower of Bliss episode in fact plays down the gendering of colonial narrative. Ann Rosalind Jones and Peter Stallybrass (1992) place Spenser's gendered colonial discourse within a wider articulation of sexual and national identities. Andrew Hadfield (1996) focuses on the sexual politics of Elizabeth I in Spenser's epic poem, where he seeks to render Elizabeth more 'masculine' in her method of governing Ireland.

Geography and Mapping

Gottfried (1939) mapped out the territory covered by Spenser in his dialogue. Bruce Avery (1990) argues that the production of a map by Eudoxus at a crucial moment in the dialogue forces Irenius to be more explicit in his descriptions, and, more important, reveals the map as 'a tool of domination' (an insight which links Spenser's text to the issues explored in Brian Friel's *Translations* (1980)). Eva Gold (1993) compares the analysis of problems of identity and geography in the *View* and *The Faerie Queene* Book VI, where Spenser fashions an identity apart from, and in opposition to, the Queen and her Court. Bernhard Klein (1995) illustrates the extent to which mapping Ireland was part of a process of English national identity formation.

Language

F. F. Covington (1922) and John W. Draper (1919, 1926) argued over Spenser's linguistics in the *View*. Roland M. Smith (1958) investigated the transformation of Spenser's language in the move from manuscript to print. Eamonn Grennan (1982) argued that Spenser's political rhetoric is enmeshed with his literary style. Fogarty (1989) has a very good discussion of etymology in the dialogue. Finally, Carroll (1996) points to the ambivalence and complexity of Spenser's relationship with the Irish language as adumbrated in his prose treatise.

Law

David Baker (1986) looked at the way that Spenser saw language as a means by which to manipulate both law and land. Diane Parkin-Speer (1992) engages with the *View* as a source of material on English law and legal trials, and echoes Brady (1989) in the belief that Spenser's criticism of English common law is the radical edge of his project. Hadfield (1994b) explores the relationship between language, law and political theory in terms of representation. Annabel Patterson (1993) gives a compelling account of justice and law in the *View* and Book V of *The Faerie Queene*, using Kafka's *The Trial* as a way into the discussion. Elizabeth Fowler (1995) looks at the ways in which the views of law and right in *The Faerie Queene* interface with those in the *View*. Walter Lim (1995) offers a comparison of the concept of justice as it is rehearsed in both the *View* and Book V of *The Faerie Queene*.

Sources, Influences, Reception and Contemporaries

E. W. Marjarum (1940) shows that Wordsworth was familiar with Spenser's treatise, and that it informed his own views on Ireland. Gottfried (1938) argues that Fynes Moryson's *Itinerary* (1617) owed a debt to Spenser's *View*. Bradshaw (1988) offered a close reading of texts by Richard Beacon and William Herbert contemporaneous with the *View*, concluding that Spenser is less representative and more reprehensible than his counterparts. Jardine (1993) shows how deeply embedded Spenser was in a culture of colonialism that drew on classical precedents, under the influence of learned patrons such as Sir Thomas Smith and Gabriel Harvey. Breen (1995) focuses on three features of the *View*, law, tanistry and degeneracy, in order to argue it was a source text for Moryson. Julia Lupton (1990) exposes the degree to which Spenser used classical sources, specifically Virgil, in order to represent his career in Ireland as both exile and home-making. Coughlan (1990) credits the *View* as 'the founding text of modern English discourse about Ireland', underlines its influence on the propaganda of the mid-seventeenth century, and argues that it offered a grounding for the Anglo-Irish nationalism expounded later by William Petty and Jonathan Swift. Willy Maley (1993) charts the impact of Ware's edition of the *View* on seventeenth-century Anglo-Irish politics.

Myth and Ritual

Patricia Fumerton (1986) offers a fascinating treatment, from a sophisticated ethnographic and anthropological standpoint, of fostering in the *View* and *The Faerie Queene*. Kenneth Gross (1985) sees Spenser's prose dialogue as replete with the same rich fund of Irish myths that he drew on for his epic poem. Judith Anderson (1987) maps out Spenser's uses of antiquity in his efforts to unravel the history behind Ireland's present state. Robert E. Stillman (1992) draws on Barthes' analysis of myth to argue that Spenser's Irish experiences forced him to construct 'an assimilationist mythology'. Smith (1944b) and Carroll (1996) examine the influence of the Irish book, *Leabhar Gabhála*, upon Spenser's mythology.

British History

An early essay by Edwin Greenlaw (1912) placed Spenser's work within the project of an incipient British imperialism. More recently, there have been some engagements with notions of Britishness as they manifest themselves in the dialogue. James Vink (1990) presents a compelling treatment of British origin myths in *The Faerie Queene* and the *View*. Andrew Hadfield (1993) conducts an equally elaborate exploration of British origin myths in the prose and poetry. Willy Maley (1996) argues that critics of the *View* who focus exclusively on its anti-Irish sentiments often overlook the extent to which Spenser's dialogue is concerned from the outset with a threatening Scottish context, including a claim that the Irish are originally Scots.

Bibliography

Anderson, Judith H. (1987), 'The antiquities of Fairyland and Ireland', *Journal of English and Germanic Philology*, 86, pp. 199–214.

Avery, Bruce (1990), 'Mapping the Irish other: Spenser's *A View of the Present State of Ireland*', *ELH*, 57 2, pp. 263–79.

Baker, David J. (1986), 'Some Quirk, Some Subtle Evasion': Legal Subversion in Spenser's *A View of the Present State of Ireland*', *Spenser Studies*, 6, pp. 147–63.

Bradshaw, Brendan (1987), 'Edmund Spenser on Justice and Mercy', *Historical Studies*, 16, pp. 76–89.

—— (1988), 'Robe and Sword in the Conquest of Ireland', in *Law and Government under the Tudors: essays presented to Sir Geoffrey Elton on his retirement*, ed. C. Cross, D. Loades and J. J. Scarisbrick, Cambridge: Cambridge University Press, pp. 139–62.

Bradshaw, Brendan Hadfield, Andrew and Maley, Willy (eds), (1993), *Representing Ireland: literature and the origins of conflict, 1534–1660*, Cambridge: Cambridge University Press.

Brady, Ciarán (1986), 'Spenser's Irish crisis: humanism and experience in the 1590s', *Past and Present*, 111, pp. 17–49.

—— (1988), 'Spenser's Irish crisis: reply to Canny', *Past and Present*, 120, pp. 210–15.

—— (1989), 'The road to the view: on the decline of reform thought in Tudor Ireland', in *Spenser and Ireland: an interdisciplinary perspective*, ed. Patricia Coughlan, Cork: Cork University Press, pp. 25–45.

Brady, Ciarán and Gillespie, Raymond (eds), (1986), *Natives and Newcomers: the making of Irish colonial society*, Dublin: Irish Academic Press.

Breen, John (1994–5), 'Imagining voices in *A View of the Present State of Ireland*: a discussion of recent studies concerning Edmund Spenser's Dialogue', *Connotations* 4, 1–2, pp. 119–32.

—— (1995), 'The influence of Edmund Spenser's *View* on Fynes Moryson's *Itinerary*', *Notes and Queries*, 42, pp. 363–64.

Brink, Jean (1992), 'Constructing the *View of the Present State of Ireland*', *Spenser Studies*, 11, pp. 203–28.

Canny, Nicholas P. (1983), 'Edmund Spenser and the development of an Anglo-Irish identity', *Yearbook of English Studies: Colonial and Imperial Themes*, 13, pp. 1–19.

—— (1987a), 'Identity formation in Ireland: the emergence of the Anglo-Irish', in *Colonial Identity in the Atlantic World, 1500–1800*, ed. Nicholas Canny and A. Pagden. Princeton, NJ: Princeton University Press, pp. 159–212.

—— (1987b), *From Reformation to Restoration: Ireland 1534–1660*, Dublin: Helicon.

—— (1988), ' "Spenser's Irish crisis": a comment', *Past and Present*, 120 pp. 201–9.

—— (1989), 'Introduction: Spenser and the Reform of Ireland', in *Spenser and Ireland: an interdisciplinary perspective*, ed. Patricia Coughlan, Cork: Cork University Press, pp. 9–24.

Carpenter, Frederic Ives (1922), 'Desiderata in the study of Spenser', *Studies in Philology*, 19 2, pp. 238–43.

—— (1922), 'Spenser in Ireland', *Modern Philology*, 19, pp. 405–19.

—— (1923), *A Reference Guide to Edmund Spenser*, Chicago: University of Chicago Press.

Carroll, Clare (1990), 'The construction of gender and the cultural and political other in *The Faerie Queene* 5 and *A View of the Present State of Ireland*: the critics, the Context, and the case of Radigund', *Criticism*, 32 2, pp. 163–91.

—— (1996), 'Spenser and the Irish Language: The Sons of Milesio in *A View of the Present State of Ireland*, *The Faerie Queene*, Book V and the *Leabhar Gabhála*', in A. Fogarty (ed.), *Spenser in Ireland: 'The Faerie Queene', 1596–1996*, *Irish University Review*, 26/2, pp. 281–90.

Carroll, Clare and Carey, Vincent (eds), (1996), *Richard Beacon: Solon his follie, or a politique discourse touching the Reformation of common-weales conquered, declined or corrupted*, SUNY at Binghamton: Centre for Medieval and Early Renaissance Studies.

Coughlan, Patricia (1989), ' "Some Secret Scourge which shall by her come unto England": Ireland and Incivility in Spenser', in *Spenser and Ireland: an interdisciplinary perspective*, ed. Patricia Coughlan, Cork: Cork University Press, pp. 46–74.

—— (1990), ' "Cheap and common animals": the English anatomy of Ireland in the seventeenth century', in *Literature and the English Civil War*, ed. Thomas Healy and Jonathan Sawday. Cambridge, Cambridge University Press, pp. 205–23.

Covington, F. F. (1922), 'Another view of Spenser's Linguistics', *Studies in Philology*, 19, pp. 244–8.

—— (1924), 'Spenser's use of Irish history in the *Venue of the Present State of Ireland*', *University of Texas Bulletin*, 2411: *Studies in English*, 4, pp. 5–38.

Draper, John W. (1919), 'Spenser's linguistics in *The Present State of Ireland*', *Modern Philology*, 17, pp. 111–26.

—— (1926), 'More light on Spenser's linguistics', *Modern Language Notes*, 41, pp. 127–8.

Ellis, Steven G. (1985), *Tudor Ireland: Crown, community and the conflict of cultures*, London: Longman.

Fogarty, Anne (1989), 'The colonization of language: narrative strategies in *A View of the Present State of Ireland* and *The Faerie Queene*, Book VI', in *Spenser and Ireland: an interdisciplinary perspective*, ed. Patricia Coughlan, Cork: Cork University Press, pp. 75–108.

—— ed., (1996), *Spenser in Ireland: 'The Faerie Queene', 1596–1996*, *The Irish University Review*, 26 2.

Fowler, Elizabeth (1995), 'The failure of moral philosophy in the work of Edmund Spenser', *Representations* 51, pp. 47–76.

Fumerton, Patricia (1986), 'Exchanging gifts: The Elizabethan Currency of children and poetry', *ELH*, 53, pp. 241–78.

Gold, Eva (1993), 'Spenser the borderer: boundary, property, identity in *A View of the Present State of Ireland* and Book 6 of *The Faerie Queene*', *Journal of the Rocky Mountain Medieval and Renaissance Association*, 14, pp. 98–113.

Gottfried, R. B. (1937a), 'The date of Spenser's *View*', *Modern Language Notes*, 52, pp. 176–80.

—— (1937b), 'Spenser as an historian in prose', *Transactions of the Wisconsin Academy of Sciences, Arts, and Letters*, 30, pp. 317–29.

—— (1937c), 'Spenser's *View* and Essex', *PMLA*, 52, pp. 645–51.

—— (1938), 'The debt of Fynes Moryson to Spenser's *View*', *Philological Quarterly*, 17, pp. 297–307.

—— (1939), 'Irish geography in Spenser's *View*', *English Literary History*, 6, pp. 114–37.

—— (ed.) (1949), *The Works of Edmund Spenser: a variorum edition*, 11 vols (1932–49), Baltimore: Johns Hopkins University Press, vol. 9, *The Prose Works*.

Greenblatt, Stephen J. (1980), 'To fashion a gentleman: Spenser and the destruction of the Bower of Bliss', in *Renaissance Self-Fashioning: from More to Shakespeare*, Chicago: Chicago University Press, pp. 157–92.

Greenlaw, Edwin (1912), 'Spenser and British imperialism', *Modern Philology*, 9, pp. 347–70.

Grennan, Eamonn (1982), 'Language and politics: a note on some metaphors in Spenser's *A View of the Present State of Ireland*', *Spenser Studies*, 3, pp. 99–110.

Hadfield, Andrew (1993), 'Briton and Scythian: Tudor representations of Irish origins', *Irish Historical Studies*, 28, pp. 390–408.

—— (1994a), 'Was Spenser's *View of the Present State of Ireland* censored? A review of the evidence', *Notes and Queries*, 41, pp. 459–63.

—— (1994b), 'Spenser, Ireland, and Sixteenth-Century Political Theory', *Modern Language Review*, 89 1, pp. 1–18.

—— (1994/5), 'Who is speaking in Spenser's *A View of the Present State of Ireland*? A response to John Breen', *Connotations*, 4/1–2 (1994/95), pp. 119–32.

—— (1996), 'The trials of Jove: Spenser's Irish allegory and the mastery of the Irish', *Bullán*, 4, pp. 1–15.

—— (1997), *Spenser's Irish Experience: Wild Fruit and Salvage Soyl*, Oxford: Clarendon Press.

Hadfield, Andrew and Mc Veagh, John (eds), (1994), *Strangers to that Land: British perceptions of Ireland from the Reformation to the Famine*, Gerrards Cross: Colin Smythe.

Harrington, J. P. (1991), *The English Traveller in Ireland: accounts of Ireland and the Irish through five centuries*, Dublin: Gill and Macmillan, 1991.

Heffner, Ray (1942), 'Spenser's *View of Ireland*: some observations', *Modern Language Quarterly*, 3, pp. 507–15.

Henley, Pauline (1928), *Spenser in Ireland*, Cork: Cork University Press.

Hulbert, Viola B. (1937), 'Spenser's relation to certain documents on Ireland', *Modern Philology*, 34, pp. 345–53.

Hull, Vernam (1941), 'Edmund Spenser's Mona-Shul', *PMLA*, 56, pp. 578–79.

Jardine, Lisa (1993), 'Encountering Ireland: Gabriel Harvey, Edmund Spenser and English colonial ventures', in *Representing Ireland*, ed. B. Bradshaw, A. Hadfield and W. Maley, Cambridge: Cambridge University Press, pp. 60–75.

Jenkins, Raymond (1932), 'Spenser and the clerkship in Munster', *PMLA*, 47, pp. 109–21.

—— (1932), 'Spenser's Hand', *TLS*, 31 (7 January), p. 12.

—— (1933), 'Spenser at Smerwick', *TLS*, 32 (11 May), p. 331.

—— (1937), 'Spenser with Lord Grey in Ireland', *PMLA*, 52 (1937), pp. 338–53.

—— (1938), 'Spenser: the Uncertain years 1584–89', *PMLA*, 53, pp. 350–62.

—— (1952), 'Spenser and Ireland', in *That Soveraine Light: essays in honor of Edmund Spenser 1552–1952,* ed. W. R. Meuller and D. C. Allen, Baltimore: Johns Hopkins University Press, pp. 51–62.

Jones, Ann Rosalind and Stallybrass, Peter (1992), 'Dismantling Irena: the sexualising of Ireland in early modern England', in, *Nationalisms and Sexualities,* ed. Andrew Parker et al., London: Routledge, pp. 157–71.

Jones, H. S. V. (1919), 'Spenser's defense of Lord Grey', *University of Illinois Studies in Language and Literature,* 5, pp. 7–75.

—— (1930), 'A View of the Present State of Ireland', in *A Spenser Handbook,* Ithaca, NY: Cornell University Press, pp. 377–87.

Judson, Alexander C. (1933), *Spenser in Southern Ireland,* Bloomington Indiana University Press.

—— (1945), *The Life of Edmund Spenser,* in *The Works of Edmund Spenser: a variorum edition,* Baltimore, MD: Johns Hopkins University Press.

Keaveney, Arthur and Madden, John (eds) (1992), *Sir William Herbert: Croftus, sive de Hibernia Liber,* Dublin: Irish Manuscripts Commission, 1992.

Klein, Bernhard (1995), ' "And quickly make that, which was nothing at all": English national identity and the mapping of Ireland', in *Nationalismus und Subjektivität, Mitteilungen Beiheft,* 2, Johann Wolfgang Goethe-Universität Zentrum zur Erforschung der Frühen Neuzeit: Frankfurt am Main, pp. 200–26.

Kliger, Samuel (1950), 'Spenser's Irish tract and tribal democracy', *South Atlantic Quarterly,* 49, pp. 490–7.

Lennon, Colm (1995), *Sixteenth-Century Ireland: the incomplete conquest,* Dublin: Gill and Macmillan.

Lim, Walter S. H. (1995), 'Figuring justice: Imperial Ideology and the

Discourse of colonialism in Book V of *The Faerie Queene* and *A View of the Present State of Ireland*', *Renaissance and Reformation* 19/1, pp. 45–67.

Lupton, Julia (1990), 'Home-making in Ireland: Virgil's Eclogue I and Book VI of *The Faerie Queene*', *Spenser Studies*, 8, pp. 119–45.

Maley, Willy (1993), 'How Milton and some contemporaries read Spenser's *View*', in *Representing Ireland: Literature and the Origins of Conflict, 1534–1660*, ed. B. Bradshaw, A. Hadfield and W. Maley. Cambridge: Cambridge University Press, pp. 191–208.

—— (1994), *A Spenser Chronology*, London: Macmillan.

—— (1996) 'Spenser and Scotland: the limits of Anglo-Irish identity', *Prose Studies*, 19/1, pp. 1–18.

—— (1996/7) 'Dialogue-wise: some notes on the Irish context of Spenser's *View*', *Connotations*, 6/1 pp. 67–77.

Marjarum, E. W. (1940), 'Wordsworth's View of the State of Ireland', *PMLA*, 55, pp. 608–11.

Martin, William Cliff (1932), 'The date and purpose of Spenser's *Veue*', *PMLA*, 47, pp. 137–43.

Morgan, Hiram (1993), *Tyrone's Rebellion: the outbreak of the nine years war in Tudor Ireland*, Woodbridge: Boydell Press.

Morley, Henry (ed.), (1890), *Ireland under Elizabeth and James I, described by Edmund Spenser, by Sir John Davies . . . and by Fynes Moryson*, London.

Morris, R. (ed), (1910), *A View of the Present State of Ireland*, in *The Works of Edmund Spenser: the Globe edition*, Macmillan: London, pp. 609–83.

Myers, James P. (ed.), (1983), *Elizabethan Ireland: a selection of Writings by Elizabethan Writers on Ireland*, Hamden, CT: Archon.

Ní Chuilleanáin, Eiléan (1990), 'Ireland, the cultural context', in *The Spenser Encyclopedia*, ed. A. C. Hamilton, London and Toronto: Routledge, pp. 403–04.

O'Donovan, J. (ed.) (1858), 'Errors of Edmund Spenser: Irish Surnames', *Ulster Journal of Archaeology*, 6, pp. 135–44.

Ong, Walter J. (1942), 'Spenser's *View* and the Tradition of the 'Wild' Irish', *Modern Language Quarterly*, 3, pp. 561–71.

Parkin-Speer, Diane (1992), 'Allegorical legal trials in Spenser's *The Faerie Queene*', *Sixteenth Century Journal*, 23/3, pp. 494–505.

Patterson, Annabel (1993), 'The egalitarian giant: representations of justice in history/literature', in *Reading between the Lines*, London: Routledge, pp. 80–116.

Quinn, David Beers (1990), *The Elizabethans and the Irish*, Ithaca NY: Cornell University Press.

—— (1990), '*A vewe of the Present State of Ireland*', in *The Spenser Encyclopedia*, ed. A. C. Hamilton, London and Toronto: Routledge, pp. 713–15.

Renwick, W. L. (1929), 'Spenser's Galathea and Naera', *TLS*, 28 (14 March), pp. 206–7.

—— (ed.), (1934), *A View of the Present State of Ireland, by Edmund Spenser*, London: Scholartis Press.

—— (ed), (1970), *A View of the Present State of Ireland, by Edmund Spenser*, Oxford: Clarendon Press.

Smith, Roland M. (1942), 'Spenser's Tale of the Two Sons of Milesio', *Modern Language Quarterly*, 3, pp. 547–57.

—— (1943), 'The Irish background of Spenser's *View*', *Journal of English and Germanic Philology*, 42, pp. 499–515.

—— (1944a), 'More Irish words in Spenser', *Modern Language Notes*, 59, pp. 472–7.

—— (1944b), 'Spenser, Holinshed, and the *Leabhar Gabhála*', *Journal of English and Germanic Philology*, 43, pp. 390–401.

Stillman, Robert E. (1992) 'Spenserian Autonomy and the Trial of New Historicism: Book Six of *The Faerie Queene*', *English Literary Renaissance* 22, pp. 299–314.

Vink, James (1990), 'Spenser's "Easterland" as the Columban Church of Ancient Ireland', *Éire-Ireland*, 25, 3, pp. 96–106.

Glossary

A large part of Spenser's text is already an extended glossary. Many of the terms below are glossed by Irenius, but often in the form of confused or false etymologies, designed to reinforce particular arguments.

Attainder   An official proclamation of treason, usually by parliament.

Bardes   Gaelic poets and chroniclers.

Bawn   A fortified enclosure.

Boolying   The practice of pasturing in the hills.

Brehon Law   A judicial system operating in Gaelic Ireland, from *breitheamh(ain)*, judge(s).

Carrows   Card players, gamblers.

Cess   A cover term for various government impositions (see Purveyance).

Churl   An Irish peasant; a word that Spenser seems to assume is Irish, but comes from Old English *ceorl*.

Concealments   One of several means whereby land claimed by the Crown, for example after attainder, was held back.

Conveyances   Another means by which escheated lands were withheld from the Crown, by transferring ownership.

Coigne and Livery, Cuddy, Coshery, Bonnaught, Shragh, Sorehin   Terms applied to diverse impositions made by Gaelic chiefs upon freeholders, all forms of exactions made by Gaelic lords and their gallowglasses.

Creete   From Irish, *crech*, *crechadh*, livestock taken as booty.

Distrayne, distraint   Seizure of goods in lieu of rent.

Erich   A means by which compensation could be paid to the victims of a crime or to their relatives.

Escheat   The reversion of lands from tenant to lord if there is no heir or if the tenant has committed a felony.

Fealty   A feudal tenant's acknowledgement of obligation to a lord.

Foeffement, feoffment   Means by which possession of a freehold estate is formally transferred.

Franci-plegium   Frankpledge, guarantee of good behaviour.

Freeholders   Land or property held by tenure.

Gallowglass   Professional foot-soldiers, mercenaries of Scottish extraction, armed with long-handled axes.

Garron, garran   A strong horse.

Glibbes   Long hair that could cover the face.

Hereditament   Inherited property.

Horseboy   An Irish youth who tended horses.

Hundreds   Subdivision of counties or shires.

Kern   Gaelic foot-soldiers, lightly armed and thus highly mobile.

Kincogish   A system whereby the landed are held accountable for their tenants and servants.

Lozell, losel   Profligate, rake, ne'er-do-well.

Mantle   A long coat or cloak worn by the Irish.

Mona-shutes, Monashul   From Irish, *mná siubhail*, vagrant women.

Mortmains   Literally, land held by a 'dead hand', from Latin *mortua manus*; in practice, property held inalienably by an ecclesiastical or other corporation.

New English   Post-Reformation Protestant planters.

Old English   Descendants of the original twelfth-century English settlement.

Pagadore   A Spanish paymaster or treasurer.

Palatines, Palatinate   An absolute local authority; a region in which royal power is effectively delegated to a local magnate.

Pale   The English Pale in Ireland, centred around Dublin, but with shifting parameters in the period.

Purveyance   A monarch's right to requisition food and transportation at a price below market value, applied in Ireland to the household of the chief governor.

Raths   Ancient hill-forts.

Redshanks   Scottish Highland soldiers allied to the Irish.

Romescot   The payment of military wages in the form of land.

Runnagates   Renegades, vagabonds.

Scythians   Spenser sees them as 'Scots', while Ware derives the term from 'shooting', but Scythians were more generally held to be inhabitants of Scythia, a region north of the Black Sea.

Seignory   Feudal lordship; a term used to refer to lands granted to undertakers on the Munster Plantation. Spenser had a seignory.

Seneschalls, seneschal   A steward of a medieval great house, here used to refer to Gaelic chieftains.

Sept   A Gaelic clan or family.

Scutage   A system by which military service was owed in return for land.

Stocah   A foot servant.

Talk-motes, Folkmotes   Popular assemblies.

Tanistry   From *tánaiste*, meaning second, referring to the nominated successor of a Gaelic chief. Succession by election rather than bloodline.

Wardship   A lord's right to guardianship over tenants who inherited as minors, including the right to arrange marriages and to administer property.

Index